The Show Must Go On

D1712813

The Show Must Go On

*How the Deaths of Lead Actors
Have Affected Television Series*

Douglas Snauffer

Foreword by Joel Thurm

McFarland & Company, Inc., Publishers
Jefferson, North Carolina, and London

LIBRARY OF CONGRESS CATALOGUING-IN-PUBLICATION DATA

Snauffer, Douglas.
The show must go on : how the deaths of lead actors have affected
television series / Douglas Snauffer ; foreword by Joel Thurm.
p.   cm.
Includes bibliographical references and index.

ISBN 978-0-7864-3295-0
softcover : 50# alkaline paper

1. Television actors and actresses — United States — Death.
2. Television programs — United States.   I. Title.
PN1992.3.U5S58   2008   791.45'75 — dc22   2008010226

British Library cataloguing data are available

On the cover: (upper left) James Garner and (upper right) David Spade joined
the cast of 8 Simple Rules for Dating My Teenage Daughter after the death
of John Ritter; (bottom, left to right) Martin Spanjers, Kaley Cuoco,
Katey Sagal, and Amy Davidson (All images from ABC/Photofest).
Front cover by TG Design.

Manufactured in the United States of America

*McFarland & Company, Inc., Publishers
Box 611, Jefferson, North Carolina 28640
www.mcfarlandpub.com*

To my family:
My Dad, Regina, Michelle, Chris, Theresa,
Tricia, and Michael

Acknowledgments

I'd like to begin by thanking those individuals who were there for the long run.

I owe a great debt of gratitude to Bob Shayne, the award-winning writer and producer of such television projects as *Simon & Simon*, *Hart to Hart*, and *The Return of Sherlock Holmes*. Bob's gracious gift of his time, talent, and wisdom, reading every word of my manuscript and offering sometimes harsh but always constructive criticism, proved invaluable. Thank you, Bob.

I also wish to express my thanks to Mark Dawidziak, television critic for *The Cleveland Plain Dealer*, and David Bianculli, respected TV historian and author, for their continued friendship and support, and for answering a myriad of questions I proposed during the writing of this book. My appreciation also extends to Gabriel Scott, former press liaison for the *Writer's Guild of America West*, who acted as a go-between in my efforts to contact many of the retired interviewees whose words are quoted in this book.

I'd also like to acknowledge Cy Chermak, also an award-winning writer and producer, whose television credits include *Ironside*, *Kolchak: The Night Stalker*, and *CHiPs*; he kindly introduced me to his agents, Mike and Susan Farris, who in turn located a publisher for my manuscript. Thanks as well to Dave McDonnell, editor of *Starlog* magazine, for providing me with journalistic opportunities without which other doors would not have opened. I'm indebted to them, one and all.

Then there are the scores of entertainers, both in front of and behind the camera, who contributed to this collection of memoirs. They are the characters in this book, the supporting players in each chapter. It's through their anecdotes that the true stories of those who are no longer with us can be told in the pages that follow. Thank you.

Table of Contents

Foreword

Douglas Snauffer has chosen as the topic for this terrific book a little explored and hardly documented area of show business, i.e. what happens when a popular star or co-star of a TV show dies. Appropriately, the title of his book is the first rule in this strange and wonderful business — the show must go on! But how does the show go on? Who decides how to continue? Who mourns? How long is the mourning period? Often, this rule is obeyed where perhaps it should have been disobeyed, and the show goes on so damaged that its life ends with a whimper.

I've had a long and exciting career in both movies and television. I served as Executive in Charge of Talent and Casting at NBC for ten years, followed by tenures at Paramount, Spelling-Goldberg Productions, and CBS Television, each for another two years, and as an independent producer and casting director on, amongst many others, such notable films as *The Boy in the Plastic Bubble*, *The Rocky Horror Picture Show*, *Grease*, and *Airplane!* On the television side, I happened to be either directly affected by or peripherally involved with replacing a deceased star on seven of the series covered in this book.

Although I did not work on *Eight Is Enough*, the first TV movie I produced was *The Boy in the Plastic Bubble*, the movie that showed the world that Vinnie Barbarino (John Travolta) from *Welcome Back, Kotter* could act. I went on to cast the movie *Grease*, followed by John's first movie failure, *Moment by Moment*, in which he co-starred with Lily Tomlin. I had worked with original *Eight Is Enough* co-star Diana Hyland for all of one day when I was the stage manager for a dreadful off–Broadway play. She showed up for the first reading and then she and the other two actors wisely quit. The next time I saw her was on the set of *The Boy in the Plastic Bubble*. The author's interview with Randal Kleiser (who directed both *Grease* and *The Boy in the Plastic Bubble*) was on-the-spot accurate and even explained to me things that were puzzling at the time regarding Diana's behavior. Please have a tissue handy when you read this chapter.

Jon-Erik Hexum was one actor I put under contract in my early years at NBC. Jon-Erik had been sent to me by his manager, Bob LeMond (coincidentally John Travolta's first manager), with the words, "I haven't a clue if he has any talent for acting, but he is drop dead gorgeous and a star." Bob was right. He was a difficult sale to most producers but an easy one to James Parriott, the producer of the NBC series *Voyagers!* (1982–83). The program, which offered Jon-Erik his first leading role, was aimed at kids — an audience that required less demanding acting skills. I never spent time with Jon-Erik outside of an office or sound stage, but adding what I knew of him to the author's writing, I now have a complete and satisfying picture.

My very first talent deal at NBC involved Nell Carter. I offered her a contract that she accepted, after which she dropped out of the second workshop for *Dreamgirls* and moved to California. We marked time by putting her on the Universal series *The Misadventures of Sheriff Lobo* in the hope she would bring some life to the show. This was a temporary measure to bide time until we could put her in a sitcom pilot. That nearly didn't happen. Brandon Tartikoff, then President of NBC and my boss, called me one day near the end of the 1981 pilot season. He said all the pilots we made that year had tanked and asked if there was anyone under contract whom we could center a half-hour comedy around. I had already been pitching Nell to no avail, but nonetheless said to Brandon, "How about Nell Carter?" Brandon asked what kind of character I thought she could play. In a sarcastic and not-to-be-taken-seriously way, I said, "Well, she could always play a maid." To which Brandon said, "Yes...like a black *Hazel*. Whom would she work for?" "Some authority figure like a policeman or fireman," I said. "Who could we get for the part?" "Dolph Sweet," I replied. Dolph was in the very first play I cast on my own as David Merrick's casting director in New York. Dolph was gentle and courtly in a manner entirely in opposition to his physicality. Nell liked and, more importantly, respected him. His untimely passing hardly helped *Gimme a Break!*

Nell Carter and I became great friends. Nell introduced me to one of her friends, Jackie Harry, who was to change her name to "Jackee" and, coming to her senses in a few more years, Jackee Harry. I was in negotiations with Jackee to co-star with Nell in a new sitcom pilot when Redd Foxx died on the set of his CBS sitcom *The Royal Family*. CBS asked Jackee to step in and take up some of the slack left by Foxx's demise, and there went my sitcom.

One of my assignments at CBS was to cast the first *Bob Newhart Show* for MTM. While there, I had seen an extraordinary actress, Barbara Colby, in an off–Broadway show that starred Judd Hirsch, *The Hot L Baltimore* (later to become a short-lived ABC series in its own right). I helped Barbara get a foothold in television by introducing her to the casting director for *The Mary Tyler Moore Show*. Barbara then got a great role as the hooker Mary spends the night with in jail. It was a no-brainer when it came to casting her in the spin-off *Phyllis* as Cloris Leachman's boss. Her unfortunate and tragic murder only weeks into production, and the numerous replacements that followed, doomed the show. On the other hand, while I was at NBC a few years later, we dealt a bit more successfully in the replacement department with Florence Halop and Selma Diamond, the wonderful bailiffs from *Night Court*, as well as Woody Harrelson, the replacement for Nick Colasanto, Coach from *Cheers*. In each of the latter cases the producers and network executives were in sync, and the shows continued and arguably were even more successful.

Douglas Snauffer's wonderful writing, research and detail in *The Show Must Go On* make this a fascinating and often heart-rending read. I trust you will enjoy it as much as I did.

Joel Thurm
February 2008

Preface

On the morning of September 12, 2003, fans of actor John Ritter were stunned to learn of the comedian's sudden death. Ritter, one-time star of the late–70s hit comedy *Three's Company*, had developed a large following which had remained loyal over time. Nearly twenty years after *Three's Company* left the air, Ritter was still going strong. In the fall of 2002 he returned to ABC in another situation comedy, *8 Simple Rules for Dating My Teenage Daughter*. This time around, instead of playing a freewheeling bachelor, Ritter was the frustrated father of three teenage children. His fans were still there, however, and still enjoying Ritter's antics. By now, many of them had children, too, an entirely new generation that had grown up with reruns of *Three's Company* and were equally taken by Ritter's on-air charisma.

But on that tragic morning in the early fall of 2003, as *8 Simple Rules* was gearing up for a second season, Ritter's devotees gathered not in front of their TV screens, but on their computers to console one another. They weren't alone. Only two years after the horrifying attacks on the World Trade Center towers and other U.S. targets, with the entire world still seemingly in turmoil, Ritter's passing managed to take center stage. CNN devoted continuing coverage to Ritter's story that day, while other media outlets chose universally to lead their telecasts with the latest on the actor's untimely passing.

As news of their loss spread, Ritter's admirers continued to come together on the Internet to mourn, share their memories, and debate the future of *8 Simple Rules for Dating My Teenage Daughter*. They weighed the pros and cons of whether the series could continue without Ritter, or indeed whether it *should* return without him. Ritter's fans felt they had a vested interest in the program. They certainly had opinions. Strong opinions. Some based on reason, some on raw emotion. But they all had a view, and thanks to their home computers, they had a public forum upon which to voice them.

They weren't the first to face such bereavement. Unfortunately, Ritter's was not the only star to fall. Other notable cases include Freddie Prinze, the 22-year-old stand-up comic who became an overnight sensation as star of the mid–70s sitcom *Chico and the Man*. His fame came too quickly and proved too overwhelming for the young man, and in January of 1977 Prinze took his own life. His fans may not have had the Internet with which to congregate and share their emotions, but they too had to be asking themselves the same difficult questions as Ritter's followers, particularly when NBC chose to continue *Chico and the Man* without Prinze.

Still many other examples abound: Dan Blocker, the gentle-giant Hoss Cartwright on the classic western series *Bonanza*, died suddenly just weeks before production began on the program's fourteenth season; Diana Hyland, the original matriarch of the Bradford clan of *Eight Is Enough*, passed away tragically only weeks into the series' run; Redd Foxx, best known as cantankerous Fred Sanford, was making a much needed comeback with the 1991 comedy *The Royal Family* when he died suddenly while rehearsing on the set; Nicholas Colasanto, the kind-hearted Coach of *Cheers*, lost a brave battle with heart disease after three seasons with the show; and Phil Hartman, the sly anchorman of the workplace sitcom *NewsRadio*, perished in a bizarre murder-suicide that shocked all of Hollywood. And still the list goes on: promising TV vehicles that experienced the loss of a star and made the decision to proceed.

While fans were questioning the wisdom of these series continuing production without their stars, it was the network executives in charge of these shows that found themselves on the hot seats. Their decisions were based not on emotion, but on economics. In the case of *Chico and the Man*, Freddie Prinze had completed nearly three seasons of work, or 62 episodes, too few to put together in a viable syndication package. Canceling the series at that point would have meant forfeiting tens of millions of dollars in future profits. Another season's worth of episodes was needed to guarantee a successful syndication berth. But at what cost to the series from a creative standpoint? By all accounts, the fourth and final season of *Chico and the Man* was a disaster, its ratings reflecting the poor quality of that year's episodes. *8 Simple Rules*, too, faced the same dilemma — did financial incentives balance out the idea of returning to work without John Ritter.

The Show Must Go On is a comprehensive look at the medium of television in its darkest hours, a stark analysis of how the death of a lead actor affects a television series, from the studio level right down to the soundstages. Each chapter is told through the eyes of those who were there and lived the experience. They include many of the most notable actors, producers, writers, and directors in television over the past five decades. Through their reminiscences, you the reader are witness to what really happened behind closed doors when network television was faced with its worst nightmares.

Douglas Snauffer
March 2008

CHAPTER 1

8 Simple Rules for Dating My Teenage Daughter
John Ritter

Mortality has always been an emotional issue to deal with, even when those we lose are simply fictional characters we've grown accustomed to as part of our weekly television viewing habits. In the fall of 1956, Danny Williams' wife Margaret passed away on *Make Room for Daddy*. In September 1976, James Evans was killed in a car crash that left wife Florida to raise their three children in the ghettos of Chicago; so much for the family's *Good Times*. A decade later, Valerie Hogan also died in an automobile accident on *Valerie*, leaving *The Hogan Family* (the series' new title) to continue without her. In each case, the real cause of death, however, was a contract dispute between an actor and studio. But the lines between fiction and reality can truly become blurred when a favorite character is lost due to the real-life death of the actor playing the role.

Never was there a more stunning example than the reality that presented itself to the public on the morning of September 12, 2003. When people turned on their televisions and radios that morning, they were hit with the news that actor John Ritter had suddenly passed away.

A day earlier, on the afternoon of September 11, 2003, Ritter had been rehearsing on the set of his sitcom, *8 Simple Rules for Dating My Teenage Daughter*, when he fell ill and was rushed to a nearby hospital. As his family, friends, and coworkers gathered, the Emmy-winning actor was rushed into an operating room, but surgeons could not save him, and he passed away that evening.

By the following morning, word of Ritter's death had spread across the country and beyond, eliciting a response that was remarkable and totally unexpected in its scope. As actress Amy Yasbeck, Ritter's widow, would later comment on the public outcry, "Can you believe it, I married Elvis."

Ritter's death beat out other world news to become the lead story on CNN (along with just about every other news outlet). That weekend, TV Land, the cable channel dedicated to classic television, programmed a twenty-four-hour marathon showcasing Ritter's past work; and on the Internet, Ritter's fans assembled en masse to share their memories and offer condolences to Amy and John's four children: Jason, 23; Carly, 21; Tyler, 19; and Stella, who had turned five on the day her father died.

8 Simple Rules for Dating My Teenage Daughter was to have been a series comeback for the versatile entertainer. The show had cast the one-time *Three's Company* star as middle-aged newspaper columnist Paul Hennessy, a devoted husband and father of three rambunctious teenagers.

After Ritter's death, one of the issues being hotly debated by fans on the Internet was the fate of *8 Simple Rules*. The series had premiered on ABC in the fall of 2002 and had quickly become one of the network's crown jewels, despite mediocre ratings. The season had not gone well for ABC; it was able to place only one scripted series, perennial favorite *N.Y.P.D. Blue*, in the top 30. Thanks to the network's creative difficulties that year, *8 Simple Rules* was quickly picked up for a second season and was set to anchor ABC's Tuesday night schedule for the 2002-03 season. But with Ritter gone, fans were split as to whether the show should continue.

The situation on *8 Simple Rules* was far different from that of *Make Room for Daddy* or *Good Times*. Ritter hadn't left the series for greener pastures. His death was real, and that couldn't be glossed over even by the best scriptwriters. If *8 Simple Rules* was to continue, Ritter's passing would have to be dealt with in a way that would satisfy his many fans and convince them that the Hennessys still had something to offer dramatically without the family patriarch, their beloved John Ritter.

Ritter was born Jonathan Southworth Ritter in Burbank, California, on September 17, 1948, to country music star Tex Ritter, the legendary "singing cowboy," and actress Dorothy Fay, who, before marrying Tex, had been his frequent leading lady. His older brother Tom, who'd been diagnosed with cerebral palsy, heeded his parents' warnings to avoid the trappings of showbiz and became a lawyer. John, however, got hooked on the limelight. As a child, he made occasional appearances with his father onstage, where he proved to be a natural. At Hollywood High School in the early 1960s he was both student body president and the class clown.

Shortly after graduation in the spring of 1965, he made his television debut as a contestant on *The Dating Game*; he won the date and a trip to Arizona. He then enrolled at the University of Southern California as a psychology major, but an acting class later steered him toward a degree in drama. While still in college, he studied acting with legends Nina Foch and Stella Adler. He excelled at comedy, appearing regularly in USC stage productions, but also proved himself a capable dramatic performer.

Even before graduating in 1970, he landed his first professional acting gig in the second episode of *Hawaii Five-O* ("Strangers in Our Own Land," 10/3/68). His next appearance was on the Burt Reynolds crime drama *Dan August* ("Quadrangle for Death," 10/12/71), which co-starred Ritter's future *Three's Company* castmate Norman Fell. Ritter also honed his craft onstage. While his father Tex was entertaining troops in Germany in the early '70s, John appeared in a series of stage productions across Europe.

Ritter's first regular television role was as the Reverend Matthew Fordwick in the popular CBS family drama *The Waltons*. "He kind of cut his teeth with us," says the show's creator and narrator, Earl Hamner, Jr. "He was a remarkably inventive and unique kind of talent, playing an unlikely preacher, a sort of fledgling young Baptist who was just trying his wings."

Ritter's character got off on the wrong foot in his premiere episode, "The Sinner" (October 26, 1972). Fresh out of seminary school, Rev. Fordwick arrives on Walton's Mountain and prepares to assume his duties. Ritter was spot-on with his fire-and-brimstone approach to the character, while at the same time presenting a youthful sense of insecurity. While nervously preparing to take the pulpit, Fordwick naively begins to sip moonshine, and by the time he appears before the congregation he's completely inebriated. His touching performance at episode's end, as a broken young man ready to abandon his life's calling, was a testament to Ritter's versatility.

Despite his dramatic turn onscreen, Hamner recalls Ritter's sense of humor when the cameras weren't rolling:

> John was a genius at comedy. He and Richard Thomas together used to keep the cast in stitches because they would do a gorilla act, they would lope around bent over scratching themselves like monkeys. It sounds horrible but they were terribly funny. It's nice on a set to have people relaxed and laughing, and John provided that.

Although Ritter's father Tex had attempted to dissuade his son from becoming an actor, he was very happy when John landed his role on *The Waltons*, which was Tex's favorite show. Sadly, it was on the set of the show that John received word, on January 2, 1974, that his father had passed away. (In 1983, John would get a star on the Hollywood Walk of Fame right next to his father's.)

His recurring role on *The Waltons* allowed Ritter to pursue other opportunities. His credits include a return engagement on *Hawaii Five-O*, as well as spots on *Kojak, Mannix, The Streets of San Francisco* and *Starsky & Hutch*. On the lighter side, he appeared on a memorable *Mary Tyler Moore* episode as the reverend who married Ted Baxter and Georgette Franklin on the evening of November 8, 1975. That led to roles on *Rhoda, Phyllis*, and *The Bob Newhart Show*. The charismatic young actor was very much in demand. In 1976 he made his first prominent feature film appearance in director Peter Bogdanovich's period musical *Nickelodeon*.

Then in 1977 Ritter's life and career changed forever when he landed his breakthrough role on *Three's Company* (which was based on an early '70s British comedy, *Man About the House*). The premise cast Ritter as Jack Tripper, a culinary student in Santa Monica desperately looking for affordable housing. He answers an ad in the local paper placed by two young women looking for a third to share expenses. Eventually, Tripper convinces the girls to rent him the spare room, with the understanding that their relationships would remain platonic. In order to make the arrangement work, however, Tripper has to convince the conservative landlord, Mr. Roper, that he's gay to assure him that nothing "immoral" will be occurring in his apartment building. The program's humor relied heavily on sexual suggestion and double innuendo.

Cast as Ritter's curvaceous roommates were Joyce DeWitt as florist Janet Wood, the level-headed brunette, and Suzanne Somers as ditzy typist Chrissy Snow (in a later episode, it was amusingly revealed that her actual name was Christmas Snow, Chrissy for short). Veteran character actors Norman Fell and Audra Lindley assumed the roles of nosey landlord Stanley Roper and his sex-starved wife Helen. Rounding out the cast was Richard Kline as Jack's best friend, used-car salesman Larry Dallas.

Series production on *Three's Company* began in January 1977. DeWitt first met Ritter in the show's rehearsal hall after everyone had been cast. She recalled:

> He was instantly adorable and accessible and marvelous. We got along very well. Our stage was a great place to come and play, and everyone played very hard there. John always said, "We aren't trying to make somebody laugh, we're trying to make somebody laugh so hard they fall off their couch laughing." So we were willing to attempt any ridiculous, silly thing if we thought it would make America laugh. Little did we know we were going to get really lucky and be able to make the whole world laugh.

John Ritter is pictured with his *Three's Company* co-stars Joyce DeWitt (above) and Suzanne Somers (below). The sitcom, which ran on ABC from 1977 to 1984, made Ritter a superstar (courtesy ABC/Photofest).

ABC introduced *Three's Company* to the public on March 15, 1977. The show was an immediate hit and would rank number 11 for the season. The show was a silly, old-fashioned, unrealistic sitcom with a little titillating sexuality (but no sex) added. The show may very well have resulted from an effort to counter-program the smarter, more literate comedies of the decade (*All in the Family, Maude, M*A*S*H, Taxi*) — the same way *Married...with Children* would emerge in light of *The Cosby Show* a decade later.

John Ritter seemed to have found the perfect role to showcase his talent (the folks on Walton's Mountain would get a new minister the following season). Ritter's physical antics onscreen made him one of the few performers who could honestly be compared to the great Lucille Ball. Ritter admitted that Lucy was one of his comic idols. (She, too, was apparently won over by him. Lucy would host a special hour-long retrospective titled *The Best of Three's Company* on May 18, 1982; Ritter would return the favor by making a special guest appearance on Lucy's ailing comedy vehicle *Life with Lucy* in 1986.)

Noted DeWitt:

> He was a total natural when it came to physical comedy. He had that sense of wild abandon to just let it happen. In order to be as funny as John was, you have to have huge courage and be willing to make a fool of yourself on occasion. You can't be always second guessing yourself or holding back, you just have to lean forward and hope it works, and sometimes that means you come up with egg all over your face. John was able to take a chance in the hope that it would bring the gift of laughter to other people.

Not only was Ritter's career now in high gear, but his personal life also changed dramatically during this period. On October 16, 1977, he married Nancy Morgan, a struggling young actress whose credits included appearances on *Lucas Tanner, Medical Center*, the mini-series *Backstairs at the White House*, and the feature *Grand Theft Auto*. Their 19-year union would produce three children: Jason in 1980, Carly in 1982, and Tyler in 1984. In 1977 Ritter also began hosting the annual United Cerebral Palsy Telethon after witnessing his brother Tom's brave battle against the condition. As official MC for the next couple of decades, Ritter managed to raise millions of dollars for the charity.

Always the doting family man, Ritter made it a priority not to neglect his family in favor of his career. At the same time, he took his acting responsibilities very seriously. It was a difficult struggle because *Three's Company* took up a great deal of his time, particularly as its popularity skyrocketed.

Ritter realized that Jack Tripper would most likely be the character he'd always be best remembered for, but he was determined to continue pursuing challenging roles. The *Three's Company* ride proved to be a bumpy one, but Ritter made the best of it, choosing to relish the doors it would open for him down the road. One of the opportunities that came Ritter's way was the chance to start his own production company, Adam Productions, in 1980 (with partner Bob Myman). One of their first projects was the TV-movie *The Comeback Kid*, which cast Ritter as a down-and-out minor league ball player who turns his life around by coaching a team of underprivileged kids.

Despite several cast turnovers, *Three's Company* continued on the air for seven seasons, ending its run in 1984 with 172 episodes. For six of those years, the show ranked among the top-ten series on television. Ritter was recognized with both an Emmy and a Golden Globe as best actor for the series' final season.

When *Three's Company* began to wind down, the producers approached Ritter about continuing the character of Jack Tripper in a spin-off. In the new show, *Three's a Crowd*, Jack and his girlfriend Vicky Bradford (Mary Cadorette) set up housekeeping together in an apartment over Jack's restaurant, much to the dismay of Vicky's conservative father (former *Soap* star Robert Mandan). The magic was gone, though, and *Three's a Crowd* was cancelled after a single season.

Ritter was ready to move on. He certainly hadn't rested on his laurels during the run of *Three's Company*. In 1982's *Pray TV* he'd played a young minister who interns for the summer with a high-profile televangelist (Ned Beatty). In director Tony Bill's 1984 comedy-drama *Love Thy Neighbor*, he co-starred with Penny Marshall (*Laverne & Shirley*) in one of her last major acting roles before becoming a full-time director. On the big screen Ritter appeared in the popular 1980 comedy *Hero at Large* as a struggling actor who thwarts a robbery while in costume as a superhero and is soon being hailed as the real thing.

Then, in 1987, Ritter decided to return to the weekly grind of a television series in producer Steven Bochco's *Hooperman*. When Bochco, best known for such high-profile dramas as *Hill Street Blues* and *L.A. Law*, and Ritter, best known for *Three's Company*, teamed up, the result was coined a "dramedy." *Hooperman* was a half-hour in length, but was not filmed in front of an audience, nor did it utilize a laugh track. Although the scripts were laced with humor, most of it somewhat dark, the show was primarily a crime drama.

Detective Harry Hooperman (Ritter) was a San Francisco police detective who, in the series opener, went after the killer who had murdered his landlady. Hooperman then inherited the woman's broken down apartment building, her temperamental terrier Bijoux, and a host of eccentric, often angry tenants. Hooperman also fell in love with Susan (Debrah Farentino), an aspiring writer who also worked as the building's custodian. She became pregnant with Hooperman's child, but suffered a miscarriage and left the series at the end of the first season. Audiences didn't know quite what to make of this new TV hybrid, and the show vanished quietly at the end of its second season.

Over the next few years, Ritter appeared in a number of movie projects. He played the lead in director Blake Edwards's 1989 farce *Skin Deep*, most memorable for a hilarious scene involving a glow-in-the-dark condom. In 1990 he appeared in *Problem Child*, playing the flustered father of a seven-year-old terror (Michael Oliver). The movie went on to gross over $50 million domestically and inspired a 1991 sequel. It was during the filming of *Problem Child* that Ritter met Amy Yasbeck, who was cast as his wife. Nine years later she would assume the same role in real life.

In 1992 he was lured back to television for another comedy, this time one that was a bit more conventional. CBS's *Hearts Afire* featured Ritter and Markie Post (*The Fall Guy*, *Night Court*) as John and Georgie Ann Hartman, a married couple working as aides to eccentric southern senator Strobe Smithers (George Gaynes). Billy Bob Thornton co-starred as John's close friend and confidant, Billy Bob Davis. Created by Linda Bloodworth-Thomason and produced by she and her husband, Harry Thomason, *Hearts Afire* was often an indictment of the political system. The Thomasons were close friends of President (and former governor) Bill Clinton and his wife (future senator) Hillary Clinton, and the couple had more than a passing knowledge of the political process. Still, the show never ventured far from the typical sitcom format.

According to David Steven Simon, the series' co-executive producer:

> If anyone typified life, if there was a definition of life in the dictionary, John's picture is there. We would film as late as one in the morning, and then we always went out to dinner afterwards, at one o'clock, two o'clock in the morning. John's brother Tom was there all the time, they were inseparable. So was Billy Bob; it was a great time.

Simon also witnessed the developing relationship between Ritter and Yasbeck, who was then a regular on NBC's *Wings*. "I knew John in two incarnations," explains Simon. "I knew him with his first wife; we used to play on a softball team. Then years later, Amy was on the set all the time. I watched John fall in love with Amy on the set of *Hearts Afire*. Talk about a match made in heaven." When word of their romance became public, it proved to be an embarrassing and painful experience for all involved. John and Nancy legally separated, although they wouldn't actually divorce until September of 1996.

After a low-rated first season, *Hearts Afire* received a makeover. The Hartmans left the employ of Senator Smithers and took to running a small-town newspaper. The show never did catch fire and was cancelled midway through its third season.

Ritter and Amy Yasbeck continued their relationship and were married on September 18, 1999.

Ritter continued to make notable guest appearances on programs like *Ally McBeal* and *Buffy, the Vampire Slayer* (as a robot looking for the perfect human family). In 1996 he also co-starred with his old pal Billy Bob Thornton in the critically acclaimed film *Sling Blade*. Thornton had penned the script while he and Ritter were still shooting *Hearts Afire*, and wrote Ritter's part specifically for him. In a moving performance, Thornton played Karl Childers, a man released back into society after serving twenty-five years in a mental institution for the childhood murders of his mother and her lover. Ritter played a homosexual man who befriends Karl. The movie was Thornton's debut as a writer-director; he won an Oscar for Best Screenplay and was nominated as Best Actor. While Ritter failed to be recognized with a major award, many considered the part to be his greatest dramatic performance.

In 2000 Ritter became the voice of *Clifford, the Big Red Dog* for PBS's award-winning animated children's program. He received four consecutive Daytime Emmy nominations for his work and won over an entirely new generation of fans.

On September 11, 1998, Yasbeck gave birth to the couple's daughter, Stella. (Back on the January 31, 1991, episode of NBC's megahit *The Cosby Show*, Ritter and Yasbeck, more than eight years before their union, played a married couple soliciting advice from obstetrician Dr. Cliff Huxtable.) Now Ritter found himself a father again at age 50. The event led to his decision to pursue work on another sitcom, which would guarantee him a stable work-week and more time to spend with his family.

Ritter began sifting through a myriad of potential offers. The search ended after he read a script from Disney titled *8 Simple Rules for Dating My Teenage Daughter*. Ritter was immediately won over by the idea of playing a beleaguered head of household and signed on.

8 Simple Rules for Dating My Teenage Daughter was based a book by author and humorist W. Bruce Cameron. When Disney bought the television rights, veteran scribe Tracy Gamble (*The Golden Girls*, *Home Improvement*) was brought in to develop it as a series. Gamble felt connected to the material and truly made it his own. For starters, he named the show's children after his own — Bridget, Kerry, and Rory. He christened Ritter's TV wife Cate in homage to his own wife Katherine. Once Gamble began writing the pilot, he used a great deal of Cameron's dialogue from the book but colored it with his own personal experiences raising his two teenage daughters.

Ritter would be playing Paul Hennesey, a sportswriter who began working at home after his wife Cate (former *Married...with Children* star Katey Sagal) resumed her career as a nurse. The new domestic situation held more than a few surprises for Paul. He soon began to realize that his daughters, 16-year-old Bridget (Kaley Cuoco) and 15-year-old Kerry (Amy

In the fall of 2002, John Ritter returned to series television as a family man in the ABC situation comedy *8 Simple Rules for Dating My Teenage Daughter*. Pictured left-to-right: Martin Spanjers, Kaley Cuoco, Ritter, Katey Sagal, Amy Davidson (courtesy ABC/Photofest).

Davidson), weren't daddy's little angels anymore. Son Rory (Martin Spanjers), 13, became his dad's only ally, although he secretly enjoyed the fact that his sisters' behavior often took the heat off his own extra-curricular activities.

8 Simple Rules for Dating My Teenage Daughter premiered on ABC on September 17, 2002, and quickly became the highest-rated new series of the season. Part of the program's charm was watching Ritter play a role so opposite Jack Tripper — a harried father protecting his daughters from the type of character that had made him a star back in the 1970s.

Gamble (along with co-executive producer Flody Suarez and the other writers) tried to keep the plots as genuine as possible. They would often borrow ideas from Cameron's book, such as an episode in which Paul agreed to chaperone one of his daughter's parties ("Cool Parent," 2/18/03). Other times Gamble would lift stories from his own life, a particular instance being a segment that found Bridget taking the car without permission ("The Drummer Boy, Part 2," 2/11/03). "That came right out of my life, except with the other daughter," laughs Gamble. "I was at the studio one day and my daughter Kerry called and said, 'Hey Dad, I miss you, when are you going to be home?' I said around six and thought it was sweet that she'd said she missed me. Then it occurred to me how suspicious it was, so I went home and sure enough she had taken the car. She was fifteen and did not have a license and had been driving around town. I confronted her and asked what would happen if she hit another car, and she said, 'Well, I'd drive away really fast.'"

Perhaps the highlight of *8 Simple Rules*'s first season was an episode subtitled "Come and Knock on Our Door" (1/28/03), a hilarious send-up of *Three's Company*. The episode had Paul dreaming that his two daughters were sharing an apartment with a boy (Billy Aaron Brown) they were both smitten with. Ritter took a riotous, good-natured turn as stuffy Mr. Roper. The set designers were able to recreate the *Three's Company* apartment to a tee, and even Don Knotts showed up in a cameo as landlord Ralph Furley.

Gamble and Ritter became close friends while doing the series. Like everyone else, Gamble was thrilled to be working with Ritter. Explains Gamble:

> John had this friendly charisma; he made you feel like you were his best friend when you'd only known him for five minutes. Stephen McPherson, then head of Touchstone (and later President of ABC Primetime Entertainment), backed the show because of John. Katey Sagal wanted to do the show even before she read the script. She was like, "Oh my God, John Ritter is doing a series and I want to work with him." John was like a father to the young actors on the show. It was like a nice cocktail.

James Widdoes (*My Wife and Kids*, *The King of Queens*) was brought on board as the in-house director after the pilot had been completed. Widdoes himself was a former actor who'd appeared in *National Lampoon's Animal House* and the freshman season of *Charles in Charge*. He remembers walking onto a show where everyone was very content:

> For me, it had all the earmarks of a great opportunity. The cast and crew who were involved in the pilot were very happy. They usually are when you go through the rigors of making a pilot that gets on the network schedule. Everybody is pretty much on a high. Then reality sets in once you begin making episodes. You begin to get a sense of the enormous expectations that the network has for the series.

Widdoes had worked with Ritter on a couple of previous occasions and appreciated his style. He knew Ritter was just right for the part:

> John was absolutely made for this role. I guess you could call it a departure depending on what previous work of John's you were drawing from. To me anyway, having known John a little bit, it didn't seem a departure at all. It was that perfect blending of the right actor at the right time in his career with the right part. John was a wonderful, loving family man, and it was great that people got to witness that side of him.

As a testament to just how important *8 Simple Rules* became to ABC in a very short time, the network upped their first season order from twenty-two episodes to twenty-eight so as to guarantee episodes would be readily available for both the February and May sweeps periods. The show was also given an early renewal for a full second season. Ritter and his colleagues wrapped their first year confident that *8 Simple Rules* was destined for a long run.

Ritter kept busy during the summer hiatus. He finished work on two feature films: *Manhood*, an indictment of suburbia; and *Bad Santa*, written, directed and starring his friend Billy Bob Thornton as a con artist who poses as a department store Santa each Christmas. He also found time to lend his voice to *Clifford's Really Big Movie*, a big-screen adaptation of his popular PBS children's series.

In early August 2003, Ritter and the *8 Simple Rules* cast reassembled at the Disney Studios to begin work on their second season. Ritter had every reason to be in high spirits: his show was not only doing extremely well, but his son Jason had landed his first regular role on the new CBS drama *Joan of Arcadia* and seemed primed to follow in the footsteps of his father and grandfather.

ABC was again pinning its hopes on *8 Simple Rules* to anchor its Tuesday night line-up. Production went smoothly on the first three episodes of the 2003-04 season. On Monday, September 8, rehearsals began on episode four, which was to feature guest appearances by two of Ritter's best friends, actor Henry Winkler (*Happy Days*) and director Peter Bogdanovich. Several days of rehearsals and scene blocking took place prior to the start of actual filming.

September 11, 2003, began as a typically hectic day on the set of *8 Simple Rules*.

For most of the country, September 11 brought back somber memories of the terrorist attacks on the World Trade Center buildings and the Pentagon that had occurred two years earlier. But personally for the Ritters it was a day of celebration, as it was daughter Stella's fifth birthday, and John wanted to make it special for her. He wasn't due on the set until after lunch and spent much of the morning at home overseeing preparations for later that evening.

Although Ritter had the morning off, the younger stars of *8 Simple Rules* had an early morning call on the set. A number of scenes for that week's episode took place in the hallway of the kids' school, so Kaley Cuoco, Amy Davidson, and Martin Spanjers arrived early to shoot those sequences. Although the series was filmed before a live audience each Friday, certain scenes, for logistical reasons, were sometimes completed the day before.

Their storyline involved Bridget's new, mysterious love interest at school. Things went smoothly and they finished in time to break for lunch.

Ritter arrived on the set around one o'clock, along with Winkler and Bogdanovich. It was to be a busy afternoon for Ritter. First on his agenda was to shoot a couple of Disney Channel promos for the United Kingdom. After those were completed, rehearsals resumed with the camera crew in preparation for shooting the episode on Friday.

Ritter's storyline (each episode consisted of two) had Paul losing his office at the paper, after which he was forced to share space with the paper's neurotic book reviewer (played by Bogdanovich).

A pivotal scene called for actor Larry Miller, who had a recurring role on the series, to come into the small office to razz Paul about the situation. Winkler, as their boss, then entered to inquire as to what all the commotion was about. The scene required a lot of movement and rhythm as the other three actors orbited Ritter at his desk. Widdoes had put the actors through their paces all week getting the scene down, but they'd enjoyed themselves, ad libbing much of the dialogue and taking great joy in breaking each other up.

Recalls Gamble: "My fondest memory of that show is that it would have been by far our funniest. [James Widdoes] had directed it perfectly and it was hilarious—the Marx brothers in a stateroom. People fell out of their set chairs laughing. I regret none of it exists on film."

But the fun soon ended.

"We got through a couple of scenes, and then John pulled me aside and said he had a bit of a stomachache," recalls Widdoes, "and would it be okay if he went upstairs to his dressing room to rest for a while. He wanted to be sure I could get along with his stand-in. I said 'absolutely.' That was around four o'clock in the afternoon. It was the last time we spoke."

Ritter went to lie down, but it didn't help. He called home and spoke to Amy a short while later, complaining of nausea. He told her he thought he might have a case of food poisoning. Shortly after that, he began experiencing chest pains, at which point he agreed to be taken across the street to Providence St. Joseph Medical Center where a doctor could examine him. He was escorted out to the parking lot where a car was waiting. Just as he was about to get in, he turned to concerned onlookers, members of the crew, and assured them not to worry. He would be fine.

At the hospital, emergency room doctors initially felt that Ritter was suffering a heart attack and began to monitor his condition. Ritter's family, along with the cast and crew of *8 Simple Rules*, who'd grown concerned, began to gather in the waiting room. Yasbeck spent a couple of hours with her husband as doctors reviewed his case. After further tests, the doctors revised their diagnosis—Ritter had an aortic dissection, a weakened blood vessel wall where the aorta leads into the heart. In John's case, it was a condition he may have had all his life that went undetected and only now was beginning to rupture. Ritter was rushed into an operating room where doctors worked for several hours trying desperately to correct the problem. Sadly, their efforts failed, and John Ritter passed away shortly after 10 P.M. He was 54 years old.

The next morning when the news broke to the entire country, Ritter's fans were in disbelief. He had become more than just a familiar TV personality; he'd become a friend to his fans. As Gamble had said, he made people feel as if they were his best friend. Parents who'd grown up with Ritter on *Three's Company* mourned alongside their children, who'd discovered his talent through reruns on TV Land and *8 Simple Rules*.

September 12 was a "hard day for everybody," says Widdoes. "We all had to get through it our own way." For most, that involved losing themselves in the wonderful memories of their friend John.

Joyce DeWitt remembers:

We all knew that John was very loved. But what we didn't know until his passing was that he was "beloved" by the American public. The way they felt about him was so powerful and beautiful. It was an extraordinary experience to go through, both a public mourning and a private mourning at the same time, particularly when you're experiencing the awareness and the impact of just how huge the affection for your lost friend was.

Tracy Gamble remembers what a caring friend and family man Ritter was:

He was just wonderful to me, and I will always appreciate that. I remember going to a Dodgers game with him. He was so proud of his kids, like when Jason got the pilot for *Joan of Arcadia*, and when Tyler got accepted into Penn, he was so proud. He was always bragging about Carly, his daughter. He'd come into work everyday telling these stories about Stella, his five-year-old, and the witty things she said. That always impressed me. I miss him.

Family, friends, and co-workers (from his many decades in the business, from *The Waltons* to *8 Simple Rules*) said good-bye to Ritter in a touching memorial service, after which he was interred at Forest Lawn Cemetery in the Hollywood Hills.

At Disney, discussions began as to how TV's Hennessy family would survive. Several divergent opinions abounded. Some felt the show could not survive without Ritter and felt that ABC should cancel the series outright. Others believed the network should hold the three completed, unaired second season episodes until November (the all-important sweeps period), then broadcast them, followed by a special tribute to Ritter. The only other option on the table was to continue the program with Katey Sagal as a single mother.

States Widdoes:

ABC was really spectacular. [Former Chairman of ABC Entertainment] Lloyd Braun was so sympathetic and supportive of us. I'm sure there were enormous pressures over at ABC, "What do we do about this? *8 Simple Rules* was going to be the jewel of this season's comedy line-up." We were on our way to being their most successful new comedy in years. And that had enormous corporate ramifications. But ABC gave us all the support we needed.

The first question they had to ask themselves was whether Katey Sagal could carry the show as its star. "Katie is a wonderful actress and a bona-fide TV star," insists Widdoes. "And while I don't know if anyone at that time was developing *The Katey Sagal Show*, we were absolutely confident that given the circumstances under which we were going to move forward that she was absolutely up to the task of being the center of this family."

ABC and Disney agreed to allow *8 Simple Rules* to resume production if they wanted to move ahead. They did, so long as one stipulation was met. Amy Yasbeck had to give her blessing. "We wouldn't have done it without Amy's okay," insists Widdoes. "We needed that." Amy gave them her blessing, certain it was what John would have wanted.

The decision was made to premiere the show's second season as scheduled on September 23, 2003, with the first of Ritter's three completed episodes; the other two would air on September 30 and October 7. Then the show would take a short hiatus before returning on November 4 with the first post–Ritter segment.

The November 4 episode, a special one-hour telecast subtitled "Goodbye," opened with the Hennessy family going through their usual hectic morning routines, except for Paul, who had gone out to pick up some milk. Then, in an emotionally charged moment, the phone rings and Cate gets the tragic news: Paul has collapsed at the grocery store and is being rushed to the hospital, where he dies. Cate and her children then had to get through the funeral and say their goodbyes to Paul. Afterwards, they had to pull together and begin to move on with

Mourning, on-screen and off. Early in the series' second season, the Hennessy family of ABC's *8 Simple Rules for Dating My Teenage Daughter* mourned the loss of their patriarch, Paul (played by the late John Ritter). Off-screen, pictured actors, from left, Kaley Cuoco, Katey Sagal, Amy Davidson, and Martin Spanjers were dealing with the real-life death of their co-star (courtesy ABC/Photofest).

their lives, just as Amy Yasbeck was heroically leading the Ritter family through their own healing process.

Actors James Garner (*Maverick, The Rockford Files*) and Suzanne Pleshette (*The Bob Newhart Show*) were added to the cast as Cate's divorced parents, who arrived to help the family through their transition. Garner would sign on as a regular, moving in with the family; Pleshette departed after the Thanksgiving episode ("The First Thanksgiving," 11/25/03). Just as the Hennessy kids had their mother for support, Garner's character gave Sagal's character someone to go to when she needed a shoulder to cry on.

Widdoes recalls:

> Jim came in with such a calm authority that he really did become this rock that the cast and everybody could lean on. Not only did he bring his professionalism and skill, but in a positive way he brought a detachment from John's death. It's not that he wasn't enormously saddened by the loss of John, but he was new to our show, so he didn't have to show up everyday on a stage where we had just spent the last year and a half with John. There was one instance where one of the girls was just overcome with emotion during a scene we were doing, and Jim, in that very quiet, deep Jim Garner voice, put his arm around her and said, "There, there, sweetie, I understand, but now it's time to do our jobs."

On the January 13, 2004, episode, "Get Real," David Spade (*Saturday Night Live, Just Shoot Me*) was introduced as Cate's wayward nephew C.J., who arrived to pay his respects and never left. The dramatic talents of Garner and the comedic talents of Spade combined to help take up some of the slack left by Ritter's absence. "David had a compassion for the show because he had been partners with Chris Farley," explains Gamble. "He told me, 'I lost somebody close to me, so I can empathize with the cast.' He just wanted to be part of an ensemble, not the star."

Even though *8 Simple Rules* continued on without Ritter, he was by no means forgotten. Many sitcoms choose to avoid references to departed characters, but *8 Simple Rules* took the more realistic route. Paul was often discussed and sorely missed. That honesty, Widdoes feels, struck a chord with viewers: "We got a lot of letters from people who actually had experienced similar things in their family. They thanked us for actually dramatizing this. For those particular episodes we were life and art as one, not imitating each other."

Viewers evidently had grown attached to the Hennessy family and continued to tune in each week even after Ritter's death. The series performed well for the remainder of the year and was picked up for a third season. Judd Pillot and John Peaslee (*Coach, Just Shoot Me*) joined the series that fall as the new showrunners, replacing Gamble, who had elected to depart over creative differences.

The new season also brought a new timeslot for the show, Fridays at 8 P.M., where it would become part of ABC's T.G.I.F. lineup, a night usually dedicated to younger audiences. That's why some viewers were surprised at a number of developments during that season: it was revealed early on that seventeen-year-old daughter Kerry had lost her virginity over the summer while in Europe. Bridget was initially upset that her younger sister had had sex before her, but by the end of the season she too had followed suit. Even Kate found romance that year with Ed Gibb (Adam Arkin), principal at the kids' high school, where Cate had taken a job as the nurse. Sagal's former *Married...with Children* co-star Ed O'Neill even showed up as a former suitor in the episode "Old Flame" (1/14/05).

Ratings began to slip in the series' new Friday timeslot, and although the numbers remained respectable, ABC chose to cancel the show at the end of the 2004-05 season. *8 Simple Rules* ended its run that summer after completing 76 episodes. While many fans

After the death of John Ritter early in the program's second season, actors David Spade and James Garner joined the cast of ABC's *8 Simple Rules for Dating My Teenage Daughter*. Pictured, clockwise from top center: Katey Sagal, James Garner, Amy Davidson, Martin Spanjers, Kaley Cuoco, David Spade (courtesy ABC/Photofest).

supported the series' attempt to continue without Ritter, some felt it was a mistake. Either way, the additional runtime secured enough episodes to ensure the show would be able to live on in syndication (thus preserving Ritter's final work in those initial 31 episodes).

In whatever role his fans choose to remember Ritter, it's clear they'll recall him fondly, like a close friend with whom they shared a lot of laughter.

In 2005, Amy Yasbeck sued Providence St. Joseph Medical Center and two physicians for her husband's misdiagnosis in the emergency room. The hospital settled out of court for $9.4 million (Yasbeck also received an additional $5 million from other parties involved with Ritter's emergency room care that day). The case against the two doctors went to court in March of 2008. Yasbeck and Ritter's four children were seeking $67 million, the amount that they allege Ritter, as the family's primary breadwinner, would have earned in the remaining years of his life and career.

On the witness stand, Yasbeck recalled Ritter being informed by a cardiologist that he was experiencing a heart attack. Frightened and uncertain, he requested a second opinion, but was told there was no time for such a consultation. Before a proper diagnosis could be rendered, Ritter's condition had deteriorated and he could not be saved.

It was also revealed in testimony, however, that Ritter had undergone a full body scan in 2001 and had been warned against the possibility of heart disease. He was advised by a radiologist to consult a specialist. While no defect in his aorta was present in the body scan, further examination of his cardiovascular system might have caught the tear years before it killed the actor. But Ritter never followed up with a cardiologist. Therefore, the jury ruled 9-3 to reject Yasbeck's wrongful death claim.

Undaunted, she has been determined to move on with her life and career. A dedicated single mother, Yasbeck is now faced with the daily task of providing her and John's children with guidance and support they need to move forward without their father. Professionally, Yasbeck has continued to act. She starred in the short-lived 1995 Fox sitcom *Life on a Stick* and has made a number of guest appearances on other series.

CHAPTER 2

Alias Smith & Jones
Peter Duel

The television landscape in the late 1950s and '60s was ruled by westerns. There were classics such as *Bonanza, Gunsmoke, The Lone Ranger, Maverick,* and *Wagon Train.* There were memorable entries like *The Big Valley, The High Chaparral, Sugarfoot,* and *Bronco.* And then there were forgettable and mostly short-lived titles, including *The Westerner, The Deputy, Custer,* and *Shane.*

But by the early 1970s the TV western had gone the way of the buffalo. CBS's *Gunsmoke* was still going strong, but NBC's *Bonanza* was showing signs of age, while the network's *The Men from Shiloh* (a retooled version of *The Virginian*) was winding down quickly. The western landscape was suddenly looking awfully bare.

NBC and CBS were more interested in moving on to more contemporary programming such as *All in the Family, Maude,* and *Sanford & Son.* But ABC, the only network that did not have a western on its schedule at that time, was ready to give the genre another chance. They did so in early 1971 by debuting *Alias Smith & Jones,* a sassy western about two free-wheeling outlaws, Hannibal Heyes and Kid Curry, who tried to put their crooked pasts behind them and go straight.

The show was light and breezy, and its characters easy to root for. The two actors chosen to play Heyes and Curry, Peter Duel and Ben Murphy, were handsome, amiable, and had great chemistry. They became two of television's most popular anti-heroes, and *Alias Smith & Jones* earned high marks with both critics and viewers.

But the fun that everyone seemed to be having onscreen was a far cry from the turmoil that was transpiring behind the cameras. *Alias Smith & Jones* was a troubled show from the very beginning, and its future was to be marred by a tragedy that would end the series' run prematurely and continue to haunt its cast, crew, and fans for decades to come.

Alias Smith & Jones was born in the mind of Glen A. Larson. Larson had written a number of hit songs during his days with the Four Preps musical group in the early 1960s, including *26 Miles* and *Big Man.* He also harbored an ambition to write for television and took a portable typewriter along whenever he toured with the Preps so he could write scripts in his free time. It didn't take long for him to sell stories to *Twelve O'clock High* and *The Fugitive.* After selling a script to *It Takes a Thief* in 1968, he was hired as a story editor and then promoted to producer in the span of only one season.

Peter Duel (left) and Ben Murphy (right) portrayed Hannibal Heyes and Kid Curry, legendary outlaws who tried to clean up their act in exchange for a pardon in the ABC western series *Alias Smith & Jones.*

By age 30, Larson had become a boy wonder at Universal Studios. *It Takes a Thief* wrapped production in 1970, at which time producer Leslie Stevens (*The Outer Limits*) hired Larson to co-executive produce the final season of *The Virginian*. The show had been re-titled *The Men from Shiloh* and consisted of three rotating segments featuring James Drury, Doug McClure, and Stewart Granger, with Larson in charge of the McClure episodes.

Working on *The Men from Shiloh* was right up Larson's alley. He grew up a big fan of the western genre; Roy Rogers was his childhood idol. When it became clear that *The Men from Shiloh* was on the verge of cancellation, Larson began to consider his next career move.

What he really wanted to do was to create and produce a series of his own, and he wanted it to be a western. It didn't matter to him that westerns were becoming scarce on the small screen. Says Larson:

> I don't know if I would say they were dying out. Obviously *Butch Cassidy and the Sundance Kid* had been one of the biggest movies of the decade, and *The Wild Bunch* and a few other pretty notable films were being made during that period. The so-called era of the western, in which every show was a western, had passed. But I don't think ABC considered a new series risky, primarily because there had been those very successful westerns at the box-office.

Larson decided to proceed with his western but decided to put a different spin on it. He wanted to focus on the American West at the turn of the century when technology was drastically altering the landscape. Larson's script centered on two outlaws, Hannibal Heyes and Kid Curry, who, as part of the notorious Devil's Hole Gang, had become highly successful at robbing banks and holding up trains and stagecoaches. The fact that they had never shot or killed anyone had made them into folk heroes rather than hated desperados. (Larson had patterned the Devil's Hole Gang after a notorious real-life bunch known as the Hole-in-the-Wall Gang, whose membership at times had included Jesse James, Butch Cassidy, and a real-life Kid Curry.)

Heyes and Curry had been able to stay one step ahead of the law, but time eventually caught up with them. The pilot episode of *Alias Smith & Jones* opened with the outlaws attempting to rob a train, only to see their carefully orchestrated plan fall into comedic disarray. The safe they encounter onboard is a new model that the boys just can't crack. Frustrated at being unable to get at the payroll loot inside, and with the threat of a posse looming on the horizon, the gang finally decides to take the safe along for the ride. Anchoring it to the saddles of three horses, they drag it off down the trail in hopes of opening it later.

This was certainly not your conventional western, but was in keeping with Larson's style of light-hearted storytelling. Heyes and Curry soon realized that the only future for men in their line of work was either prison or a premature grave. So they turned to their old friend Lom Trevors, a former member of the Devil's Hole Gang who now wore a sheriff's badge.

The boys wanted to go straight and were seeking amnesty for their crimes. Reluctantly, Trevors approached the governor with Heyes and Curry's proposal. The governor, who'd been under pressure from the railroads and the banks to do something about the two outlaws, took the bait. After all, he couldn't catch them, and with an election year approaching it was to his advantage to solve the problem one way or another. The governor made a counter-proposal — Heyes and Curry could have their amnesty if they could first go straight for one year. If they managed to live upright and honest lives for twelve months, they'd get their pardon.

The catch was that until then their arrangement would be a private one. The governor didn't want to be embarrassed if Heyes and Curry failed to live up to their side of the bargain. The boys reluctantly accepted the deal and began their lives anew. The series would deal with their attempts to live down their reputations, keep one step ahead of the law, and fight off temptation whenever they encountered an easy mark.

The premise of *Alias Smith & Jones* sounded very familiar to critics and the viewing public alike. In *Butch Cassidy and the Sundance Kid* the two protagonists also approached an old cohort turned lawman with talk of amnesty. Making the comparison even more damning was the casting of stars Pete Duel and Ben Murphy. Murphy, in particular, was a dead ringer for Paul Newman.

But Larson, a well-read scholar of history, defends the premise:

> They all figured this was sort of a parallel to *Butch Cassidy and the Sundance Kid*, although it was truly based on some factual things that happened with the Hole-in-the-Wall Gang. Butch Cassidy and another member of the gang were offered amnesty by the government if they'd stop robbing trains, and then they were going to give them jobs guarding them. They figured that would be a good way out. My device was that they had to deserve it, to keep their noses clean for about a year without telling anybody that they have a deal. Meanwhile, people are taking shots at them. So it made for a good storyline, and it was historically accurate.

ABC rushed the series into production because they needed a quick replacement for the faltering Vince Edwards drama *Matt Lincoln* on Thursday nights. Unfortunately, by inheriting *Matt Lincoln*'s timeslot, *Alias Smith & Jones* also inherited that series' curse, being slated against NBC's top-rated hit *The Flip Wilson Show*. On a positive note, with such tough competition, nobody really expected *Alias Smith & Jones* to dominate the time period. The bar was substantially lower, which meant, to survive, Heyes and Curry would simply have to hold their own.

Veteran producer Jo Swerling, Jr., who'd been hired to oversee the day-to-day operation of the series, recalls that problems began to arise behind the scenes almost immediately:

> Glen actually created the show and produced the pilot for Universal under the command of [Head of Production] Frank Price. Glen started preparing scripts as soon as ABC bought the pilot, but things were not going quickly enough. Glen was still involved with *The Men from Shiloh* at the time, and Frank was worried that Glen was a little too new at the game to be actually producing two shows at once.

So Price turned to veteran producer Roy Huggins to take the reins. Huggins was considered one of the most talented and capable show-runners in the business. His credits included *Cheyenne, Maverick,* and *77 Sunset Strip.* (He also created *The Fugitive* for producer Quinn Martin.) *Maverick* had relied on the same kind of humor that ABC was looking for in *Alias Smith & Jones.* Continued Swerling:

> Roy was perfectly happy to have Glen working with him. When the first season started out, Glen prepared a batch of scripts and Roy prepared a batch of his own. Glen would produce every other episode and I would produce the others, and we were both working for Roy. Now I wasn't inside of Glen's head so I don't really know what was going on, but my guess is that he didn't really care to be reporting to somebody else on a show he created.

It wasn't that Larson disliked Huggins; in fact, he admired him greatly. As Larson explains:

> It was kind of like having two cooks in the same kitchen. It kind of rankled me that I didn't have more to say about my own show. But I was barely thirty. I created the show and got it on the air and I wanted to have a little more input into what direction we were going to take. So it wasn't as much fun for me.

Huggins immediately made one change to the show's concept that was in direct conflict to Larson's way of thinking. Explains Larson:

> Roy believed there were only two types of westerns — those set in the Old West, and the "bastard westerns." Roy just felt that the idea of being close to the turn of the century constituted a "bastard western." You couldn't do that as far as he was concerned. One of the great things about the pilot, in my opinion, was the era and how the Old West was modernizing and how it was one of the hardest things for outlaws to deal with — bigger safes, Western Union, telephones, and the Pinkertons. But Roy decided to roll it back to the 1880s.

While Larson was struggling with the idea of playing second fiddle, Huggins was obviously enjoying his tenure on *Alias Smith & Jones*. Of the 14 episodes shot for the series' first season, Huggins would receive a story or teleplay credit on 10 of them. He would remain equally prolific throughout the show's run.

When writing, Huggins would often use the pseudonym John Thomas James (which was derived from the first names of Huggins' three youngest sons). He did so much writing under the pen name that many believed them to be two separate individuals. John Thomas James was even given his own parking space. Agents would routinely call the production office hoping to sign him as a client; Huggins would delight in leading them on, saying John was a wonderful writer but hated agents.

Huggins also had an unusual modus operandi when writing. He would climb into his car and take road trips, disappearing sometimes for days or weeks at a time. He'd drive into Arizona and New Mexico, or sometimes up to Oregon and Washington, and dictate detailed stories into his tape recorder. An assistant would transcribe the tapes, which were then handed to a freelance writer who would get started on the script. "Roy was such a lousy driver," laughs Swerling, "that each time he drove off we all prayed we would see him again."

Casting for the series went fairly smoothly.

Pete Duel was born and raised in New York and briefly considered studying medicine. His father, grandfather, and great-grandfather had all been physicians. But the acting bug infected Duel and he moved to Hollywood in 1963 where he started out doing guest spots on series like *Combat!* and *Gomer Pyle, USMC*. He soon landed co-starring roles in two short-lived ABC comedies. The first was *Gidget*, starring Sally Field, which premiered in 1965 and ended after only a single season. In 1966 he played opposite Judy Carne in *Love on a Rooftop*, a TV version of the play-turned-movie *Barefoot in the Park*. It, too, was cancelled after a single year, but Duel garnered great reviews and was signed to a seven-year contract by Universal Studios.

One of Duel's first projects at Universal was *The Young Country*, a pilot movie written and directed by Roy Huggins. The project teamed Duel with actor Roger Davis as a couple of adventurers in the Old West. The movie aired on ABC on March 17, 1970, and tied as the highest-rated TV-movie of that season, but the network passed on ordering it up as a series. Its failure cleared the way for Duel to be cast in *Alias Smith & Jones*.

Ben Murphy was born in Arkansas and grew up in Memphis and Chicago. His acting ambitions led him to Los Angeles where he also became a contract player for Universal. He had small roles in the films *The Graduate* and *Yours, Mine, and Ours*, and was a regular on the NBC series *The Name of the Game*. His remarkable resemblance to Paul Newman helped him land his role as Kid Curry in *Alias Smith & Jones*.

After months of preparation, the show kicked off with a special 90-minute sneak preview on the evening of Tuesday, January 5, 1971. That extended episode set up the premise, allowing Hannibal Heyes and Kid Curry to make their amnesty proposal to the governor through Sheriff Trevors. While waiting for Trevors to return with a reply, Heyes and Curry's old gang wanders into town and begins to case the local bank. Realizing that if the bank gets robbed they'll most likely be blamed and lose any chance at amnesty, the boys take jobs as tellers in order to protect the vault. The premiere telecast attracted a sizeable audience.

The series then settled into its regular timeslot beginning on Thursday, January 21, at 8 P.M. As expected, the show failed to overtake *Flip Wilson*, but ratings were strong enough that insiders felt the series had the potential to remain an asset to the network for several years to come. Duel and Murphy became instantly recognizable to the young demographic that the network was aiming for. The series was able to stay afloat that spring, and ABC ordered 24 new episodes for the 1971–72 season.

Overall the show was operating as well as could be expected. Westerns are much more difficult to shoot than contemporary series, but Huggins and Swerling had solid backgrounds in the genre and knew what to expect. Says Swerling:

> Stagecoaches are difficult to work with. They're not like cars where you do a run-by and if you need another one the guy just turns around and comes back. With a four-up, you get to the end of the road and it takes five or ten minutes just to turn the damn wagon around. But the powers-that-be didn't look upon it with those kinds of specifics in mind. It was just an hour show to them. Those elements of difficulty equated to stress, and that equated to tempers and tantrums.

Fortunately, flare-ups on the set were infrequent. Swerling found both Pete Duel and Ben Murphy to be consummate professionals. After awhile, however, Duel began developing the bad habit of showing up late for work. Once he was on the set he was perfectly fine, always knew his lines, hit his marks, and did great work. But his tardiness began to irritate his coworkers and, even worse, started to rub off. Soon Ben Murphy was arriving late as well. Murphy would routinely show up about twenty minutes late, and Duel would then clock in about ten minutes after him.

One day while shooting at the Fox Ranch, Swerling decided to address the problem. The cast and crew were busy shooting the episode subtitled "The Bounty Hunter" with guest star Louis Gossett, Jr., and, as usual, Duel and Murphy had shown up late. Swerling first approached Pete Duel.

"Pete, this really isn't fair," Swerling began. "We have a very distinguished actor as the guest star and he's here early and he has to sit around and wait until you show up. And you're not endearing yourself to the crew because they want to go home, they don't want to be working overtime because the star is late in the morning."

"We get along fine, the crew loves me," Duel shot back defensively.

"Sure they do, but it doesn't make them happy when you come in late," Swerling countered. "It's not professional and it doesn't look good. Please, get here on time. Is there anything we can do to help you get here on time?"

Duel walked away muttering, obviously upset at the exchange. At this point, Swerling was not looking forward to a similar encounter with Murphy, but now that he'd broached the matter with Duel he had no choice. A short time later, he sat down with Murphy and repeated his concerns. Swerling remembers it as a defining moment between the two men. After Swerling finished saying his piece, Murphy paused for a moment and then replied:

> Let me explain something to you, Jo. I am not as good an actor as Pete Duel. I rely very heavily on the chemistry that he and I have together, both on and off the set, for my performance to work. My relationship with Pete requires that I like him, because I have to feel the same way

about him that Kid Curry feels about him. If he comes in late and I'm there on time sitting around waiting for him, I'm going to get pissed off and I'm going to start disliking him, and whatever chemistry that you guys have been happy with up until now is going to disappear. I can't really let that happen, so I come in about ten minutes before he does so I don't have to wait on him. If he's a half hour late, then I'm twenty minutes late. If he's an hour late, I'm fifty minutes late.

Swerling sat there for a moment, perplexed.

"How the hell do you do that? How do you figure out what time to get here?' he finally asked.

"I have an instinct about it," Murphy answered simply. "But you understand if I don't do that, I'm going to start hating him. I just don't want that."

Swerling just stood there nodding his head in agreement. "I had no answer for that," says Swerling. "I thought it was such a flawless argument. At the time, I didn't even realize that Ben was that thoughtful a guy. I never said another word to him about it. I just kept on Pete, trying to get him there on time."

It was true that Pete Duel was well liked by the crew of *Alias Smith & Jones*. So much so that Duel's mood often set the tone for how everyone else on the set would feel. According to Swerling:

> Pete tended to be moody. He would come in on some days and be very up. He was a very charming guy and he would lift everybody's spirits. Then there were days he would come in and be very depressed. He wouldn't be mean to anybody, but you could tell that he was just depressed. And by osmosis that would drag the morale of the crew down a notch.

Swerling noticed that Duel was extremely sensitive, to the point where he would allow other people's problems to greatly depress him. Even things he'd only hear about on the news would get him into a deep funk. "He would be depressed because he couldn't cure that which was evil in the world," elaborates Swerling. "He would suffer for other people's woes. The guy had a heart as big as Texas and he took all these things as if they were a personal failure of his. Pete was just a very emotional guy who felt empathy for everybody."

Duel and Murphy got along well, although they didn't socialize outside of work. Even when situations arose that could have driven a wedge between them, they worked through it. Money once became such an issue.

When the show first started Pete Duel was being paid three to four times as much per episode as Murphy was making. The reason was that Duel had starred in *Love on a Rooftop* and some other things, and was much more of an established actor. Murphy was a contract player at Universal, which many equated to being a resident slave. So when they cast them on the series together they had to pay Duel a great deal more.

Eventually Murphy began resenting the fact that he was being paid so much less and approached Universal Business Affairs to give him a raise. At first, Universal stonewalled Murphy. The situation could easily have blown up if Huggins had not found out about it and interceded. He personally approached Frank Price and went to bat for Murphy.

"Look, you've got to give this guy a raise," Huggins said. "This is not right. He has a very valid point and he's a very important part of the show. I'm not suggesting you pay him the same money you're paying Pete, but he should have more parity with his co-star. He should get a very healthy salary increase."

Murphy got his raise. He also demonstrated his professionalism in that throughout the ordeal, even when he felt he was being slighted, he never became bitter towards Duel. He couldn't let that happen.

The show continued to perform well during the early months of its second season. But as summer turned to fall, Duel continued to grow more distant and depressed. Glen Larson recalls taking a trip with Duel to Catalina Island where he witnessed first-hand how emotionally detached the young actor was becoming from the world around him:

> We went over to Catalina Island and I thought we were having fun. We visited a few of the boats in the harbor. Kids came up to Peter all over the island and treated him very much like a hero. But he didn't seem to feel that was something of significance. He was very nice to the kids, he wasn't arrogant or stand-offish, but there were issues in his life that wouldn't allow him to fully appreciate what he meant to them.

Duel openly criticized the quality of the show on many occasions and hoped to get out of television altogether. He wanted to make motion pictures, movies of substance. But with *Alias Smith & Jones* consuming so much of his time and establishing him as a small-screen leading man, that goal seemed less and less attainable.

Despite the success of his ABC western *Alias Smith & Jones*, actor Peter Duel continued to suffer from depression in his personal life, which many believe led to his suicide in the early morning of December 31, 1971.

Duel was also experiencing difficulties in his personal life. He had been dating a woman named Diane Ray, but their relationship was troubled. To deal with his depression, Duel turned increasingly to alcohol. In June of 1971 he was arrested and pled guilty to felony drunk driving. He was fined and sentenced to two years probation.

The walls seemed to be closing in.

Pete Duel, who could not help but agonize over the pain and suffering of complete strangers, was now drowning in his own problems. Life seemed to be pulling him under, and he was quickly losing whatever grip he had.

In the early morning hours of December 31, 1971, he thought he had found the solution.

Duel had spent most of the previous day, Thursday, December 30, at Universal Studios shooting scenes for an upcoming episode of *Alias Smith & Jones*. He went home that evening and watched another episode of the series on TV (episode 29, subtitled "Miracle at Santa Marta"), which he hated. He had been drinking heavily and was very depressed.

According to a police statement given by Diane Ray that morning, she and Duel were in bed together until approximately 12:30 A.M., when she heard Duel get up and leave the room. A few minutes later she heard a "pop" coming from the living room.

She called his name but received no reply.

Concerned, she climbed out of bed and went to investigate. Her concern turned to horror as she entered the living room. There she discovered Duel's nude body lying next to the Christmas tree, a bullet wound in his head and a .38 caliber revolver nearby.

A police report would later note two bullet holes in the room: one in a wall approximately 15 feet from Duel's body, and another in a window approximately 12 feet away. For this reason police at first investigated Duel's death as a homicide. Later it was learned that Duel had fired one of the shots a month earlier after receiving a telegram informing him he had not been chosen to serve on a board at the Screen Actors Guild. He had taped the telegram to the wall and fired a shot through it.

Duel was pronounced dead at the scene. A telegram was dispatched to his parents in Penfield, New York, at 6:19 A.M.

Early that morning, Jo Swerling, Jr., was home in bed. He and his wife had plans to go to San Francisco that weekend to celebrate New Year's Eve. At about 3:30 A.M. Swerling received an urgent phone call from a young woman named Dorothy Bailey, who was Roy Huggins' assistant and had also had a brief romantic relationship with Duel. Bailey was inconsolable.

Recounted Swerling:

> I could barely get out of her the essence of what had happened. So I told her I'd be right over. I went to her apartment and got her calmed down. She had a relative who worked in a factory on the swing shift who had heard it on the radio. So I'm at her place by 5 A.M. and we call Roy Huggins and woke him up. He was concerned about the crew and wanted to shut down production. It was too late to prevent people from coming in to work, but once they were there we would explain the situation, if they hadn't already heard, and allow them to go back home.

Swerling called the production office and notified them of what to do when employees began to report for work. Then he and Dorothy went over to Ben Murphy's apartment and broke the news to him. As Swerling remembers it, "Ben's initial reaction was sort of strange. His first reaction was anger. He said, 'That damn son-of-a-bitch, I knew he'd pull something like this.' Then he got more sentimental. But his initial reaction was anger."

As the news of Duel's death spread across town, Swerling drove to Universal Studios where he met Huggins and Frank Price. A flurry of meetings between studio brass and ABC executives took place that morning. Roy Huggins wanted to cancel the show right then and there, but he was met with strong resistance.

As Swerling recalls:

> ABC said, "No way!" They said, "You have a contract to deliver this show to us, and you will continue to deliver the show as best you can on schedule or we will sue you." Hearing those words, Universal didn't hesitate for a second to instruct us to stay in production. We were already a little bit behind the eight ball on airdates. So we contacted everybody, including Ben, and told them to come back in. The entire company was reassembled and back in production by one o'clock that day shooting scenes that did not involve Peter — only twelve hours after his death.

The company was midway through production on an episode subtitled "The Biggest Game in the West," which had been scripted by Roy Huggins. The plot had Heyes and Curry acquiring a large satchel of counterfeit money that they then use to get into a high-stakes poker game. Director Alexander Singer had been helming the episode. He was on his way to the set when he learned what had happened. "I was driving early in the morning in the Hollywood Hills listening to the radio, and the news came on and there was a description of the suicide of one Peter Duel the night before," recalls Singer. "I pulled over to the side of the road and just stopped for a few minutes. It was too hard to pay attention to driving. I was going to be seeing him in a few minutes."

Singer then drove to the production office and waited until official word came down from the Black Tower, the Universal Studios administrative building. He was shocked when he learned that production was to commence immediately. "What we did that day was absolutely ghoulish and quite extraordinary," states Singer, "and we did it because we were ordered to do it." For the rest of the afternoon, the cast filmed whatever pick-up shots they could manage without Duel being there.

Recalls Singer:

> I got together with the crew and we moved like people underwater. Usually I was very aggressive in driving towards that first set-up and watching the clock and pushing everybody and making sure the next shot was prepared, but everybody worked as if we were in slow motion. Nobody said a word about it, but they knew that this was a particularly repellent gesture on the part of management. The day ended early and I went home, and I wondered what they would do. I assumed they would cancel the show and that would be the end of that. I got a call that weekend that they had recast the part with Roger Davis.

Roger Davis was one of those actors whose face was familiar without people being able to necessarily recall his name. He had supporting roles in a number of TV series, *The Gallant Men* (1962–63), *Redigo* (1963), and, most notably, a three-year stint from 1967 to 1970 on the gothic soap *Dark Shadows*.

Davis and Duel had a history together: Davis was originally cast as the lead in *Love on a Rooftop* but dropped out to do another pilot; the *Rooftop* gig then went to Duel. The two men then co-starred in Huggins' *The Young Country* pilot. Later, Davis had been an early contender for the role of Hannibal Heyes. Huggins, impressed with Davis' work in *The Young Country* opposite Duel, was ready to offer him the part. But Davis was on location in Acapulco starring in the pilot for an updated version of the late 1950s/early '60s adventure series *Adventures in Paradise* (being produced by Aaron Spelling) and therefore was not available to begin work on *Alias Smith & Jones*, once again abdicating a lead series role to Duel. Huggins did hire Davis to do the voice-over narration for the opening titles of the show, and even cast him as a villain in one episode ("Smiler with a Gun," 10/7/71).

Davis was on his way to Aspen on the afternoon of December 31, 1971, when Roy Huggins tracked him down. Davis recalls:

> I was switching planes in Denver to go to Aspen, and some security people from the airline were asking everybody if they were Roger Davis as we got off the plane. I was taken to a phone, and Roy told me that Pete had shot himself and asked me if I would come and replace him. I said, "Well, for how long?" because I was up for a picture at that point, the lead role, an important time for me. And he said, "Well, Roger, Pete has shot himself and he died. So you would have to consider this for some time into the future if the show is picked up." I owed Roy Huggins a big favor because he had done a lot for me. So I accepted on the basis of my loyalty to him.

On Sunday, January 2, 1972, a memorial service was held for Pete Duel at the Self-Realization Fellowship Lake Shrine in Los Angeles, attended by hundreds of co-workers and fans alike. Afterwards, Duel's body was flown back to Penfield, New York, for burial near his family's home.

The press was brutal in their criticism of how Universal and Roy Huggins had handled Duel's passing. As Swerling notes:

> When Pete's funeral was written up in the trades, we were pretty badly treated by the press. They thought we were morbid to be back in production. They forgot the old adage about how the show must go on. They didn't know what the essential facts were, so it was Huggins and I who got the

blame. We were like Simon Legree whipping the crew back to work on the same day. But like they said at Nuremberg, we were just following orders.

In hindsight, Swerling feels that Duel may very well have showed signs of being suicidal:

> None of us at the time had the slightest idea that he had any kind of suicidal tendencies. But people who are struggling with the idea of committing suicide are under a great deal of stress for a period of time, but once they make the decision to do it, it kind of lifts all that stress away. The decision's been made. Where maybe they had been depressed for a period of time, all of a sudden the depression appears to have gone away, and they're up and happy and kind of manic. You think that they're out of the depression, when in fact the next thing they're out of is the window. On that last episode that we never actually finished with him [#34, "The Biggest Game in the West"], we had several days of dailies that were in our opinion the best work he had done on the series.

The transition from Duel to Davis was literally overnight. Davis spent Saturday, January 1, 1972, at Western Costume Company with Swerling getting fitted for his period outfit, and then reported to the set on Monday morning where he assumed the role of Hannibal Heyes.

Instead of starting on a fresh episode, the decision was made to go back and complete the episode "The Biggest Game in the West." Explains Singer:

> We had two days of footage that we had already shot and we needed to salvage, but to do so we had to figure a way to work around Peter Duel's presence in those scenes. There was a particularly complex master scene that we had completed with Peter in it. Then we had to shoot close-ups of all the actors in the scene so we could cut away to them. When Roger came on board, we had to re-stage the scene and shoot close-ups of Roger to edit into the scene in place of Peter. So you'd see Roger in a close-up, then in the master you'd be seeing Peter's back.

The entire company was extremely affected by the situation. The following day, when the company broke for lunch, Singer headed over to watch dailies and suddenly found Davis walking along beside him.

"Can I walk with you to the projection room?" Davis asked.

"Sure," Singer replied. "How are you holding up?"

Davis just shrugged his shoulders. He had tears in his eyes.

"I have a feeling this is all going to work out," Singer assured him.

"I really love this part. I was up for it. I was one of the possibilities for the lead. When Peter got it I was very irritated, very annoyed. But I didn't want it this way."

Singer felt for Davis in those early days after Duel's death. "I don't think he ever got over the shock of stepping into the role the way he did," says Singer. "It was as though a ghost came attached to the role. He was fine, he recovered, but it was very hard because it's your nightmare, you get the part but the guy's dead."

Davis was trying to keep a positive attitude, despite his misgivings. Says Davis:

> It was very unusual and difficult to pick up and do the show from my perspective. Everyone was trying to convince me that everything would be fine, but I knew from the start that it was unlikely that everyone would just live happily ever after. A lot of people seemed to feel they had to take sides — to say, "Well, I liked Peter so I guess I can't like Roger Davis." But I did feel good about those first four episodes. I think we got some momentum going.

Since Ben Murphy was the only other regular cast member, it really fell to him whether to accept or reject Davis in the role of Heyes. Although Murphy and Duel had not been close

After the suicide of *Alias Smith & Jones* co-star Peter Duel late in the show's second season, actor Roger Davis assumed the role of reformed outlaw Hannibal Heyes. Above (left), he is pictured alongside Ben Murphy (courtesy ABC/Photofest).

friends off the set, Murphy took his co-star's death very hard. "It's a very difficult thing to pin a human being down," Murphy states of Duel. "He was very likable, very down-to-earth and human. Obviously he had his foibles or he wouldn't have committed suicide."

As for accepting Davis, Murphy explains:

> I liken it to rolling over in bed one day and your wife is gone and there is a new woman in bed. You're saying the same words to that person and you're trying to pretend it's the same feelings, but it's not. And that's what it was like for me as an actor to go to work. And it wasn't easy for Roger Davis because he had to be the new person.

With Davis in place, production was completed on that season's slate of new episodes. The series finished the year ranked 46th in the Nielsens. ABC saw enough potential in the teaming of Murphy and Davis that they renewed *Alias Smith & Jones* for a third season.

But there were definitely mixed messages being sent to the cast and crew as production started back up. On the one hand, ABC had ordered only 13 episodes for the coming season instead of a full-season order of 24. They also scheduled the series in a new timeslot, Saturday nights at 8:00 P.M. against the powerhouse *All in the Family*. Job security was certainly questionable for those involved with the series that fall. But on the other hand, Universal had agreed to up the budget significantly, allowing Huggins to move the entire production from the Universal back lot to Moab, Utah. The scenery there was beautiful; the price tag monumental.

Glen Larson left the show before the third season began to take a job as showrunner on NBC's *McCloud*, with Dennis Weaver. But Roy Huggins was more dedicated to the series than ever before. He personally wrote the plotlines for every episode that season, as well as writing the teleplays for many of them as well. Unfortunately, his efforts seemed to be in vain. The series kicked off its third season on the evening of Saturday, September 16, 1972. When the ratings were announced the following week, *Alias Smith & Jones* placed 65th out of 65 programs. It was the beginning of the end.

Even before the season had begun, ABC had made the decision to tinker with the show's timeslot. Every fourth week the network would preempt *Alias Smith & Jones* for an episode of *Kung Fu*, a new martial-arts drama that wouldn't premiere full-time until later that season.

As the weeks passed, ratings continued to fizzle. It was becoming clear that Saturday night television viewers were more interested in tuning in to Archie Bunker's antics than they were in Heyes and Curry's quest for clemency. By the time November sweeps ended, no additional episodes of *Alias Smith & Jones* had been ordered. ABC had concluded that the best way to compete with CBS's popular comedy line-up, which also included *The Mary Tyler Moore Show* and *Bob Newhart*, was to introduce a few comedies of their own.

The final original episode of *Alias Smith & Jones* aired on January 13, 1973 ("Only Three to a Bed"). Two weeks later, on January 27, two new half-hour comedies premiered in its place: *Here We Go Again*, with Larry Hagman, and *A Touch of Grace*, starring former *Hazel* lead Shirley Booth. ABC's strategy failed: neither program managed to attract much attention, and both were cancelled after 13 weeks.

Alias Smith & Jones co-stars Roger Davis (left) and Ben Murphy (center) are joined in this third-season publicity photo by guest star Frank Sinatra, Jr. (right) (courtesy ABC/Photofest).

Initially, many held out hope that *Alias Smith & Jones* might still have a future. Despite its low ratings in the United States, the series was a huge hit overseas, particularly in England. At one point, the BBC approached Universal with a proposal to continue production for first-run syndication. As a result, when the show first went on hiatus, all of the series' props were set aside in a storage trailer. The plan called for production to resume that summer in Spain. In the end, however, Universal opted out of the complicated venture, and the show was officially cancelled.

Few programs that end production with only 50 episodes are able to successfully compete in the syndication market. But *Alias Smith & Jones* developed a loyal cult following that has allowed it to play somewhat steadily in reruns for over thirty years. Sadly, when people think of the show, it's Duel's suicide that comes immediately to mind, a perpetual dark cloud that continues to overshadow an otherwise well-crafted, entertaining series.

Ben Murphy has managed to come to terms with that period in his life and career:

> My preference would be that Peter had not killed himself and that he'd be around to enjoy reminiscing about the show today. But once he killed himself, he was gone, and the chemistry was gone. I've never found that great a chemistry with another actor. When you do your first series, there's nothing like it. So maybe that kind of clouds it and makes me think how great it was. But I remember it as a lot of fun and a lot of hard work, and it was just an exciting time in my life.

Murphy *would* go on to star in a number of short-lived TV series: *Griff* (1973), *The Gemini Man* (1976), *The Chisholms* (1980), *Lottery* (1983), *Berrenger's* (1985), and *Dirty Dozen: The Series* (1988), but he would never recapture the potential success that *Alias Smith & Jones* once promised. Roger Davis made a number of prime-time guest appearances but never landed another regular series. He had better luck as a voice-over artist for commercials. He later turned to real estate, buying old properties, including homes in Beverly Hills and aging hotels, and made millions.

Alias Smith & Jones continues to play in syndication to the delight of its fan base. The show had come along at a transitional time in television history — when cowboys on TV were a dying breed. Despite its tumultuous run, the series earned a lasting place in television history alongside other classic westerns. Likewise, Pete Duel will be remembered by his fans as the eternally youthful, ever optimistic Hannibal Heyes, the outlaw with a wide grin and all his problems just a pardon away.

CHAPTER 3

Bonanza
Dan Blocker

In the fall of 1959 there were thirty western series on in prime time. The previous season, seven of the top-ten television programs had been westerns, and with good reason. They were being tailor-made for everyone: hours, half-hours, anthologies (*Zane Grey Theater*), straight dramas (*Gunsmoke*), those with humor (*Maverick*), and a few for the kids (*The Lone Ranger*). Even with the glut of westerns on the air at that time, they were still a network's best bet for achieving a hit.

Yet westerns were also increasingly under fire for the amount of violence they presented to viewers. Eager to protect their cash crop, network executives began looking for shows that portrayed less gunplay. Thus came the idea of the "domestic western." Not set in a sheriff's office or on the trail, this type of show was designed to portray families trying to survive in the Old West. In 1958, ABC had premiered *The Rifleman*, starring Chuck Connors as Lucas McCain, a former gunfighter turned family man, now a widowed father to a young son (Johnny Crawford). The show was an instant hit.

The following season NBC decided to follow suit by developing a family-themed western of its own. They turned to producer David Dortort (*Climax!*, *The Restless Gun*) to develop the project. Dortort's idea, *Bonanza*, was unusual in several ways. Besides being filmed in color during an era when few color TV sets were in use, the show's patriarch, Ben Cartwright, was a wealthy land baron presiding over his huge ranch, the Ponderosa, on the banks of Lake Tahoe in the 1860s. Such a character was traditionally the villain in most westerns. But Ben was a levelheaded, self-made man who ruled over his domain with a stern but righteous hand.

Ben had three grown sons: Adam, Hoss, and Little Joe. But like Lucas McCain, he was a widower raising his sons alone. It seemed nuclear families just didn't have a place in the Old West, usually at the expense of the women. Ben had actually been widowed on three occasions; each of his sons had a different mother. The three Cartwright boys had no more luck at achieving a long-term relationship than their father, as falling in love proved to be fatalistic for all of them during the series' run. The Ponderosa was littered with the graves of the women they'd loved.

Bonanza premiered on NBC on Saturday, September 12, 1959, at 7:30 P.M., during the family hour. Nestled among those other twenty-nine westerns, and scheduled opposite CBS's top-ten hit *Perry Mason*, *Bonanza* failed to make much of a dent in the ratings its first season. But the following year it landed at number 17, even with its formidable competition, causing NBC to note the show's potential.

For its third season, beginning in the fall of 1961, the show was moved to Sunday nights at 9:00 P.M. against less threatening competition, ABC's *Bus Stop* and CBS's combination of *G.E. Theater* and *The Jack Benny Show*. *Bonanza* finished the season as the number two show on television. It would remain there, a Sunday-night fixture, for the next nine years, never rating below tenth place for any season. From 1964 through 1967 it ranked as number one.

The show became a national phenomenon that drew families together one night a week. It also made superstars of its cast: Lorne Greene as Ben Cartwright; Pernell Roberts as oldest son Adam, college-educated and worldly; Dan Blocker as Eric, better known as "Hoss," a gentle giant of a man; and Michael Landon as "Little" Joe, the young, impulsive brother. The Cartwrights became like an extended family to millions of American TV viewers. The show still offered its share of violence, but it was significantly toned down. The storylines were a mixed bag. While often a serious western, the show had more than its share of comedic episodes. Hoss and Little Joe were usually at the root of those misadventures, while Adam, although intended as the voice of reason, would more often than not end up getting conned and roped into the situation as well.

It wasn't until the spring of 1972, after thirteen seasons, that events would unfold leading to *Bonanza*'s cancellation. Still a top-ten series at the time, the program fell victim to both network politics and a behind-the-scenes tragedy that shattered the happy Cartwright family and left viewers equally numb. Dan Blocker, dearly loved by viewers, died under tragic circumstances. Despite a valiant effort by the cast and crew to reassemble and continue the show, it seemed fate had finally turned against the Cartwrights themselves.

David Dortort's vision for a family western became one of television's all-time classic series of any genre. "It wasn't as much a western as it was a show about a family," explains Dortort. "I tried to keep violence to a minimum. I had to use it occasionally but not in a gratuitous sense. That is why entire families were able to watch."

Bonanza differed from most other series of the late '50s and early '60s because it was filmed in color. "There was relatively no color television at the time, it was a black and white world," laughs Dortort, "but I said I think color is coming out of the left. It's a little early in the game but I think it's the wave of the future." Initially, the network was dumbfounded by his request. "I knew I wanted to go to Lake Tahoe and shoot, and wanted to get all the splendid colors of the landscape," he explains. "Everybody who bought a color television set was automatically a viewer of our show."

The four leads — Greene, Roberts, Blocker, and Landon — fell into their respective roles seamlessly. From their very first scene together, they were completely believable as family. Dortort had personally cast each of them, and credits their performances as the key to *Bonanza*'s ongoing legacy.

Dortort's first job as both writer and producer was on the NBC western *The Restless Gun*, starring John Payne. Recalls Dortort:

> We had a young man named Michael Landon in the pilot, and somewhere in the first year I put a call out for some tall, rather large extras because I had a certain script in mind. Dan Blocker came in, walked right over to us and said he had to have this job. He and his wife and four children were living in a hotel room on Sunset Boulevard, had run out of resources and if he didn't find work immediately he was going to have to take them back to Texas, where he had a teaching job.

The original cast of NBC's long-running family-oriented western, *Bonanza*. Pictured from left: (front) Dan Blocker, Lorne Greene, (back) Michael Landon, Pernell Roberts (courtesy NBC/Photofest).

Blocker was born on December 10, 1929, in Texas and grew up in poverty. He weighed a whopping 14 pounds at birth, and by age 13, in 1942, he tipped the scales at 200 pounds. That year he joined the Texas Military Institute, and later graduated from Sul Ross State College. He had originally enrolled as a physical education major but switched to drama after landing a role in the play *Arsenic and Old Lace*. During the Korean War he was a non-commissioned officer who led a charge up Pork Chop Hill, an agonizing battle in which many of the men under his command were killed. When he returned to civilian life, he took a job as a high school teacher, but after a year he packed up his family (wife Dolphia, identical twin daughters Debra Lee and Danna Lynn, and sons David and Dirk) and headed for Hollywood. His first professional acting role was in an early episode of *Gunsmoke*. Soon afterward he had his fateful meeting with David Dortort.

Fortunately, Dortort saw something in the desperate young man that convinced him to give Blocker a break. "When we did the show I asked the cameraman and my director to get some close-ups of him, and he was wonderful," recalls Dortort. "So I told Dan, 'I can't promise you anything but I'll try to write some additional parts, next time maybe with some dialogue.'" Dortort kept his word, and Blocker began to appear semi-regularly on *The Restless Gun*.

The following season NBC hired Dortort to create a series of his own, and *Bonanza* was born. Even as he was developing the concept, Dortort was envisioning not only the beautiful Nevada landscape but also the actors he'd like to see riding against that backdrop. "When I wrote *Bonanza* I couldn't help but think of Michael and Dan. So I wrote the parts of Little Joe and Hoss with Michael and Dan in mind." Hoss's name was actually Eric, but Dortort wanted to give him a nickname that would reflect the personality of the character. "The show takes place in the middle of the 19th century, so I wanted something that would have actually been part of the vernacular of the era,

Dan Blocker spent thirteen years playing the gentle giant of a man, Hoss Cartwright, in NBC's classic western series *Bonanza*. His untimely death in the spring of 1972 greatly contributed to the program's cancellation the following season.

as well as something that would possess a slight note of respect to it."

Lorne Greene's authoritative voice had served him well in the 1940s as a commentator with the Canadian Broadcasting Company, updating listeners nightly about the war in Europe. He later moved to Hollywood and appeared in a number of supporting movie roles before shifting to television and being cast as Ben Cartwright. Pernell Roberts was a young unknown who'd made guest appearances on series such as *Sugarfoot* and *Have Gun, Will Travel*.

Over the years, *Bonanza* proved both a source of unending pride and constant frustration for Dortort. Few producers in Hollywood get to create a classic series. But winning the war in delivering *Bonanza* to the public each week meant that Dortort had to fight a series of unnerving smaller battles on a regular basis — some with the network, some with his cast. For the most part, the show's set was happy and harmonious, but inevitably obstacles would arise.

Dortort really enjoyed doing comedy, even after igniting a bit of controversy after submitting his first humor-filled script to NBC.

"This is a comedy," a shocked NBC executive pointed out.

"I realize that, so what?" Dortort replied.

"You can't do comedy."

"What do you mean I can't do comedy?"

"You're doing a western."

"Oh, and westerns can't have comedy? I'm producing the number one show in the world; don't tell me what to do."

Dortort laughs at the brassy comment made some forty-five years earlier. "Fortunately, I had the sponsor to back me up. Chevrolet loved the comedies. General Motors loved them. After all, we were all trying to reach those families. I had a very happy relationship with the sponsors."

But Dortort also had to deal with occasional uprisings from the cast as well. As he explains:

> I had some problems with Lorne in the beginning. He was a Canadian and he had been broadcasting out of the Canadian Broadcasting Company, delivering a news program during the beginning of World War II when the Germans were invading Europe. He would come on and he was known as the Voice of Doom. With his deep, serious voice he could be a little scary, and loud. Then when he came on the *Bonanza* set he was using the same voice.

"Lorne, you don't have to shout."

"I don't shout."

"Well then, let me put it this way, you put more volume into it than is necessary. See that little microphone over your head, that can pick up any sound, even a little sigh, so speak a little more softly."

But Greene had trouble adapting. Continues Dortort:

> So one day I got so angry with him that I stopped production and took him to the projection room. We ran some dailies, and he could see that he was coming through like a shouting madman. I said, "See what you sound like, you don't have to yell like that." Well, then he lowered his voice so that it was barely a whisper, so I was back to square one. It took awhile, but he eventually adjusted. He had exceptional warmth as an actor, especially in terms of his relationship with Michael Landon.

Landon was the youngest member of the cast, only twenty-two when the series began production. He was also a lot like his character — impulsive, eager, and perhaps a little cocky. But he was also extremely talented and anxious to learn the craft of television production — not just acting, but also producing, writing, and directing. He wanted to do it all. For Landon, the set of *Bonanza* became more of a home than a workplace, with the cast and crew his adoptive family.

Eventually, Landon wasn't satisfied with simply acting. As Dortort remembers:

> First he wanted to write. He asked me if he wrote a script if I'd read it, and I told him of course I would. So he writes this script that is 28 pages long [an average script for an hour-long program is 60 pages.] I said, "Michael, it's an hour-long show; you've only written half an episode, so you haven't told an entire story here." So I began to teach him, to coach him, even how to spell properly. You don't want people to see you can't spell these simple words, you have to have more pride in yourself, and he took it well. So I let him write a couple of scripts.

Writing kept Landon at bay for a few years, but soon he was once again knocking on Dortort's door. This time he asked for a chance to direct. Dortort wasn't surprised. He knew how driven Landon was, and knew that the young man needed to continue growing creatively:

> When he came to me and said he wanted to direct, I had already been watching him. He had spent a lot of time observing and learning, and there wasn't an aspect of production he didn't understand. I said, "OK, I'll let you direct under this condition: I hire one of our regular directors and he will be there and will be paid his full salary. If he feels at any point you're not cutting it, you're not doing it right, that there is something lacking, he will either tell you what he thinks or

suggest a whole new way of doing it." I had a very fine director, William Claxton, stand there and give him a couple of insights. But Michael knew all about the camera, he knew about everything involving the cameraman and the director. He had really learned the process. So he wrote, directed, and acted for me.

By the end of the series' run, Landon would add producing to his list of talents. Although not officially credited as such, it was no secret that Landon pretty much ran *Bonanza* the final two seasons it was on the air. He and William Claxton would begin a collaboration that would include Landon's two follow-up hit series: *Little House on the Prairie* and *Highway to Heaven*.

Dealing with Pernell Roberts, on the other hand, proved to be a much more difficult proposition. Besides being upset with the quality of the show's scripts, Roberts felt the show was holding him back, preventing him from becoming a big-screen leading man. He often asked Dortort and NBC to release him from his contract, but they'd refuse, afraid his departure might upset the program's chemistry.

Says Dortort:

Pernell Roberts, when he wanted, could be brilliant; but when he did not want to be, he would sort of walk through the entire process. Pernell was the last one I cast. I was still shooting *The Restless Gun* at Republic, and he was shooting a *Wagon Train*. I went down to the set to look at him. They were doing a fencing scene. I remember he had all this big black hair, a handsome guy, and he seemed to move beautifully and handle himself very well. So I told him about the show and he was agreeable. I was really happy because I finally had my cast.

But a week later Dortort got his first taste of what was to come. Roberts came into his office one afternoon and confronted the producer.

"You know, this thing on my head, I don't want to wear it," Roberts stated.

"What are you talking about," Dortort asked.

Roberts yanked a hairpiece off his head, and suddenly Dortort was staring at a man who appeared twenty years older. He was shocked.

"When I cast you," Dortort protested, "you were wearing that piece, and it makes you look good. As long as you're doing this show you must wear it."

So started the war.

Roberts has been notoriously tight-lipped over the years about the circumstances surrounding his departure from *Bonanza*. When he did speak, it was to express his dissatisfaction with the scripts and with his character. He once described Adam Cartwright as a "middle-aged teenager" still living at home, dependent on his father for financial support and fearful of confronting him when things went wrong. When his contract finally expired in 1965, Roberts refused to re-sign and departed the show, giving up millions of dollars in future earnings.

Dortort remembers it differently. He alleges it all finally came to a head one evening during *Bonanza*'s sixth season. As Dortort tells it, his wife had just called the production office to remind him they had a dinner reservation, and he assured her he'd be home by seven o'clock. Just as he hung up the phone, it rang again. It was an assistant calling to say there was a problem and he was needed on the set immediately.

The cast and crew were assembled on the backlot at Paramount. Dortort had chosen Paramount as the location because it was one of the few backlots at the time that contained a western set that was at least two stories high, and Virginia City had been the largest Metropolis west of the Mississippi. (Today, Paramount is one of the few studios without a backlot.)

It was a cold and windy February evening in 1965.

With the departure of co-star Pernell Roberts after six seasons, actor David Canary was added to the cast of NBC's hit western *Bonanza* as ranch hand "Candy" Canaday. Pictured from left: Canary, Dan Blocker, Lorne Greene, Michael Landon (courtesy David and Maureen Canary).

Laughs Dortort:

I had always said if it's a small problem don't call me, just work it out. If it's a big problem I'll come down. So it's a big problem. I come down and there's a disagreement over some lines of dialogue between Michael and Lorne. Michael would sometimes tease Lorne; he'd say, "You don't want to read lines like that, Lorne." This particular night, Michael had such a problem. He was insisting Lorne read a line a certain way, but Lorne was happy with his delivery and didn't want to change it. When I got there I went right up to Michael and said, "Why are you doing this, why are you making such a problem with everybody?" He said, "Why do you feel I'm doing that?" I answered, "Because you know you're doing it, you know you are." Anyway, it was like a family, everybody knew how to push everyone else's buttons. By the time I got through handholding and babysitting this crowd it's close to midnight. I'd missed dinner and I was cold.

Just as Dortort was about to leave the set, Pernell grabbed his arm and said he needed to speak to him.

"OK, what do you want to talk about," Dortort responded.

"Why are you holding me back?"

"Wait a minute, wait a minute. Are you going to give me that again?"

"Sure I'm going to give you that again."

"You say I'm holding you back, from what?"

"I could be making movies if it weren't for this show."

Frustrated, cold, and hungry, Dortort stared at Roberts for a moment, then said calmly, "You know, Pernell, I've heard this now for so many years. As of this minute, you are free to go wherever you like. I don't even want you back."

"You don't mean that," Roberts responded.

"I've never meant anything more in my life," Dortort insisted.

Dortort left the set. The next morning he received a call from Roberts' agent at the William Morris Agency.

"Pernell says that you let him off the show," the agent said urgently.

"Yes, I did," Dortort responded.

"Why did you do it?"

"Because I don't want to be reminded again that I'm holding back his career."

Roberts' agent asked Dortort to take him back for the remainder of the season, perhaps in the hope that during that period they would be able to work out their differences. There were only six more episodes of *Bonanza* to film that spring.

Explains Dortort:

I said on one condition — that he not tell me that he wants to be the biggest star in Hollywood. He agreed to that, we did the six shows, and we said goodbye. He really did have potential and could have been a very, very big star. I think he made a terribly foolish mistake. He should have listened to me. This was only the end of the sixth year; we went on for eight more, with big salary increases each year. He could have been independently wealthy.

Whichever version actually played out that spring, Pernell Roberts left *Bonanza*. He continued to work regularly in television, making guest appearances. In 1979 he returned to the weekly grind as the title character of CBS's *Trapper John, M.D.*, which ran for seven seasons.

Dortort thought very highly of the entire cast, but felt Dan Blocker was the foundation of *Bonanza*. He found him to be an honest, decent person and a dedicated family man. He could, at the same time, be a man of many excesses and extremes.

Recalls Dortort:

There was one incident in the early '70s. We always started the season up in Lake Tahoe before the tourists came so I could get the hotel spaces. Dan didn't like to fly, so he drove up. This particular spring he arrived in a brand new Lamborghini. He was fond of racing cars, and sat with the guys at the Indianapolis Speedway. So he comes up in this gorgeous, fire engine-red sports car. I told him how much I admired it and he said, "Well, boss, let's take a ride." So I said ok and got in the car. Now you have to realize that the roads around Lake Tahoe are very narrow and wind-ing, and there we were in this Lamborghini. We hit those curves and all the tires would squeal, we were making a horrible racket. We were going ninety miles an hour, which was like nothing in this car.

"I said, 'Dan, you better slow down.'"

"Why?"

"Because you're driving way over the speed limit, that's why. We start shooting tomor-row; I don't want to be in some jail."

"Oh, don't worry."

"What do you mean, don't worry? You're crazy, you're risking both of our lives, and dis-turbing the peace of all these people with their lakeside homes. Slow down, slow down!"

But Blocker was too caught up in the moment. He was like a big kid with a shiny new toy. Then Dortort noticed the flashing red lights in the rear view mirror.

"Now you're going to get it. I told you to slow down," he chastised Blocker.

But even then Dan refused to slow down. Soon he and Dortort's scenic drive around Lake Tahoe had turned into a high-speed police pursuit. Dortort panicked.

"For God's sake, what are you trying to do?"

"Don't worry, boss."

Finally, a few miles down the road, Blocker pulled over. The cops roared up behind them, jumped out of their cruiser and began approaching the car with their guns drawn.

Dortort continues:

They were so angry you wouldn't believe it. We rolled the windows down, and one of them starts giving Dan the business, every blue word in the book. And Dan just said, "Oh, I'm sorry, officers. I just wanted to show my boss here my new wheels. He's David Dortort, the man who produces *Bonanza*." And the cop looks at him and says, "What?" And then he looks at Dan and says, "Hoss!" And you had to be there to believe it. This cop went from angry and belligerent and almost to the point of violence to soft spoken and apologetic. He said, "Oh, sorry, we just got so many complaints from people. Can you slow down a little?" They let us go. So we start to drive back and Dan says, "I told you not to worry." He was off the hook.

Blocker's excesses sometimes concerned Dortort:

Dan was a great eater and also a great drinker. I remember once having breakfast with him, and for breakfast he had a big T-bone steak and a six-pack of beer. He was carrying a lot of weight. One year he weighed about 280 and was about 6'4"; he was a big man. Then he and his wife went to Italy, and he came back about fifty pounds heavier. I said, "Dan, what did you do to yourself?" He said, "Boss, that pasta, I ate my way from the top of Italy to the bottom."

Blocker's doctor finally warned him that if he didn't lose some weight and drastically change his lifestyle, he could be facing some major health problems in the future. He was already experiencing problems with his gallbladder that would eventually require surgery.

Young actor Mitch Vogel had been added to the cast of *Bonanza* in 1970 as Jamie Hunter, a young orphan taken in by the Cartwrights. Eventually, Ben adopted him. Vogel and Blocker shared an interest in playing snooker, a variation on pool. Blocker had a snooker table at his house and would sometimes invite Vogel over to play. Vogel recalls:

One night he invited me over, and he was on a diet because his doctor told him he needed to start losing weight. As we played he had this large bowl nearby full of green Jell-O, and next to that he had a six-pack of club sodas. That was his diet. I remember him munching on it that night as we played. He was serious, though, about losing weight.

During *Bonanza*'s twelfth season, actor Mitch Vogel joined the cast as Ben Cartwright's adopted son Jamie. Pictured from left: Michael Landon, Lorne Greene, Dan Blocker, Mitch Vogel (courtesy NBC/Photofest).

Blocker was the same caring and dependable friend off-screen as Hoss was onscreen. Wally McCleskey was a native Texan who, like Blocker, had come to Hollywood to work in the entertainment industry. McCleskey worked as a stand-in and extra on *Bonanza* for many years, and became a close friend of Blocker's. Perhaps one thing that drew them together, at least initially, may have been their excessive intake of alcohol.

McCleskey credits Blocker with saving his life. States McCleskey:

Dan got me off whiskey in 1972. Dan drank a lot of whiskey, something like three fifths a day. But all of a sudden he just quit. I was still drinking, and at one point I was drunk for almost three months, day and night. One day I'm sitting at a bar, and in walks Sunshine Parker, an old pal of Dan's who'd been staying with him. I could see that Dan's big old Mercedes Benz was parked out there in the loading zone, and I said, "What the hell are you doing here, boy?" Shine said, "Dan wants to see you." I thought, "Oh shit, I'd rather see a gorilla than see Dan right now." Shine grabbed my arm and said, "Well, come on, goddammit, Dan said if I didn't find you then I can't come back. And shit, I ain't gonna have no place to live if you don't come along."
    So I went with him, I went up there and I walked up those old steps. Dan lived in this big old two-story house. I walked in and Dan is standing there in the door. He always wore an old pair of engineer's overalls and an engineer's cap. And his shoulders were hairy and he looked just like a goddamn gorilla with a cap on. He was standing there with his hands on his hips looking down at me, and he says, "Well, you silly son-of-a-bitch, have you figured out you can't drink at all?" I said, "Dan, I tried my best." He said, "Come in here." He knew I was in bad shape. I was shaking, I was really bad.

Blocker was preparing to leave for Switzerland, where he planned to meet with actor Kirk Douglas and purchase a script that the *Spartacus* actor owned based on the acclaimed best-selling novel *One Flew Over the Cuckoo's Nest*. Blocker planned to produce and star in the film version during his hiatus from *Bonanza,* playing the lead role of Randle Patrick Murphy (which would eventually land Jack Nicholson an Oscar in 1976). Explains McClesky, "He said he had a part for me as an Indian," but added, "you have to get over the goddamn whiskey. While I'm gone, you stay here in the house and get straight. He looked at Sunshine and said, 'You better keep this son-of-a-bitch in the house until I get back.'" Blocker's family was already in Switzerland at the time. He was flying to Paris and then going on to join them.
    McCleskey continues:

He was on a big diet because he had to lose a lot of weight to have a gallbladder operation. For two goddamn weeks I walked the floor. I wanted to drink so bad I couldn't stand it. But I said, "No, I told Dan I wouldn't." And sure enough I didn't. When he got home I was about halfway over the shakes and I could eat a little. He told me that while he was flying over there that Michael Douglas was talking to his Daddy in Paris, and Kirk told him he was selling the script to Dan Blocker, and Michael said, "No, keep it, I want to do it myself." So by the time Dan got to Paris, Kirk had changed his mind and let Michael have it. And sure enough, Michael made it and made a ton of money off it. But Dan got me to go straight during that period.

Losing his opportunity to produce and star in *One Flew Over the Cuckoo's Nest* was a big blow for Blocker. He had confided in McCleskey and others close to him that he feared *Bonanza* was nearing the end of its run. The studio had recently bought out all of the actors' rerun residuals. That meant they were in the early stages of preparing the series for syndication. FCC regulations in place at that time stated that a series could not enter syndication until it had ended its network run. For Blocker, it was a clear signal that the end of the series was at hand, and he was concerned about what was next. *Bonanza* had supplied him with a steady and sizeable paycheck for thirteen years, had allowed him to move his family into a mansion, and had provided his children with the very best of everything. That was important to Blocker, who'd grown up in near-poverty.
    He did have two aces up his sleeve. He had a project in development titled *The Wilson Boys*, and had landed the role of Roger Wade in the upcoming Robert Altman film *The Long Goodbye* (Sterling Hayden would eventually play the part). Altman had directed some early

episodes of *Bonanza*, and he and Blocker had remained friends. And, of course, *Bonanza*, for the time being, was still on NBC's schedule. It had been renewed for the upcoming 1972–73 season.

But first on Blocker's agenda was his health. Blocker had managed to lose twenty-five pounds before entering the hospital to have his gallbladder removed in early May of 1972. The surgery was elective at the time, but he was in a lot of pain and wanted to get it over with before production began on the new season of *Bonanza*.

The surgery went smoothly. McCleskey and Sunshine Parker visited Blocker in the hospital in the days afterward. States McCleskey:

> He was in the hospital for nine days and had the finest surgeon in the country. That was before they had that system where they could go in there and bust that thing up with lasers. They had to go in there and cut a hell of a gash across his stomach. Well, Shine and me went up there a few days later to see him, and when we walked in the door, he looked at us and said, "You son-of-a-bitch, don't you tell me no goddamn jokes, I can't laugh." I saw that scar across his stomach, it was a big one. He wanted them to do a check on his liver while they were in there because of all the drinking he'd done over the years, and his liver was perfect. But it left a hell of a scar. After nine days he came home, and that next night I went over to see him and he looked fine; his cheeks were shiny and he looked like a brand new baby.

But later that night Blocker began having trouble breathing. His condition continued to worsen until finally, early on the morning of May 13, 1972, his wife Dolphia rushed him to the emergency room. Dan passed out in the car on the way. In the ER, doctors tried to track down the cause of his breathing difficulties. Only too late did they realize a blood clot had formed, most likely as a result of his surgery, and traveled to his lungs. He was rushed into surgery, but it was too late. Dan Blocker died of heart failure before doctors could remove the clot. Blocker was 43 years old.

Later that morning, Wally McCleskey again made his way slowly up the front steps of the Blocker home. He was still in shock. Inside, family, friends and colleagues had gathered. Lorne Greene and Dolphia Blocker sat together in the breakfast nook. Greene was devastated and couldn't stop crying. The only person missing that day was Michael Landon, and everyone understood why. Landon had difficulty expressing his feelings openly, a result of his troubled childhood. He and Dan had been like the brothers they'd portrayed onscreen for so many years. Landon had to deal with his feelings privately.

Blocker was later interred at DeKalb Cemetery in his home state of Texas.

A mere three weeks later the cast and crew of *Bonanza* reassembled at Lake Tahoe to begin work on the show's fourteenth season. There was never any doubt that production would continue without Blocker. Everyone involved with the show had become like family, and they needed each other now more than ever. Originally, the first episode scheduled to be shot was subtitled "Forever," and was a poignant episode in which Hoss fell in love and was married, only to have his fiancée brutally murdered. The normally sweet and gentle Hoss was then to go on a rampage and track down her killers. Michael Landon had written and was going to direct the episode. But after Blocker's passing, another script was substituted to allow Landon time to go back and rewrite "Forever." In the revised version, it was Joe who would lose his young bride. Landon also wrote the loss of Hoss into the episode. It was never explained just how Hoss had died, only that Ben and Joe were still dealing with his death.

Going back to work without Blocker did prove to be difficult. The first episode to be shot in place of "Forever" was "The 26th Grave," guest starring actor Ken Howard (*Manhunter, The White Shadow*). Remembers Howard:

> I got there and it was the first show of the season after Dan Blocker died. We shot the episode, and Michael Landon was really funny, he just had this wonderful humor about everything, kidding me about this mustache I was wearing and how I was trying not to scrunch my upper lip. He just made everybody laugh all the time. We finished the episode, and I had a really wonderful time with him. And when it was over, Michael got up and gave a speech, and he broke down during it. What he was saying to this group, to this crew that had been together forever, was that we all know it's not the same, and never will be. And that's when he lost it and his voice broke. That was the first time that they'd been together after Dan died, and it was very moving and very touching, and I felt like I was part of a piece of history—and sadly so. There were jokes and stories and this wonderful sort of acknowledgement of the man who wasn't there.

To help take up some of the slack left by Blocker's absence, Landon first called actor David Canary. Canary had become a regular on *Bonanza* in 1967 after then-producer Robert Blees felt the show was beginning to become a bit repetitive. He wanted to shake things up a bit by adding a new character. Canary was added as a rough ranch hand, "Candy" Canaday. "They brought me on just to give one other facet to the story," explains Canary, "that of a hot-headed guy who loved to get into fights and didn't like to talk as much as he liked to hit." Canary clicked with viewers and remained with the series until 1970, when he left the show after the producers refused to grant him a pay raise.

Landon asked Canary to return to the show as Candy. Landon told Canary he'd see to it that he was given the raise he'd been denied two years earlier when he left the show. That never happened, but Canary didn't care. He was just happy to be back.

Joining Greene, Landon, Vogel, and Canary that year was actor Tim Matheson, who was brought in to play new ranch hand Griff King. Matheson got off to a bad start. He explains:

> I made a horrible tactical mistake when I came on the show. *TV Guide* interviewed me about the state of westerns, and being sort of a green show-biz kid, I said, "*Bonanza* is of the older generation of shows, and it's time for a new generation of shows." And I was quoted saying something like that in the fall premiere issue of the magazine, and immediately got a call directly from Michael Landon, who was very upset because I was speaking in disparaging tones in public about *Bonanza*, which was not very bright. Once Michael took a position on something he never changed his mind. He was always cordial to me, but he was never very open to me after that. I learned a lot from making a stupid remark like that in the press. Michael was right to feel the way he did, but he wasn't very forgiving.

Trouble continued to plague Matheson while on location at Lake Tahoe:

> I do remember Lorne had a huge Mercedes, a big, old, long, semi-stretch Mercedes that he drove, and I remember it being parked at the motel where we all stayed. And I thought, "A Mercedes, wow!" It had one of those little hood ornaments that's flexible, on a wire, so in case they get bumped they don't get broken. I went to play with it one time as I walked by, and it broke off. I went, "Oh my God! I've broken Lorne Greene's hood ornament. Shit." So I took it and I balanced it back up on the hood. I can imagine him getting in and slamming the door and the thing falling over. I never told him. Joining the show was tough, but it was a fun experience.

As the cast and crew of *Bonanza* struggled to move forward, forces were at work against them. As Dan Blocker had suspected weeks before his death, NBC was eager to get the show into syndication. The network also seemed to agree with Matheson's assessment that the series was aging, although it had ranked number 10 in the seasonal Nielsen ratings the previous year.

By that time, Michael Landon was running the day-to-day operations of *Bonanza* as an un-credited producer. During shooting, if Landon saw something in the script he didn't like, he'd simply shut down production and retreat to his office to personally rewrite it while the cast and crew waited. He utilized a great deal of outdoor location filming to give the show a more realistic feel, and also exercised a free hand in developing storylines more in tune with the early '70s, including drug addiction ("The Hidden Enemy," 11/28/72), spousal abuse ("First Love," 12/26/72), and mental illness ("The Hunter," 1/16/73).

Before the 1972-73 season began, NBC delivered another huge blow to the show when it announced it was moving *Bonanza* out of the Sunday night 9:00 P.M. timeslot it had occupied for the past eleven years and placing it on Tuesdays at 8:00 P.M. Among its new competition would be *Maude* and *Hawaii Five-O*, two of those "new generation" shows the networks were then embracing. In another blow, *Bonanza* lost its long-time sponsor General Motors. As expected, when the show bowed that fall on Tuesdays, the ratings plummeted. Still, the show had been so good to NBC for so many years that those involved felt certain that the network would weather the storm with them.

Then one eventful afternoon in October, early in *Bonanza*'s fourteenth season, co-star Mitch Vogel was at home in Burbank unloading things from the trunk of his family's car. Just a teen, Vogel was mostly unaware of the backstage problems plaguing the show. Despite the loss of Blocker, he'd been very happy with the direction the series had taken that season. Ben had adopted his character Jamie, so Vogel was now officially a Cartwright. Several episodes had been written specifically for his character. An episode was even in the planning stages in which Jamie was to get his first gun, a sign of manhood in the Old West.

Then someone tapped him on the shoulder.

"Are you Mitch Vogel?" the man asked.

Vogel was handed a Western Union telegram. He opened it there in the driveway and learned that *Bonanza* had been cancelled. He immediately called the production office to verify the news. At the studio, Dortort, producer Richard Collins, and Landon had just received the news. Lewis Allen, a frequent director on the series, was also on hand. He'd been there doing prep work for the following week's episode.

Landon took it upon himself to drive out to the location where the crew was busy shooting the season's fifteenth episode, subtitled "The Marriage of Theodora Duffy," with guest stars Karen Carlson and David Soul. The episode revolved around Matheson's character Griff King and his make-believe marriage to an undercover government agent (Carlson) in order to lure in a gang of outlaws. They were busy filming scenes at an exterior location where Matheson and Carlson had set up housekeeping when Landon arrived.

"Well they did it, they pulled the plug," Landon announced. "This is the last episode of *Bonanza*."

Landon returned a short time later, accompanied by members of the press. He praised the series and the years of hard work that had gone into it. "It was really sad," remembers Matheson, "because all these people had been together so long and had become like a family."

After thirteen-and-a-half seasons and 430 episodes (including the two-hour "Forever"), *Bonanza* ended its original run on the evening of Tuesday, January 16, 1973, with the episode subtitled "The Hunter" (which was the next-to-last episode filmed). Perhaps appropriately, the episode had been written and directed by Michael Landon, and guest-starred Tom Skerritt. It contained very little dialogue and was basically a character study of two men: Skerritt as an insane war veteran hunting down Joe Cartwright (by this time he was no longer "Little Joe") through the desert. Landon and Skerritt were the only two actors with significant roles: a hunter and his prey, neither of whom spoke to one another, only engaging in a desperate game of cat and mouse. When it faded out, so did the saga of the Cartwright family.

Future attempts would be made to revise *Bonanza* in the form of made-for-TV movies, but never with the original cast.

Lorne Greene had just signed to return as Ben Cartwright in a reunion movie when he died of pneumonia on September 11, 1987. His daughter Gillian joined Michael Landon, Jr., in the TV-movie *Bonanza: The Next Generation* (4/20/88), while Landon, Jr., and Dirk Blocker, son of Dan Blocker, appeared together in two more small-screen revival efforts, *Bonanza: The Return* (11/28/93) and *Bonanza: Under Attack* (1/15/95). In 2001 the PAX network brought the original characters back to life in a new series called *Ponderosa*, on which Dortort served as an executive producer and consultant. In that series, a young Ben Cartwright (Daniel Hugh-Kelly) and his three sons, Adam (age 21), Hoss (age 17), and Joe (age 12), first settle on the Ponderosa ranch. The show lasted only a single season.

After *Bonanza* left the air in 1973, Lorne Greene continued to act in both movies (*Earthquake*) and series television (*Battlestar Galactica*). In 1986 he reunited with Michael Landon in an episode of Landon's *Highway to Heaven*. Landon starred in two more long-running series, *Little House on the Prairie* and *Highway to Heaven*, both for NBC. When his *Highway* co-star Victor French was diagnosed with terminal cancer at the beginning of the series' fifth year, Landon closed the series down rather than continue without him. Landon had just shot the pilot for another series, *Us,* when he was diagnosed with cancer himself in 1990. He died on July 1, 1991. Pernell Roberts remains the lone surviving original cast member of *Bonanza,* but he still refuses to discuss the series. The other actors live on, however, through *Bonanza,* which has run continually in syndication all over the world for more than thirty years.

CHAPTER 4

Cheers
Nicholas Colasanto

When 30-year-old Brandon Tartikoff was handed the reigns of NBC Entertainment in 1980, the network was floundering. What few hits they had, including *Little House on the Prairie* and *CHiPs*, were beginning to age, and new titles such as *Supertrain*, *BJ and the Bear*, and *Hello, Larry* were being panned by critics and ignored by viewers. Two years after Tartikoff took over, the network was still struggling. During the 1981-82 season, NBC failed to place a single program in the Nielsen top-twenty.

The Yale-educated Tartikoff had joined NBC as a programming executive in 1977, and in 1980 succeeded Fred Silverman at the head of the table. There was tremendous pressure on the young man to fix NBC's broken prime-time schedule. He realized he had to act fast or would be out the door. The strategy Tartikoff chose was to rebuild NBC as the home of quality television. Instead of looking for new shows that would become runaway hits straight out of the gate and dumping everything else, Tartikoff decided to cultivate more upscale series, then step back and allow them time to develop a following. While high-octane projects like *Knight Rider* and *The A-Team* would continue to fuel NBC, the network would soon be able to boast of such titles as *St. Elsewhere*, *Family Ties*, *Fame*, and *Remington Steele*.

In the spring of 1982, NBC made a surprise move by picking up the Emmy-winning comedy *Taxi* after ABC unceremoniously dumped the series after its fourth season. The network then proceeded to sign two of the program's Emmy-winning writers, Glen and Les Charles, to an exclusive development deal. The brothers had honed their talents on such classic comedies as *The Mary Tyler Moore Show* and *Bob Newhart*. Tartikoff offered them creative autonomy to create and produce a sitcom, and guaranteed them a full season on the air. The result was *Cheers*.

The concept for *Cheers* was decidedly simple, exploring the interactions of the employees and patrons of a sports-themed Boston pub called Cheers. Ted Danson was cast as the bar's owner, Sam Malone, a former pitcher for the Boston Red Sox and a recovering alcoholic notorious for his womanizing. Shelley Long landed the co-lead as Diane Chambers, a graduate student who, in the pilot episode, is jilted by her fiancé and must take a job waiting tables at Cheers until she can pull her life back together. The sexual chemistry between Sam and Diane would be the cornerstone upon which much of the comedy would be built.

Rounding out the supporting cast of *Cheers* was Rhea Perlman as acid-tongued waitress Carla Tortelli, and character actors George Wendt and John Ratzenberger, as Norm Peterson and Cliff Clavin, two barflies who spent more time at Cheers than at their own homes.

The sole remaining character that needed to be cast was bartender Ernie Pantusso, fondly known to the gang at Cheers as "Coach." He was to be *Cheers*' "dumb" character — dimwitted but loveable, and admirable for the honest, naive way he approached life. Coach was Sam

The original cast of the NBC comedy *Cheers*, clockwise from left: John Ratzenberger, Nicholas Colasanto, Rhea Perlman, George Wendt, Shelley Long, Ted Danson (courtesy NBC/Photofest).

Malone's best friend, a pillar of his support system. He'd been a former pro baseball coach and manager. But whereas Sam was still having trouble letting go of his glory days, Coach was happy with his life at Cheers, glad to have friends and a place to go each day at his age. Many well-known comedic actors tested for the role before Nicholas Colasanto walked through the door.

It was Colasanto, the consummate veteran, who would prove an inspiration to his young costars with his determined attitude during *Cheers'* low-rated early seasons. Later, he would demonstrate even greater courage and strength as he battled declining health in an attempt to continue doing what he loved most — performing.

Colasanto was born in Providence, Rhode Island, on January 19, 1924, one of seven children. He dropped out of high school and joined the Navy during World War II, and was awarded a number of medals for service in Europe and Africa. He left the military after the war ended in 1945 and continued his education, eventually earning a degree from Bryant College and becoming an accountant. In his late twenties he became enamored of acting and began doing local theater in Phoenix, Arizona, where he'd relocated. He later returned to New York, where he excelled at both acting in and directing off–Broadway plays (including *A Hatful of Rain*). He also earned a reputation for being a prominent acting coach.

In 1965 friend Ben Gazzara coaxed Colasanto into moving to Los Angeles with an offer to direct an episode of Gazzara's NBC TV series *Run for Your Life*. More work soon followed. In '68 Colasanto's name appeared on a list of possible directors handed to veteran Hollywood producer Dean Hargrove, who was then overseeing a show called *The Name of the Game*. Colasanto got the job, and he and Hargrove became close friends.

Hargrove, a prolific producer, would often call upon Colasanto when looking for a director. This led to Colasanto landing two choice assignments on the high-profile '70s detective series *Columbo*, with Peter Falk. The first of the *Columbo*s was subtitled "Etude in Black" (9/17/72), which cast avant-garde director John Cassavettes as a murderous maestro. Recalls Hargrove:

> Cassavettes was particularly uncooperative during that episode, and if it weren't for Nick the show wouldn't have gotten done. First of all, Nick knew acting very well, and he always cast excellent actors and knew how to work with them, which is at least half the battle. Secondly, Nick had an extremely strong visual sense, and his shows always had a very definitive look.

One interesting side note to "Etude in Black" is that many viewers believed that Nicholas Colasanto was merely a pseudonym adopted by Cassavettes when he directed for television. The rumor was particularly prevalent in Europe, where to this day many hard-line Cassavettes fans still refute that Nicholas Colasanto was ever a living, breathing human being. Despite the production turmoil, "Etude in Black" became one of *Columbo*'s most noted episodes, as was Colasanto's other *Columbo* venture, "Swan Song" (3/3/74), with guest villain Johnny Cash.

Hargrove also employed Colasanto as an actor:

> He appeared in a short film I directed called *The Home Movie*. He also did a pilot I shot in 1976 called *The World's Greatest Detective*, starring Larry Hagman. Nick was playing a nervous police detective, and on the set he would occasionally have difficulty memorizing his dialogue. Once, we were outside and losing our sun, and I wanted him to be nervous in the scene, so I took away his cue cards and told him he had to get the scene right before we lost the sun. This made Nick extremely anxious, and it played that way in the scene and was quite hilarious.

Although Colasanto was primarily known for his dramatic acting, Hargrove was able to recognize the full range of his talent. "It wasn't until he landed the role on *Cheers* that he was really given credit for his comedic skills," offers Hargrove. "ABC rejected Nick for a pilot I was doing a few years before he started *Cheers* because they didn't think he was funny." As for his expertise behind the camera, Hargrove recognized Colasanto's abilities early on. "He actually preferred to direct," explains Hargrove. "In fact, one of the things that always amused me was when we would bring actors in to read for parts, I would invariably wind up watching Nick rather than the actor who was auditioning because he was so compelling."

Colasanto was clearly talented, but at the same time very demanding on the set. He was a hard drinker and had a bad temper, which, when compounded by his fierce desire to do things his own way, branded him as difficult in the eyes of many producers. Hargrove is quick to jump to his defense:

> Nick was a colorful guy. I don't believe his drinking was a problem in as much as it never interfered with his work. But sometimes Nick had very definite opinions about what he wanted as a director, and he would occasionally run into conflicts with crew members or with producers because he had a very singular vision as to what he wanted. But I couldn't say, and wouldn't say, that it had anything to do with his drinking.

Colasanto remained a sought after director and actor throughout most of the '70s. Toward the end of the decade, however, he began to secure fewer directing jobs. One of the problems may have been his declining health. Colasanto had been diagnosed with heart disease in the mid '70s, and the cumulative affect of that and his alcoholism was destroying his health. Eventually he realized he had to get help and joined AA, after which he would remain sober for the rest of his life. He stepped away from directing in 1977 and only acted occasionally. His role as mob boss Tommy Como in 1980's Oscar-nominated *Raging Bull* was to be his last, and perhaps best remembered, big-screen appearance.

By the time *Cheers* came along in 1982, Colasanto was all but ready to retire, but the opportunity to do a sitcom appealed to him. It meant steady work on a soundstage, in a controlled environment, as opposed to the varied locations and productions schedules prevalent on most feature films and hour-long episodic television shows. For the Charles brothers and director James Burrows, Colasanto was the perfect fit as the absent-minded but loveable Coach.

His *Cheers* castmates were thrilled to be working alongside Colasanto. "It was his sweet naiveté, innocent love, and caring that was really the heart of the show," says Ted Danson. "All of the other characters were sort of absorbed in themselves, and he was always the center of this sweetness." Adds Shelley Long: "There was a kind of surrender that the character had that made him seem like a pal. He looked up to Sam. Sam was his hero. What Sam said is what Coach did. He had a very loving heart, he wasn't out to trick anybody or seduce anybody. He was just doing his job and made a lot of friends in the effort."

Colasanto was a very private man and didn't talk much about either his personal life or his professional accomplishments. He possessed an immense modesty for someone who'd achieved so much in his career. But as the cast became closer, Danson and the others did learn more about the man and his life. Says Danson:

> He was the oldest member of the cast, but he fit right in with us. He was in AA, and he had stopped drinking. I hadn't known him before, but I'd heard people say that he could be a really angry man during his drinking days. When somebody in life deals with that in a really responsible way or is in the process of dealing with it, to me that person is in a powerful place, has gone to hell and back, and has something very powerful to offer to those around them.

Colasanto seemed to savor the opportunity to tackle such a difficult character as Coach. Joining the cast of *Cheers* was his opportunity to remain active in the industry he'd loved and given so much of himself to. The genuine approach he took to his work, and his life, inspired and infected those around him. As Rhea Perlman recalls:

> He was never false. He was one of the best actors I've ever met. He really loved his craft and was so good at it. He'd had a past before us, where he was in AA and all that. That was a very big deal to him, and he took it very seriously. He felt like he had really screwed up in the past when he was drinking a lot, and now he was just way mellowed.

Cheers premiered on September 30, 1982. In accordance with Tartikoff's strategy, NBC touted their Thursday prime-time schedule as a night of top-quality entertainment. The evening was anchored by *Fame* at eight o'clock, followed by *Cheers* at nine, the transplanted *Taxi* at nine-thirty, and the critically hailed *Hill Street Blues* at ten.

Tartikoff's campaign achieved the desired effect with critics, who were quickly won over by NBC's new docket. The viewing audience wasn't so easily recruited, however. Despite glowing reviews, only the network's new Friday night action entré,

A veteran television and film director, Nicholas Colasanto turned to acting in his later years. He is best remembered as Coach on NBC's hit comedy series *Cheers* (courtesy NBC/Photofest).

Knight Rider, seemed to click with a mass audience. Thanks primarily to competition from CBS's top-ten hit *Simon & Simon*, Thursday nights on NBC became something of an abyss. *Cheers*, in particular, performed dismally in the Nielsen ratings. If it hadn't been for the full season guarantee that Tartikoff had so generously given Glen and Les Charles, it's most likely *Cheers* would have closed up shop at midseason.

By January the situation had deteriorated to the point that Tartikoff had to take action. After examining his options, he relegated *Taxi* to Saturday nights, while on Thursdays he moved *Cheers* into the 9:30 P.M. timeslot, where its new lead-in became the Nell Carter comedy *Gimme a Break!* The changes had little effect, and when the dust had cleared that spring, *Cheers* finished its first season ranked 75th, the lowest-rated comedy on television.

Producer Ken Estin, who was at that time running *Taxi*, as well as writing the occasional script for *Cheers*, sums up the tumultuous events of that first year:

> If the series had aired in the current television environment, it would never have made it through the first season. But they had that full season commitment, and at the end of the season they received Emmy nominations, which established *Cheers* as an exceptional show. So it took the combination of critical praise along with that commitment for the entire year to keep the show from being cancelled very early on.

Estin himself was responsible for garnering the series some of its critical recognition. Although he and producing partner Sam Simon were busy running the day-to-day operations of *Taxi*, Estin found time to write an early script of *Cheers* titled "The Coach's Daughter"

(10/28/82). The episode featured Allyce Beasley (the future rhyming receptionist Agnes Dipesto on *Moonlighting*) as the Coach's daughter Lisa, who comes to town to introduce her fiancé Roy to her father. Coach finds the man (Philip Charles MacKenzie) totally obnoxious and is unable to tolerate the way Roy treats his daughter. Coach later learns that Lisa doesn't truly love Roy, but due to her plain-Jane looks and disposition in life, she fears he may be the only opportunity she'll ever have to marry and have a family.

The episode had a profound effect on the entire cast and crew. "It was Nick's favorite episode, pretty much all of ours," offers Danson, who describes the scene in which Coach finally confronts Lisa as one of the most powerful moments ever shot for the series. Continues Danson:

> She came to the bar with this sleazy fiancé. She was getting married because she was very plain and didn't feel she could do any better, and Nick took her aside in the scene and told her, "You're not plain, you're the most beautiful woman in the world." And she said, "No I'm not, I look exactly like mom." And Coach says, "That's what I'm saying, you're the most beautiful woman in the world." It was just a beautiful scene.

Glen and Les Charles had wanted to submit "The Coach's Daughter" for Emmy cosideration in the category of Outstanding Writing in a Comedy Series. Estin declined, feeling that since he was a showrunner on *Taxi*, if he were going to submit a script for consideration, it should be for that series. When Emmy nominations were announced, *Cheers* was recognized in most of the major categories in comedy: Ted Danson for Outstanding Lead Actor, Shelley Long for Outstanding Lead Actress, Nicholas Colasanto for Best Supporting Actor, Rhea Perlman for Supporting Actress, Glen and Les Charles for writing the pilot, James Burrows for directing the season finale, "Showdown (Part 2)" (3/31/83), and *Cheers* for Outstanding Comedy Series. Even the show's theme song, "Where Everybody Knows Your Name," by Gary Portnoy and Judy Hart-Angelo, was nominated for an Emmy (it was later released commercially).

Tartikoff couldn't have been happier with *Cheers* from a creative standpoint. In the course of one season it had become one of the most celebrated programs on television. When the Emmys were handed out that fall, on September 25, 1983, *Cheers* won as Best Comedy; Shelley Long, a virtual unknown a year earlier, took home the trophy for Best Comedic Actress; Glen and Les Charles triumphed for their pilot script; and James Burrows accepted honors for directing. Colasanto lost out to *Taxi*'s Christopher Lloyd in the battle for Best Supporting Actor in a Comedy, Variety, or Music Series. Under these circumstances, Tartikoff overlooked the series' poor performance in the ratings and renewed *Cheers* for a second season.

Cheers continued to struggle in the ratings during its second season, although the award nominations continued to roll in. *Cheers* would again win the award for Best Comedy Series for the 1983-84 season, and Rhea Perlman would take honors as Best Supporting Actress in a Comedy. By this time, the cast had gotten to know one another and had grown very close. Shares Perlman: "The set was a very happy place, kind of like camp. We were like idiot kids, very carefree in a ridiculous environment. Nick fit right in, even though he was much older than the rest of us. He was always part of the gang."

Colasanto also offered Danson valuable career advice. He realized that although Danson was part of a large, talented ensemble, he was still the star, and that required a little more of him. Says Danson:

> Nick really helped me find direction. I had been a character actor who had worked in New York and done three films, but I was by no means a pro, and I had never been the tall guy, the leader,

in anything. And Sam Malone was the leader, he owned the bar, and that was very foreign to me. And Nick kept quietly insisting that I behave like a leader. He would always demur to me and make me stand up and take a position. It was there on screen in the relationship of the characters, but he did it to me in life as well. He really encouraged me to stand up straight, which I will be forever indebted to him for.

The cast not only became comfortable with each other but with their characters, so comfortable that they tended to do less and less acting as time went on and spent more time just being themselves, having melded their true-life personalities with the make-believe people they so loved portraying.

All the hard work the cast and crew were putting into *Cheers* finally began to pay off during the series' third season. By the time the 1984-85 season got under way, Thursday night was television's most competitive night. CBS had been ruling the evening with its hits *Magnum, P.I.* at eight o'clock, followed by *Simon & Simon* at nine, and *Knots Landing* at ten. All three series placed in the top-20. While ABC had fallen on hard times, NBC struck gold that fall with *The Cosby Show*. Anchoring NBC's evening at eight o'clock, *Cosby* was an immediate hit, ranking number three its first year on the air. Its remarkable success paved the way for the rest of NBC's schedule that evening. The network's under-performing *Family Ties* was moved from Wednesdays into the eight-thirty timeslot, where, playing off *Cosby*'s lead-in, it shot up to number five. *Cheers*, which had been moved back to the nine o'clock spot, suddenly found its audience, tying with ABC's *Hotel* at number twelve that season. Following *Cheers*, the sophomore comedy *Night Court* finished the season at number 20, while *Hill Street Blues* continued to perform well in 30th place.

Tartikoff's plan to reinvent NBC had worked, and the Thursday night line-up was largely responsible for that victory. While the contributions of *The A-Team*, at number 6, certainly can't be denied, at least Tartikoff never felt the need to apologize for *Cheers* or *Hill Street Blues*.

Although things were finally falling into place for *Cheers* during the fall of 1984, privately Nicholas Colasanto was trying his best to hide his failing health from his co-stars. His heart disease had worsened, and although the cast and crew of the show were aware of his condition, they didn't realize how severe his illness had become. When he had returned to work for the third season, he'd lost weight. Colasanto, never one to share his problems with others, didn't broach the subject. Everyone initially chalked the weight loss up to perhaps a new medication or diet plan meant to aid in his fight against his heart condition.

Colasanto continued to show up for work and gave his all in each performance. His spirits also remained relatively high, although at times his fuse was a little short. He would often complain about the temperature on the stage being too low. He realized if he were to catch a bad cold it could easily develop into pneumonia. Finally, right after the holidays, he wound up in the hospital with water on his lungs.

Recounting the episode "Teacher's Pet" (filmed in December 1984 and aired January 31, 1985), Danson says:

The last episode he did was this one where I was trying to get my high school equivalency, and he was helping me through geography. Nick just couldn't remember a line, and what we didn't realize was that his heart just wasn't able to pump enough, he wasn't getting enough oxygen to his brain, and so it just became harder and harder for him to remember his lines. And then he got the flu during one of our breaks. We had a week off, but he didn't return afterwards. We went to the hospital to visit him.

This was the first time Colasanto had missed production of an episode. Even so, his cast-mates had every reason to believe he'd return to the show. But after being released from the hospital, he still wasn't cleared to return to work. One afternoon in early February he showed up at the production offices unexpectedly and tried convincing producers he was ready to return for the season finale. Unfortunately, without a doctor's approval, their hands were tied. Colasanto wandered down to the stage, where the cast was busy rehearsing the episode "The Belles of St. Cletes." He sat in the bleachers and quietly watched the others.

Recalls Shelley Long of that afternoon:

> I think we were all in denial. We were all glad he was there, but he had lost a lot of weight and it was kind of scary to see him. It was the last time I saw him. I remember looking up and he was in the stands for a while watching us rehearse. Then the next time I looked up he was gone. Looking back on it I wish I had spent more time with him that day.

Adds Perlman: "He wanted to be there so badly, he came in and watched from the stands. It was hard for him. He didn't want to be sick. He couldn't breathe well, it was hard, he was laboring all the time."

On the evening of February 12, 1985, Nicholas Colasanto sat down in his favorite easy chair in his living room and died of a heart attack. The cast was devastated: "I was not surprised because we had seen him so ill and looking so thin," says Long. "I was horrified but I wasn't surprised. I was more heartbroken than horrified. I just loved Nicky so much, he was a dear soul and it was terrible to lose him."

Colasanto had never married or had children, but he valued family. "He was very Italian, and family meant a lot to him; he was very close to his family, his nieces and nephews," says old friend Dean Hargrove. "He liked women, but I think he found as he got older that his choices were becoming narrower and he wasn't becoming any more desirable, and he adjusted to the fact of living alone. I never heard him express any regrets about that." It was no secret that he regarded his *Cheers* castmates as family. Remembers Rhea Perlman: "I had one kid who was born after the first year, and I was pregnant with my second kid during that third year, and he loved my kids. He was just so sweet. I still miss Nick, especially when I watch the old shows."

His *Cheers* family was determined to see that Colasanto would not be forgotten on the series. The actor had a little cubby hole in his dressing room where he'd displayed a photo of Geronimo, the famous black and white shot of the Apache leader down on one knee holding his rifle. When Colasanto died the cast went to his dressing room and removed the photo so it could become a permanent fixture on the *Cheers* bar set, hung on stage near the piano, "so it would always be there," says Danson. "Later, when we were shooting the very last episode, after Sam walks back and says we're closed, our director James Burrows blocked it so on my way back out of the bar I stop and straighten the photo, so that Nicky was represented right to the end."

The importance of that photo was an affirmation of how bravely Colasanto faced the many trials in his life. Observes Danson:

> I think he'd lived his life at times being a curmudgeon, that gruff, sort of in-your-face type of person. That combination of being sober and having heart disease obviously took its toll. AA is humbling in a wonderful way. Maybe that picture was Nick's way of saying, "Maybe I still have a Geronimo in me. I may be on one knee with some white guy taking my photograph, but don't count me out."

Colasanto's body was flown back to the east coast where a funeral was held on February 16, 1985, at Holy Cross Church in Providence, Rhode Island. He was buried in a cemetery in Cranston. "He was a very urban guy, and although I think he adjusted to living in Los Angeles, he always felt that back east was where he wanted to be in his heart," says Hargrove.

Memorial services were held in both Los Angeles for his show business colleagues and on the east coast for his friends and family. Condolences came in from fans who were heartbroken over the loss of the beloved Coach. Colasanto's alma mater, Bryant College, honored the late actor by naming one of the institution's common rooms "Nick's Place," complete with a memorial plaque and a framed apron once worn by Colasanto on *Cheers* and autographed by the cast.

When Emmys were presented for the 1984–85 season, *Cheers* would again receive a nomination for Best Comedy Series, but the award would go to *The Cosby Show*. The entire cast would receive nominations in the Best Acting categories, with Colasanto, George Wendt, and John Ratzenberger all competing for the Best Supporting Actor statue. Posthumously, it would be Colasanto's third consecutive nomination. That September, however, actor John Larroquette would take home the prize for his role as sex-obsessed assistant D.A. Dan Fielding in *Night Court*.

The *Cheers* writing staff reassembled right after Memorial Day 1985 to begin discussing ideas for the show's fourth season. The first decision that had to be made was how to deal with the absence of Coach. Thoughts of having him move away were quickly tossed aside. Coach would never have abandoned his friends at Cheers. Besides, the entire viewing audience knew that Colasanto had died, and the decision was made to handle the onscreen situation in a more honest way. After all, the people on *Cheers* were more than just characters. The actors and their screen personas had become one. So it was decided that Coach's death would be addressed in the season opener, and a new character would be added in the process.

Peter Casey and David Lee took over as supervising producers that year. Casey recalls how Glen and Les Charles approached the task of saying goodbye to one beloved character and introducing another:

> They wanted someone who was going to be innocent like Coach, and who might be a little dimwitted like Coach, but the thing they wanted to make sure they did was to go younger with the character. They wanted to add a really young character into the cast. So they created the character of this kid out of Indiana who had always dreamed of being a bartender and had struck up a pen pal relationship with Coach. Coach had always told him if he ever got to Boston to stop in and see him. And, of course, when Woody shows up he finds out that Coach is dead.

Ironically, the character of Woody was created without any particular actor in mind. As Casey laughingly recalls:

> Glen and Les had to create the character and write the episode first before we could begin casting the part, and they had already named this character Woody. So we read the script, and, as always, Glen and Les just did a fantastic job. Everyone thought the character was great, so we started doing casting. Woody was written as such a sweet, kind of aw-shucks Midwestern guy. The actors who came in were these sweet-looking young guys. We read lots of actors for that role, and there were some people who were pretty good, but it wasn't like anybody came in and we went, "That's the guy!"

The casting process for the character of Woody Boyd went on for several weeks, during which the producers tested dozens of actors. Then one day, already exhausted by the process, the producers finally found their man. Continues Casey:

They brought in this guy to read for the part, and they introduced him as Woody Harrelson, and we're going, "This is weird, you know, this guy's name is Woody." I remember being there when Woody walked in and thinking, "This guy is so not right for the part." He comes in, he's wearing basketball shorts and a sleeveless T-shirt; he's got high-top basketball shoes on that are unlaced, and he's shuffling in. He looked so not like a sweet, innocent guy. He had a face that made him look like kind of a tough guy, someone who could be a little aggressive. So I think the initial feeling in the room was that they might have brought in the wrong guy to read for this part. But when he started reading he did something that none of the other actors had done in any of the readings. When he got to the part where Sam has to tell him that the Coach had passed away, he began crying. And that was Woody's choice, it wasn't in the script. And all of a sudden you just realized, "Hey, you can't judge a book by its cover." He's playing it so sweet, so heartfelt. And I think that was the moment, because when that reading was over everybody seemed to feel that we had found our guy.

Woodrow Tracy Harrelson was born in Midland, Texas, on July 23, 1961, to Charles and Diane Harrelson. He was unruly from a young age and eventually had to be enrolled in a school for children with behavioral problems. In 1968 his father deserted the family, and a short time later was convicted in a murder-for-hire plot and sent to prison. The ordeal sent Woody's life spiraling even more out of control. In 1974 Diane moved the family, including Woody's brother Brett, to Lebanon, Ohio, where Woody became involved in the local church.

After the death of Nicholas Colasanto, fledgling actor Woody Harrelson (pictured) was cast as the new bartender at *Cheers* (courtesy NBC/Photofest).

At one point he even envisioned becoming a priest one day.

In 1978, however, his world shook once again. Charles Harrelson was released from prison, then just months later he was indicted again, this time for assassinating a federal judge. The drug dealer behind the slaying cut a deal with prosecutors for a lighter sentence by agreeing to turn Charles in. Oddly enough, it was at that point that Charles reached out to his son Woody and asked his son to come and visit him in jail while he awaited trial. Woody reluctantly agreed but never spoke publicly about what was said between the two. In 1982 Charles was convicted and sentenced to two life terms. The news sent Woody out of control. He left the church and turned increasingly to drugs and alcohol to deal with his emotional turmoil.

Fortunately, by then he had enrolled at Hanover College in Indiana, where he was able to find solace on stage as part of the school's theater arts program. He excelled as a performer and was soon landing the lead roles in such productions as Tennessee Williams' *Cat on a Hot Tin Roof.* His newfound love of acting gave the young Harrelson a new direction in life. (Woody would later make peace with his father. He even financed Charles' failed 1997 attempt at an appeal. Charles Harrelson died of natural causes in March of 2007 in a Colorado Supermax prison.)

After graduating from Hanover in the early 1980s, Woody headed to New York to pursue a career in acting. There, he struck up a relationship with Nancy Simon, daughter of playwright Neil Simon, and in the spring of 1985 was working as an understudy in Simon's hit play *Biloxi Blues*. Landing the role of Woody on *Cheers* provided him with his first professional acting job. Shortly after winning the part, he and Nancy married on June 29, 1985, although the marriage would end just a year later.

Casey says that the cast of *Cheers* was very accepting of Woody:

> People really adored Nick, and I'm sure they were still missing him but I also know that they were very warm and welcoming to Woody. I do know that Woody was absolutely terrified because he knew whose shoes he was stepping into and he really didn't have a big resume to draw from. Everything was working, and now he had to take the place of this really beloved character, and he was thinking, "Am I going to be the one to screw it up?"

The cast, too, was concerned, although they weren't about to place all that weight on Harrelson's shoulders. The young actor, who had only completed a handful of episodes by that point, had proven himself a talented addition to the cast. Whether the loss of Colasanto would disrupt the chemistry that had made *Cheers* a hit was yet to be seen, but if so, nobody could pin the blame on Harrelson. The series' ensemble would rise or fall as a group; that cohesion was their strength as well as their weakness.

Concedes Perlman:

> I think we were all concerned about that. We didn't know what would happen, because the show was so balanced character wise. That was the most amazing part about Woody coming in. Woody wasn't the same as Nick, but there was something about him, it was almost like he had taken some of Nick's spirit and was using it.

Woody was introduced to the public in the series' fourth season premiere, "Birth, Death, Love, and Rice" (9/26/85). The episode opened "Months Later," and quickly established that Coach had passed away. Just as quickly, Woody arrived in Boston from Indiana and learned of the Coach's passing. He then decided to stay on and tend bar at Cheers. The exchange wasn't dwelt upon or analyzed, but handled in a melancholy style. It helped that the episode also served as the resolution to a cliffhanger ending from the pervious spring, in which Diane and Frasier Crane (Kelsey Grammar, whose character had been introduced as Diane's psychiatrist during the third season) ran off to Europe to marry. Sam had spent the summer not only dealing with Coach's passing but also with the departure of Diane. She, of course, was to return, unwed. Any fears about how the audience would react to Woody were soon dispelled: fans universally accepted him, and *Cheers* continued to grow in popularity.

Off-screen, Harrelson quickly adapted to the Hollywood lifestyle. Each December a Christmas party would be held on the stage at *Cheers*, with the set being turned into an actual working bar. Food would be catered in, and executives from NBC and their families invited. Supervising producer Peter Casey has vivid memories of Harrelson's first holiday on *Cheers*:

> Woody knew how to party hard, and he decided to take on Brandon Tartikoff in a drinking contest. They decided to do matching tequila shooters. They were chewing a lime and then taking a shot of tequila, and this was going back and forth, back and forth, and they were going at it pretty hard. And I remember it wasn't long before both of them were standing on the bar there on the *Cheers* set with their shirts off, bare chested, swinging their shirts over their heads. And I remember thinking, "Okay, I can see that from Woody, but the President of NBC?"

An eighth-season cast photograph from the NBC comedy series *Cheers*. Pictured from left: (back row) Rhea Perlman, Woody Harrelson, Kelsey Grammer, Bebe Neuwirth, (front row) George Wendt, Kirstie Alley, Ted Danson, John Ratzenberger (courtesy NBC/Photofest).

After Harrelson's marriage ended in 1986, he dated a bevy of Hollywood starlets, earning him a reputation as a real-life Sam Malone. Laughs Ted Danson: "He was twenty-five and single, so us married guys, as soon as he'd walk in the door on Monday, we'd go, 'Sharing, sharing...'" Adds Perlman:

On set, they were always sharing these kind of guy jokes, and the women weren't really a part of that, but we would watch. They were always casting beautiful girls because Ted's character was a womanizer, so every time there was a casting session all the guys would disappear, and they would go up to where they were casting to check out who they were going to use. They made sure there were great looking extras around.

Despite his wild lifestyle, Harrelson took his craft very seriously, and as time passed he took more control over his character. As Casey explains:

Obviously the writer that creates the character has the initial vision, but if you get a good actor they're obviously going to bring something of their own to it. Jimmy Burrows and Glen and Les Charles certainly had a very strong opinion of how this character would fit into the cast and what purposes he would serve. In the early days, Woody was willing to be guided by them, but as he got more comfortable with it I think he brought some of his own ideas to the character.

Harrelson continued to grow as an actor. His feature film credits have included *White Men Can't Jump* (1992), *Indecent Proposal* (with Robert Redford and Demi Moore, 1993),

Natural Born Killers (1994), and Milos Foreman's *The People vs. Larry Flynt* (1996, for which he received an Oscar nomination for Best Actor). In addition, he received five Emmy nominations for his role as Woody on *Cheers* (with a sole victory in 1987). Outside of acting, he created a bit of controversy by becoming a leading advocate for the legalization of marijuana. He eventually settled down a little in his mid-thirties. In early 1998 he married for a second time, to Laura Louie. The couple had three daughters, Deni Montana, Zoe Giordano, and Makani Ravello. Harrelson remained with *Cheers* until the bar eventually shuttered its doors.

Cheers remained a top-ten show for the remainder of its run, finally taking the number one position for the 1990-91 season. The program came to a close in 1993 after 11 seasons, 273 episodes, 111 Emmy nominations, and 26 wins. The series aired its finale, "One for the Road" (a 90-minute special), on May 20, 1993. (It featured a special guest appearance by Shelley Long, who had left the series in 1987. Actress Kirstie Alley had then been added to the cast as the bar's new manager, Rebecca Howe, who served as both a comedic foil and potential love interest for Sam.)

The finale was followed by a 90-minute special, televised live from Boston's Bull and Finch pub, which had been used as an exterior location for *Cheers* and become an international tourist attraction in the process. *Cheers* truly went out with a bang, one of the highest-rated TV finales in history. In addition, the character of Frasier Crane was spun off into his own series, *Frasier*, which would match *Cheers*' run of eleven seasons and feature guest appearances by many of the stars of its parent series. *Cheers* was sold into syndication around the world, guaranteeing that viewers would continue to visit that homey little tavern "where everybody knows your name."

CHAPTER 5

Chico and the Man
Freddie Prinze

The life of Freddie Prinze had all the makings of a classic Hollywood story—at times happy, at times sad, often uplifting but ultimately tragic. His life could have been billed a fairy tale if not for the fateful final act that left everyone wondering just what could have gone so horribly wrong in such a short period of time. But to those on the inside there was a clear consensus that summed it up perfectly...the fame.

Freddie Prinze was born Frederick Karl Pruetzel on June 22, 1954, and grew up in Washington Heights, an impoverished area of upper Manhattan. He was an overweight child who struggled academically but excelled at making people laugh. He dropped out of high school at sixteen to take a job at New York's Improv Club, where he honed his comedy skills, eventually changing his last name to Prinze as part of his claim to the title "The Prince of Comedy."

By 1973 he had become a sensation by developing comedy routines that poked fun at his heritage. In his comedy acts, Freddie would often refer to himself as being "Hungarican," which led many to believe he was of Puerto Rican and Hungarian decent. In actuality, Freddie's father was German, his mother Spanish and Italian.

That December he was featured on *The Tonight Show*, and the audience went wild. After Freddie finished his act he was invited by host Johnny Carson to sit down and talk, a move unheard of for comics on their first appearances.

Within a year, Freddie had earned a co-starring role on the hit NBC sitcom *Chico and the Man*. The series took Freddie to new heights, his fame crossing all racial boundaries. When he wasn't busy on the series, he took his stand-up routine to Las Vegas, recorded a comedy album, and taped a special for cable TV.

But as his success grew, so did his demons. The pressures that accompanied becoming an overnight sensation began to take their toll on the young performer. His occasional drug use turned into hardcore addictions to Quaaludes and cocaine; rumors abounded about his bizarre sex life; and he became seriously depressed. It would all culminate early one morning in January 1977 in a shocking act of desperation that would rock Hollywood and cause many to rethink the price of stardom.

Ironically, Freddie Prinze's success would not have been possible ten years earlier. Even five years before the premiere of *Chico and the Man*, his odds of becoming a star would have

Freddie Prinze (left) was only nineteen years old when he was cast in the NBC comedy series *Chico and the Man* opposite veteran character actor Jack Albertson (right). Prinze became a super-star overnight, but the fame proved to be his downfall.

been long indeed. Rural comedies had dominated the television airwaves for much of the 1960s, allowing little room for minority characters. CBS, in particular, had built its prime-time line-up on the sturdy pillars of programs such as *The Andy Griffith Show, The Beverly Hillbillies, Petticoat Junction,* and *Green Acres.*

It was also CBS that, in the fall of 1971, essentially put the genre to rest by canceling the few remaining remnants of that era, including the aging *Hillbillies* and the *Griffith* spin-off *Mayberry R.F.D.*

Although CBS would find one of its greatest successes of the 1970s in the folksy charm of *The Waltons,* the decade to come would truly belong to a new style of programming being pioneered by producer Norman Lear.

All in the Family was a gritty new-age style of sitcom that included frank discussions of sex, politics, and religion. Lear had come up with the concept by taking the unusual step of adapting a British series titled *Till Death Us Do Part* (created by Johnny Speight) for American audiences. In the winter of 1971, CBS reluctantly added the controversial mid-season series to its nighttime schedule. To the network's surprise, the series became an overnight sensation.

All in the Family told the story of the Bunkers, a lower-middle-class white family in Queens, New York. The head of the Bunker household was bigoted Archie Bunker, who, as portrayed by Carroll O'Connor, was soon to become one of TV's most memorable characters. The interplay between Archie and his liberal, young son-in-law Mike Stivic (played by Rob Reiner) was to change the face of comedy.

The series' unexpected success also paved the way for a number of similarly styled sitcoms built around minority characters. CBS's *Julia,* with Diahann Carroll, in 1968 was the first sitcom to feature an African-American lead; but although groundbreaking, the series still followed many of the same network-established ground rules as other sitcoms of the time.

In January 1972 Lear and his production partner Bud Yorkin hit another home run by adapting a second British sitcom, *Steptoe & Son* (created by Ray Galton and Alan Simpson) into the hugely popular *Sanford & Son* on NBC. Bawdy stand-up comic Redd Foxx starred as Watts junkman Fred Sanford, while relative newcomer Demond Wilson played his son Lamont, who dreamed of escaping the ghetto. The Sanfords' weekly misfortunes were told in the same candid manner as *All in the Family,* and the show was met with the same overwhelming acceptance from American viewers.

The TV landscape was definitely changing. Norman Lear had blazed a brave new trail, and his success encouraged other producers to follow suit. One of those who chose to follow Lear's path was James Komack.

James Komack was a former stand-up comic who had become a highly successful TV writer and director during the 1960s, with credits that included *The Dick Van Dyke Show, Get Smart, Combat!,* and *Star Trek.* Onscreen he played Uncle Norman in *The Courtship of Eddie's Father,* the 1969–72 Bill Bixby dramedy on which Komack also served as executive producer.

Komack's talents were soon in great demand. By 1973 he had teamed with legendary TV producer David Wolper (*Police Story, Roots*) to develop new programming for all three of the major broadcast networks. Together the two men were looking to duplicate the success that Norman Lear had found with *All in the Family, Sanford & Son,* and *Maude.* Komack and Wolper wanted to introduce programs which would capture both critical praise and viewer attention while at the same time pushing the envelop of conventional television.

One summer day in 1973 Komack read a short story written by two young Chicano writers, Ray Andrade and David Garcia. The piece was actually an autobiographical account of Andrade's friendship with Howard Steinler, owner of the Main Street Gym in downtown Los Angeles in the early 1960s. As Andrade recalls, "I was seventeen years old and had no place to go. I couldn't stay with my mother because she had a house full of kids, and there was no way she could take care of me without taking away from the other kids. So I was pretty much on my own and had run out of money."

One evening a homeless Andrade slipped into the Main Street Gym and hid out after closing to avoid sleeping on the streets. When Steinler came in the next morning he found Andrade sleeping on a massage table and demanded an explanation. Embarrassed and searching for an excuse, Andrade said he was there to clean the place. Steinler was irate at first, but Andrade wouldn't take no for an answer. Recalls Andrade:

> Eventually, I was able to cut a deal with Howie. I would clean the gym, pick the cigarette butts out of the urinals, pick up the booze bottles and throw them away, and take out the trash. Howie said, "The minute I catch you stealing something you're out of here, because I know you fucking spics love to put shit in your pockets." I said okay. I was happier than hell that he didn't kick me out of the gym. Plus I could train there.

Despite their cultural differences, Andrade and Steinler would go on to become close friends, and when Andrade became a professional boxer a few years later it was Steinler who came up with his ring moniker, "Chico" Andrade. (Chico, translated from Spanish, has two meanings: literally taken it means "small boy," while also serving as a nickname for Francisco.)

Komack was immediately taken with the idea. It was just what he and Wolper had been looking for — the opportunity to do a racially diverse inner-city sitcom in which topics such as poverty and racism could be explored, allowing people to laugh freely without losing sight of the message.

Komack spent the rest of the summer hashing out a revised concept, basically turning the intense drama of Andrade's early life into a TV comedy. Instead of a gym, the old man, Ed Brown, would now run a dilapidated service station, and the young man, Francisco Xavier "Chico" Rodriguez, would be an ace mechanic. The whole premise would play out in the Barrio of Los Angeles where these two disparate characters would struggle to overcome their prejudices and become friends.

James Komack's original title for the project was *Spic and Span*, which didn't sit well with Andrade:

> I told Jimmy I didn't think that was going to wash. It had a double entente: Spic for the kid, and Span for the old man's age span. I said, "This is not the time to do this. Some people will be offended." Jimmy was insistent on it, but I said, "No." Finally he came up with *Chico and the Man*, and I said, "Alright, I'll go for that."

The veteran scriptwriting team of Don Nicholl, Michael Ross, and Bernie West, who were then writing for *All in the Family*, and would later create and produce *The Jeffersons* and *Three's Company*, collaborated on the pilot script for *Chico and the Man*. That fall Komack set the project up at NBC.

Veteran character actor Jack Albertson was the first to be cast, as grumpy Ed Brown. Character actor Burgess Meredith had actually been offered the role first but was unavailable. Albertson was a well-known and beloved figure in the show business world. He had worked in vaudeville, burlesque, movies, television, and Broadway, and been rewarded for his efforts with the triple crown of Emmy, Oscar, and Tony Awards. His Oscar and Tony Awards were actually for the same role, that of John Cleary in *The Subject Was Roses*, which Albertson performed on Broadway and later re-created for the 1968 motion picture.

Casting the other lead role proved to be more of a challenge. At the time there was not exactly an abundance of well-known Chicano leading men in Hollywood. There had been so few opportunities for such minority actors up to that point that it became necessary for NBC to hold open auditions in an effort to successfully cast the one role. Hundreds of hopefuls from across the country converged on Los Angeles for a shot at landing the coveted part.

By December of 1973, after months of callbacks, three candidates were still in the running, but Komack and executives at NBC were at an impasse. Komack was firmly behind Freddie Prinze; the network had two other actors in mind altogether, New Yorker Lazaro Perez and East L.A. native Isaac Ruiz. Both had previous acting experience, yet neither could boast the degree of recognition that Freddie Prinze had earned with his *Tonight Show* appearances and stand-up comedy routines. Eventually, both sides agreed to withhold a final decision until all three candidates could screen test with Albertson.

As it was, Albertson was performing with Sam Levine in a production of *The Sunshine Boys* at the Alexandra Theater in Toronto and could not return to Los Angeles for the auditions. The only option was to fly everyone to Toronto.

The screen tests were taped on January 2, 1974. The day of the auditions, "Freddie was slick," Ruiz says. "Jimmy Komack wanted Freddie to get the part, so he spent a lot of time with Freddie personally coaching him. Then right away Jack fell in love with Freddie. So it was almost a done deal right there in Toronto. I didn't have a chance, and neither did the other guy."

A few weeks later Freddie officially signed to play Chico opposite Albertson's the Man. At NBC's urging, Komack gave Ruiz a recurring role on the series as Mando, one of Chico's friends. Scatman Crothers rounded out the cast as Louie, the neighborhood junkman.

With the leads now cast and a script written, NBC gave the go-ahead for production of a pilot episode. All the pieces had fallen into place (if not neatly) for what would become one of the decade's most groundbreaking, inspiring, and ultimately tragic stories.

Director Peter Baldwin (*Sanford & Son, The Bob Newhart Show*) was brought on board to direct the pilot episode. But even before the cameras began rolling, he and Komack would have their share of problems to address.

Initially, members of the Latino community voiced concerns about the casting of Freddie Prinze because he was not of true Mexican heritage. Andrade maintains that Komack himself, in an effort to draw attention to the series, was actually blowing these protests way out of proportion. "One day there was a very small group of people who protested the show," he says. "In the meantime, I was receiving mail from Hispanics all over the country who were enjoying the series."

Andrade offered to speak to Paul Macias, the man who had organized the protest against the show. He and Macias had actually worked on campaigns aimed at ending stereotypical portrayals of Hispanics on TV. But Komack interceded. Laughs Andrade:

> Jimmy said, "This is beautiful, I couldn't pay ten million dollars for such publicity, let it happen." He loved the idea that it was controversial. The press got hold of it, and Jimmy was right, the series became a hit. Most Chicanos loved the show.

Other concerns would prove more daunting. Shortly before production was to start, Komack and Baldwin learned that Freddie had drug and alcohol problems. Illicit drugs were certainly not new to Hollywood, and, particularly in the 1970s, cocaine use was widespread within the industry. The initial take on the matter was that Freddie's drug use was not out of control or life threatening, but still might affect his performance. Nobody wanted to replace Freddie at that late date; he was too promising a talent. Instead, Komack and Baldwin approached him and tried to work out a plan to prevent his drug use from escalating. Recalls Baldwin:

> We had learned about the drug problems he had as we were about to start the pilot. To keep Freddie clean, Jimmy and I split up the week in order to spend all but his sleeping hours with Freddie. We would go to his house, have dinner with him, and accompany him to the coffee shop. Then when Freddie would go to bed, we would go home. Jimmy and I alternated nights all the way through the pilot. We pointed out to him, "Freddie, this pilot can make you a superstar, don't fool with this or treat it lightly. That's why we're hanging with you, because we don't want you to get yourself in trouble." Freddie was clean during that period, and it showed. He was electric. The drugs later came back, or maybe they never left, but around the time of the pilot he was clean.

Shooting the pilot for *Chico and the Man* was one of veteran director Peter Baldwin's most rewarding experiences. Traditionally there are two performances: a dress rehearsal in the afternoon and an evening show referred to as "the Air." Both are taped before a live audience, and the best moments from each performance are edited together into the end product.

The pilot for *Chico and the Man* brought Ed and Chico together. Ed wants nothing to do with the young Chicano who continues to ignore his insults and keeps showing up for work each morning until he finally endears himself to the old man, mirroring the early relationship between Andrade and Steinler.

Baldwin recalls:

> We knew we had a good script and Freddie was really funny. We tried to prepare him because he was new to working in television in front of a studio audience, which is different from doing stand-up. We tried to explain to him, "Watch out for the laughs. We know this is a funny line, so don't start talking yet until you get the laugh started, and then you can ride it and time your next line accordingly." But even we didn't expect these huge laughs and these huge interruptions by the audience. Jack Albertson was just shocked by it. He just kind of went numb because he didn't realize that there was going to be this kind of an audience reaction. We almost had to totally throw out the afternoon show because the timing was so screwed up.

Between the afternoon and evening tapings, everyone got together in an effort to better prepare for the evening show. They managed to go back and track which lines had gotten the biggest laughs so everyone in the cast and crew could adjust their timing. Marvels Baldwin:

> But then with the evening show the laughs got even bigger. But at least now we were a little more prepared for it. There were still some mistakes. Albertson was oddly a little nervous. He realized it wasn't going to be just a soundless rehearsal. But we got through the first act and things were going really well.

Then came the first-act break, which in itself led to a number of problems. Explains Baldwin:

> The pilot was interesting because of where the act break occurred. It occurred when Jack Albertson told Freddie to get out of the garage. When the second act starts Freddie has totally cleaned it up and organized it. Now, with an audience you can't take too long between an act break, and we had a lot of work to do to get that place cleaned up.

Due to the problems they'd had with the afternoon taping, Baldwin and his crew took a few moments at the act break to appraise their progress. That's when Baldwin was approached by lighting director Lon Stucky.

"Were you really happy with that?" Stucky asked.

"Well yeah, it was pretty good," Baldwin replied.

"Remember, we're going to have to clean everything up now, so nothing is going to match again if you need to go back. If you're not totally happy with something, now is the time to get it."

Baldwin heeded Stucky's warning.

"You're right, we've got to do this again. It's a pilot, we've just got to make sure we have it all."

By this time, the curtain had come down, and James Komack was out with the audience under the impression that the garage was being cleaned and the second act would soon be ready to tape. Baldwin went out onto the stage, walked up to Komack and cupped his hand over the microphone.

"What the hell is this?" a shocked Komack asked.

"Ask them if they'd like to see it again."

An astonished Komack shot back, "Are you sure? It'll ruin the momentum."

Baldwin assured him it was indeed necessary. So Komack turned back to the audience. "Do you mind if we do it again?"

The audience erupted in applause. "So we did it again," says Baldwin. "Then afterwards, the second act really soared."

There had never been any doubt in the minds of the producers or NBC that Jack Albertson would come through. But that night Prinze managed to dispel any fears. When the curtain closed that night Baldwin knew he'd been a part of television history. "At that moment, I turned around and said, 'This show is a hit, this show is sold.' Everyone in the room knew it, from the NBC people to David Wolper."

Chico and the Man premiered on Friday, September 13, 1974, following NBC's hit *Sanford & Son*. That Sunday Freddie served as Grand Marshal of the Hispanic Day Parade at Disneyland. Producer Alan Sacks accompanied Freddie to the event. "Remember, the series had just premiered a couple of days earlier," Sacks recalls. "We got to Disneyland early in the morning and it was absolute pandemonium. I had never experienced anything like that. It was Beatlemania time."

Sacks, who the following year would co-create (with Gabriel Kaplan) and produce *Welcome Back, Kotter* for James Komack, was concerned about how Freddie would handle the instant fame:

> People at Disneyland had all obviously seen the show, and we were experiencing the power of television. It was huge, and thereafter his life changed. He didn't react well. He was happy, of course, but it was way too much, way too fast. He became a superstar literally overnight.

Producer Ed Schaarlach worked with Freddie on *Chico and the Man* during the series' first season and was thrilled to see Freddie get the recognition he deserved. But he, too, was worried whether it had come too quickly:

> Everyone was excited both about the popularity of the series in general and that of Freddie personally. He had a very mature, grown-up comedy style, yet he was still appealing to the kids, especially the young girls. He was far ahead of his years in terms of his bright comedy routines.

This photo, dated December 8, 1974, features Freddie Prinze (left) alongside *Chico and the Man* executive producer James Komack (center) and future *Welcome Back, Kotter* star Gabriel Kaplan (right) (courtesy Photofest).

Freddie and co-star Jack Albertson hit it off and became good friends. Initially there was concern that their age difference could deter a close relationship and might even create a rift that could damage their onscreen chemistry. But the opposite couldn't have been more true. "They got along beautifully," says Schaarlach. "Jack was like a dear uncle to Freddie. They were very close." Baldwin agrees: "I think Jack in a way took Freddie under his wing. I don't think he could have helped him with the drugs, but it seems to me he had a kind of 'arm-around-the-shoulder' feeling for Freddie. I never saw them clash."

When *Chico and the Man* got the green light from NBC to go to series, David Wolper rewarded Freddie with a brand new Corvette. What Wolper had failed to realize was that

Freddie, as a native New Yorker (and an impoverished one at that), had spent his life riding the subway and had never learned to drive, let alone pilot a power car like the Corvette. In no time, Freddie managed to crunch both the front and rear bumpers in efforts to parallel park, not to mention a myriad of other incidental dents and scratches.

Ratings continued to climb as *Chico and the Man* progressed through its freshman year. The show finished its first season the third highest-rated series on television, right behind *All in the Family* and *Sanford & Son*.

As Freddie's popularity grew, so did the demands on his time. In addition to *Chico and the Man*, he continued to perform stand-up routines and had an extremely popular show in Las Vegas. He released a best-selling comedy album titled *Looking Good* in 1975. He was also booked for a string of guest appearances on variety programs like *The Midnight Special, Dinah Shore*, and *The Tony Orlando and Dawn Show*.

On a personal note, Freddie had a very active social life and dated a string of Hollywood beauties. For a brief time he was engaged to Kitty Bruce, daughter of controversial comic Lenny Bruce. Even during that period he was known to spend a lot of time with other women. After he and Kitty broke off their engagement, Freddie went wild and began dating a bevy of Tinseltown's most high profile female entertainers, including Pam Grier, Raquel Welch, and Aretha Franklin.

Then, in 1976, while in Las Vegas during his summer hiatus from *Chico and the Man*, Freddie met Kathy Cochran and fell head over heels in love. He immediately called all his friends and told them he'd found "the one." "When he described Kathy he was like a little kid," recalls Ruiz. "I would have to tell him, 'Freddie, slow down man, are you okay?' Kathy, without a doubt, captured this young man's heart and soul. He wanted and loved her." They were married in August, just before Freddie returned to Los Angeles to resume production on *Chico and the Man*.

Several changes occurred backstage prior to production on the show's second season. James Komack sold *Welcome Back, Kotter* to ABC, and much of his time was spent getting that show up and running. Director Peter Baldwin also departed *Chico and the Man* for other projects, leaving the door open for veteran sitcom director Jack Donohue (*The Lucy Show, The Odd Couple*), who was brought on-board as the new in-house director. Ray Andrade also left, concerned that the pressure of working on the show was destroying his marriage. He took a job directing daytime television at ABC.

It was during the second season that Freddie's drug use began to escalate. To cope with the pressure of his sudden fame, Freddie began using Quaaludes and cocaine in alarming quantities. Things were going so well that the producers chose to look the other way so long as Freddie's performances didn't suffer. "Freddie had this routine," explains Andrade. "He would coke up in the day to stay awake and be alert, and then Quaalude at night to calm down. He got away with it because he could get loaded all night and the next morning he'd come in and still know his lines."

That fall Freddie also learned that Kathy was pregnant. Ruiz recalls that Freddie would often call to talk about his impending fatherhood: "Freddie was ecstatic and couldn't wait for his son to be born. He would call to tell me how the baby was moving in Kathy's stomach and would sound so elated." Freddie Prinze, Jr., was born on March 8, 1976. Freddie handed out cigars and became a doting father.

Chico and the Man finished its second season with a small decline in ratings. As the show, still a bona-fide hit, moved into its third season in the fall of 1976, Komack took steps to prevent any further audience erosion by bringing in producer Hal Kanter to shore things up.

Kanter was to bear much of the weight of the series that season due to Komack's many other commitments. Kanter had not been a fan of *Chico and the Man*, and had only watched a few episodes, but he had strong opinions on why the show seemed to be stagnating after only two seasons on the air. Kanter insists:

> The ratings had dropped because Jimmy and the network had fallen victims to the Spanish-speaking community that kept saying that the show was an insult to them. As a result, NBC pulled the teeth out of it. There were very few Mexican or Spanish-speaking jokes. It was so homogenized that, for all intents and purposes, if anybody had tuned in and never seen the show or knew nothing about it, they would never have known that Chico was Mexican.

Kanter's solution was to steer the series back to its comedic roots. Kanter joined the show "on one condition, that I could make Chico Spanish again." He explains:

> I told them, "We've got to go back to doing those harsh jokes that Jack Albertson did about the Spanish kid." They said, "Go ahead, do whatever you can to help bring it back up." I did that, and the ratings did pick up. I don't know if they ever came back to where they were the first year, but they were considerably improved.

He also gave Jack Albertson a new antagonist by adding actress Della Reese to the series as Della Rogers, Ed's brassy new landlady and owner of a local lunch wagon. Reese's character could call Ed Brown on his behavior and shout it out with the old man in ways that would have seemed disrespectful coming from the young Chico. Their banter added a new dimension to the series.

As the third season progressed into the fall of 1976, outwardly the show seemed to be back on track. But Kanter saw things going on behind the scenes that concerned him. Primarily, he was concerned with Freddie:

> I knew that he smoked a little marijuana here and there. He wasn't alone there. Scatman smoked it all the time. But I didn't realize Freddie was so heavily into other drugs. I think he was also having some trouble at home, and that seemed to depress him.

Freddie would often call Ruiz when he was feeling down. Recalls Ruiz:

> He told me he was having problems with his marriage, and that he had made a mistake and gotten married too soon. He would call me, and I could tell he was on some kind of drug because he would be slurring his words, and then he would inadvertently hang up. When he would call me again, he wouldn't even remember that he had called before.

Freddie and Kathy eventually separated, with Kathy taking custody of Freddie, Jr. Citing his erratic behavior, Kathy obtained a restraining order against Freddie, cutting him off completely. Freddie became increasingly depressed about his failing marriage and being isolated from his son.

To cope, he began turning more heavily to drugs, anything he could get his hands on — cocaine, Quaaludes, marijuana, alcohol. "Obviously he was depressed," offers Alan Sacks. "He was always up late working on material. I think he became fearful of who was around him and started to become reclusive."

Kanter recalls Freddie's wild mood swings:

> I remember at one point he was very depressed, and then I got a call from Washington and they wanted to give an award to Freddie and Jack. They wanted to know when they'd be available to

come and get it. I called Freddie and explained what it was, and he was so delighted and happy for the next few weeks. He was a joy to be around when his attitude was that way.

Other members of the cast and crew were also keenly aware of what was happening. Comedian Danny Mora had also been added to the cast during the series' third season in the recurring role of Salvador, a part-time handyman and mechanic who helped out around Ed Brown's garage. Mora's supporting role called for him to appear every few weeks or so, and he never knew what to expect when he showed up on stage. As Mora recalls:

> Each time I went back I felt more and more comfortable with the cast and crew. Everyone treated me great. The only problems, ironically, were Freddie's. One week I would see him, and he'd be whistling and singing and happy, and the next time, in the middle of rehearsal, he would punch a hole through a set box. There'd be arguments between he and Jimmy [Komack], problems with his wife, and run-ins with the law. Arguments became more common. We'd get there in the morning, and we'd sit around the table, and there would be two empty seats, Freddie's and Jimmy's, and then Jack would get up and start pacing. So whatever personal problems Freddie was having would be reflected on the episode we were doing, and the rest of us would end up tiptoeing around trying to avoid the issues.

Until then, Freddie's problems were a closely guarded secret known only to those around him and working on the show. That changed on November 21, 1976, when Freddie was arrested for driving under the influence of drugs and alcohol. The incident was reported in papers across the country, and suddenly the public had an inkling of what was going on behind the scenes with Freddie. They had no idea, however, how deep it ran or where it was about to lead.

With Freddie's DUI in the papers, NBC began to put pressure on Komack to rein in his star. Komack already had concerns of his own. Since returning to work after his arrest, Freddie had been more deeply depressed, only now it was showing in his onscreen performances. His timing was off, and he was noticeably distracted, sometimes requiring the other actors to compensate by overstepping their marks to remain in frame with him.

By this time, Freddie's career — and his life — was being micromanaged, and he was frequently inaccessible to both friends and coworkers. Freddie's public image still seemed intact, however. In January 1977 he was invited to attend the Inaugural Ball of President Jimmy Carter in Washington, D.C. It would turn out to be his last public appearance.

On the evening of Thursday, January 27, 1977, the cast of *Chico and the Man* gathered on the show's main stage at NBC Studios in Burbank for a dress rehearsal. Isaac Ruiz was not scheduled to appear in that episode but stopped by the set with his wife Francine and infant son Gabriel. Ruiz had simply been worried about his friend Freddie and stopped to wish him the best.

As Ruiz sat with his family and quietly watched the rehearsal, he became alarmed at Freddie's appearance. When the rehearsal ended, Ruiz got up and started towards Freddie, but he was immediately cut off. Freddie's handlers surrounded the young star and began to escort him off stage. "I couldn't get close to him," recalls Ruiz. "I felt helpless and frustrated."

At the last moment, Freddie happened to glance over and saw Ruiz standing there. He broke free and crossed the stage to him. Ruiz recalls their brief meeting tearfully: "Freddie came over and hugged me, and just stared at me for a moment. Then one of his bodyguards yelled over, 'Freddie, let's go.' And he snapped back, 'I'm busy with my friend.'" Then he said to Ruiz, "You're my only true friend."

Freddie turned and took Gabriel out of Francine's arms and began hugging him and breaking into tears. "I knew he was thinking about Freddie, Jr.," Ruiz says. "He held him for the longest time, then finally handed him back to his mother. His bodyguards were calling to him again, and he turned and walked off the stage with them. That was the last time I ever saw him."

The following morning Ruiz's phone rang at 5:30 A.M. He picked up the call from his brother Manuel.

"Isaac, turn on your radio," Manuel instructed him.

"It's 5:30 in the morning."

"Isaac, Freddie shot himself," Manuel announced.

Ruiz jumped up in bed.

"Don't even joke like that, Manuel. I was with him last night. How could you even joke like that?" Ruiz yelled into the phone.

Despite his angry words, Ruiz was suddenly filled with a sense of dread; he remembered Freddie's state of mind the previous evening.

"Isaac, put on the radio," Manuel pleaded.

"That's how I found out," says Ruiz.

Earlier that morning, January 28, 1977, Freddie had put a .32 caliber handgun to his head and pulled the trigger.

The night before, after the *Chico and the Man* rehearsal, Freddie had returned to his apartment at the Beverly Comstock Hotel and become irrational. High on drugs and alcohol, and deeply despondent, he called his accountant and friend Martin Snyder, who arrived at the apartment around 2:00 A.M.

Freddie continued to make phone calls — to his parents, his personal secretary, his agent, his psychiatrist — and was clearly out of control. Snyder was trying to calm him down and reassure him. Around 4:00 A.M., Freddie pulled a handgun from under one of the couch cushions, raised it to his temple, and uttered his final words: "I can't go on." Before Snyder could react, Freddie fired the pistol and fell forward on the couch, mortally wounded. He was rushed to UCLA Medical Center where he lay in a coma until the next day. His parents Karl and Maria, wife Kathy, and a few close friends and coworkers (including Isaac Ruiz, Ray Andrade, Tony Orlando, James Komack, and Ron DeBlasio) were present throughout the ordeal. After being declared brain dead, Freddie Prinze was disconnected from life support and died on Saturday, January 29, 1977. He was only 22 years old.

The startling news sent out shockwaves, which not only devastated Freddie's fans but also trickled down to just about anyone who'd ever heard of the young comedian. How could someone who appeared to be so full of life and who possessed such a wonderful gift for making others laugh commit such a drastic act of self-destruction? Few had been witness to the slow path of drug abuse and depression that had led Freddie to that life-shattering moment.

Freddie was buried at Forest Lawn Memorial Park in the Hollywood Hills in the Sanctuary of Light mausoleum.

The industry's elite, including such comedic idols as Lucille Ball and Bob Hope, attended his memorial service. Recalls Hal Kanter:

Jack Albertson was a basket case because he had what appeared to be an abiding love for Freddie. He called me and asked me if I would write a eulogy that he would be delivering at the funeral, which I did. When he was reading it at the end of the service, he broke up and could hardly finish it.

Freddie's death was initially ruled a suicide, but many believed that it had been a terrible accident. At the forefront was Freddie's mother Maria, who insisted that her son would not have intentionally ended his own life. Among her supporters was Ruiz, who has remained a close family friend. He states:

> Freddie did not commit suicide. His mother fought in court for two years. They interviewed me, and I told them that Freddie didn't mean to take his life. He accidentally pulled that trigger. Freddie just wanted somebody to help him; he was reaching for help without knowing how to get it.

The court agreed with them, and the official cause of Freddie's death was changed from suicide to accidental shooting.

With Freddie's family, friends, and fans still in mourning, inevitably the decision had to be made about the future of *Chico and the Man*. Only 18 episodes had been completed for the series' third year, and if the show was going to continue, NBC would need four more original episodes to finish out the season. The decision was made to shoot those remaining episodes and then make a decision concerning the following year.

In the show, it was explained that Chico had gone to Mexico to spend some time getting to know his father, who had been introduced in a recent episode, "Chico's Padre." The touching episode had guest-starred Cesar Romero as Gilberto Rodriguez, the father who had abandoned Chico as a child. Gilberto had asked Chico to leave the garage and come back to Mexico with him, but ultimately Chico had declined in favor of remaining at Ed's Garage. The episode aired on February 4, 1977, after Freddie's death. Now with the need to explain Freddie's absence, the producers revisited the premise.

Events had unfolded so quickly that there had been no time to rewrite scripts before production resumed. All of Freddie's lines in the next two scripts, "Gregory Peck Is a Rooster" (3/18/77) and "Louie's Can-Can" (4/1/77), were given to Danny Mora's character Salvador. Remembers Mora:

> One of the first scenes we had to shoot, without an audience, involved Jack shaving. Jack was only dressed toward camera, only had shaving cream on one side of his face. Remember, the lines had originally been written for him and Freddie, but now he was talking to me, Salvador. One side of his face, the Ed Brown side, facing camera, was this cantankerous garage owner delivering these lines, but the Jack Albertson side literally had tears coming down his cheek. It was an unsettling moment. I'd never seen anything like that.

Mora recalls how difficult it was just returning to the NBC stages for those first days of work following Freddie's death:

> When we went back, there was this awe that filled the set, this quiet that burdened everyone. I mean, how do you pretend it didn't happen, how do you go on? Does it get real corny, like, "He would have wanted us to go on?" Do you start mouthing phrases like that? You start asking yourself, "Who really wants this to happen, why is this really happening?" It was a horrible day. Part of the pain was the broken heart of Jack Albertson. That first table we did after Freddie was gone was painful. We were all feeling it, but Jack was devastated; he was severely shaken by Freddie's demise. He was a very emotional man. Jack had a daughter but not a son. I think Jack had wanted to help Freddie in a very paternal way. He felt pain in a very paternal way when Freddie died.

NBC then cornered Komack and wanted to know exactly how he planned to handle Chico's absence should they renew the series for a fourth season. A lot was on the line. With only 66 episodes completed, *Chico and the Man* would not be able to play in syndication, which would cost Komack and Wolper millions of dollars in lost revenue. Plus, it would mean that all of Freddie's performances would also be lost if the series was simply left to collect dust in a vault somewhere.

"As I recall, I think the network wanted it to go on if Jimmy could prove to them that he could maintain the premise," says Kanter. "As long as Jack Albertson was willing and able to work, we felt the show had a chance."

Several ideas were considered. One was to have Ruiz, whose character Mando had proven to be very popular, take over full-time as Ed Brown's assistant at the garage. Another thought was to bring in a young girl, but NBC had trouble with the possible "moral implications" of such an arrangement. Eventually, Komack made the decision to bring in a young Chicano boy who would be adopted by Ed.

NBC still wanted to see how it would work before committing to a fourth season. There was still one more episode that had to be shot for the third season, so Komack used it to introduce this new character. The episode was titled "Who's Been Sleeping in My Car?" and was scripted by series staples George Bloom and Beverly Bloomberg.

As the episode opened, Ed and Louie returned from a fishing trip to find a 12-year-old Mexican boy named Raul stowed away in the back of their truck. Despite his efforts to return the boy to Mexico, Ed eventually takes him in. Then, in a touching moment at the end of the episode, he inadvertently refers to the boy as "Chico."

NBC was impressed enough with the episode to order another season of *Chico and the Man*. The transitional episode, "Who's Been Sleeping in My Bed?" would be held back and used to open the series' fourth year that fall.

Gabriel Melgar, who at age eleven was an experienced entertainer, played the part of Raul. Melgar came from a musical family. He had two brothers and three sisters, and was fluent playing the marimbas and drums. They would spend their weekends performing at fiestas and fairs. In 1973 Melgar danced onstage at Lake Tahoe with Sammy Davis, Jr., as one of "Sammy's Kids."

Melgar had watched a few episodes of *Chico and the Man* but was not really a fan. So it was ironic that in the spring of 1977 he was chosen to join the cast of the series. As Melgar remembers it:

> My dad used to have a corn-on-the-cob shop in Los Angeles, and I used to play there on weekends with a Feed-the-Kiddy Box. One Sunday I was playing, and these two ladies came over. They were Pat Amaral, who became my agent, and Joyce Selznick, the casting director for the show. They saw me play and said there was a show that they wanted me to interview for.
>
> The next thing you know I'm doing the series. The first show we did I was throwing up I was so nervous. At that time, I still didn't know anything about Freddie Prinze, but then

After the suicide of star Freddie Prinze, NBC elected to continue production of its hit comedy *Chico and the Man*. Young newcomer Gabriel Melgar (pictured) was added to the cast.

I got to meet people who had known Freddie. One of these guys was Chuck Hoffa, who used to be Freddie's personal wardrobe dresser, and he told me a lot of inside stories that made me realize what the hell was going on.

The fourth and final season of *Chico and the Man* opened on September 17, 1977, at which time viewers were introduced to the new "Chico." No longer was there any mention of Freddie's character. Ratings for the season premiere were good, as viewers tuned in out of curiosity; but just as quickly, they began to tune out in the weeks that followed.

Poor ratings were only one of the show's problems. Komack and NBC were aware viewers might reject the show without Prinze. What they weren't prepared for was a brutal backlash instituted by fans of the late actor, who targeted their rage at young Melgar.

Says Melgar:

When I became part of the show I got a lot of disgruntled letters from Freddie's fans. Now, I was a 12-year-old boy, and I didn't understand what the aggression was against me. It was hard for people to understand that I wasn't replacing Freddie, because you can't replace a 22-year-old man with a 12-year-old boy. One time I went to the Orange Bowl in Florida where there are mainly Cubans and Puerto Ricans, and I was on a float and they were all booing me. Imagine that as a 12-year-old. What price do you have to pay for something you didn't do?

Melgar had no one on the set his age with whom to bond. Fortunately, he was able to strike up a close friendship with co-star Scatman Crothers:

I used to spend weekends at Scatman's house. He was actually the first adult who ever really helped me and really cared. My parents were Mexican and very hardcore. I used to get all this detrimental fan mail, and so I'd turn to Scatman about it. One time, I was over at Scat's house and he was helping me with the major scales on the piano, and at one point he just looked down at me and said, "I wish this never would have happened to you." I said "Why?" and he replied, "You'll know later." And I know why—it ruined my whole life. It wasn't until I was in my early thirties that I got married and my wife Christina helped me to get over it and leave those things behind.

As *Chico and the Man* approached mid-season, the overall situation was worsening. Della Reese had been growing increasingly disgruntled. She had been promised her own spin-off, but it was becoming increasingly apparent that it wasn't going to happen. She finally left the show after completing the season's first 15 episodes. Ironically, she would go back to work for Komack the following season as a substitute teacher on *Welcome Back, Kotter* in an effort to fill the void left when star Gabriel Kaplan walked off the series in a dispute over the direction that show was taking.

Ratings continued to plummet for *Chico and the Man*. In an effort to revitalize the program, Komack announced a special one-hour episode that would finally deal with Freddie's death. Komack hoped that the episode would provide closure, and help fans move on and accept the new premise.

Episode number 78 was subtitled "Raul Runs Away." It dealt with Raul learning that there had been another "Chico" before him, a young man who had died. Under the assumption that Ed only took him in as a way of holding onto Chico's memory, Raul runs away to Mexico.

The finale of the episode had Ed catching up with Raul in a small Mexican chapel, where he not only confronts the young boy but his own long-suppressed feelings about Chico's death. Ed assures Raul that his feelings for the boy are genuine and all his own. He explains that he never told the boy about Chico because it was too painful for him. He offers to tell Raul more about what happened, but the boy declines. It was never revealed how Chico

The fourth-season cast of NBC's comedy series *Chico and the Man*. Pictured clockwise from top left: Scatman Crothers, Della Reese, Jack Albertson, Gabriel Melgar (courtesy NBC/Photofest).

actually died on the show, but we're left with the impression that he died the same way Freddie did in real life.

NBC had hoped the special episode, which aired on January 20, 1978, would give the series a needed boost, but it failed to generate the degree of interest they had hoped for. An additional episode aired the following Friday, January 27, 1978, almost a year to the day since Freddie's shooting, after which NBC put the show on hiatus.

But Komack, ever the optimist, wasn't ready to throw in the towel just yet. NBC had contracted for an entire season of new episodes, which meant even though the series had been taken off the air, Komack still had seven additional segments to deliver. His last-ditch effort to save *Chico and the Man* involved adding an element to the series that had been missing since Freddie's death — sex appeal. In this case, female sex appeal. Actress Julie Hill was added to the cast as Ed's 18-year-old niece, Monica. For that final batch of episodes, Ed was routinely pitted against the teen angst of his two young wards, Raul and Monica. Komack hoped Hill's presence would bring back the young male demographic that had idolized Prinze.

By April of 1978, the additional episodes had been completed. Komack began to lobby NBC to give the series another opportunity to find an audience. But NBC by then had given up on the show. *Chico and the Man* still hadn't returned to the airwaves when NBC announced its new fall schedule in May of 1978. However, the network did pick up *Grandpa Goes to Washington*, a one-hour comedy-drama developed for Jack Albertson.

Chico and the Man did return to NBC briefly that summer, airing for the last time on July 21, 1978. That fall the series' 88 episodes entered the television afterlife by way of syndication. Because of the lackluster final season, the show never achieved a great deal of success in reruns; domestically, it played primarily on smaller independent stations.

In 1979 a TV movie aired titled *Can You Hear the Laughter: The Story of Freddie Prinze*, starring *The White Shadow*'s Ira Angustain. Freddie's true legacy, however, is his son and namesake Freddie Prinze, Jr., who was raised in Albuquerque, New Mexico, by his mother and maternal grandmother, out of the public eye.

When he was old enough to make the decision for himself, Freddie, Jr., chose to continue in his father's footsteps. He began acting in 1994 and soon landed roles in a number of successful feature films, including *I Know What You Did Last Summer* and the live-action *Scooby Doo*. In the fall of 2005 he headlined his own ABC sitcom, *Freddie*. He saw little of his paternal grandmother, Maria Pruetzel, until 2002 when he married actress Sarah Michelle Gellar (*Buffy the Vampire Slayer*) and took his new bride to meet his grandmother in Puerto Rico. He has rarely spoken publicly about his father, but accepted an award on behalf of his dad and *Chico and the Man* at the Second Annual TV Land Awards in the spring of 2004. Most importantly, Freddie, Jr., seems to have avoided the pitfalls of fame that led his father to such a tragic end.

CHAPTER 6

Cover Up
Jon-Erik Hexum

From the beginning, success seemed a foregone conclusion for Jon-Erik Hexum. He was not only blessed with the type of picture-perfect good looks that get a person noticed in Hollywood, but he also possessed the insatiable drive and ambition it takes to get to the top. Only months after arriving in Los Angeles, Hexum landed the lead role on a network television series and was soon gracing the covers of just about every entertainment magazine in the country. The actor's chiseled features, along with his humble story of growing up in near-poverty to become a star, made him a media darling, while his charisma both onscreen and off made him one of television's most sought-after leading men.

In Hollywood, it seemed Hexum had been handed the keys to the kingdom. Most new-comers would have been happy with a fraction of Hexum's success, but he was conflicted. Each time he walked through a door, he was painfully aware that his looks had paved the way. He wanted to be taken seriously and began to work that much harder to prove himself. He knew he'd have to play the game but looked forward to the day when he'd be in a position to call the shots, and he never doubted that day would arrive. Even when his first series failed to ignite, Hexum knew that something better awaited him. He believed success came from within, and he believed in himself. Growing up, Hexum hadn't had much, but he never lacked for confidence.

Hexum was born in Tenafly, New Jersey, on November 5, 1957, to Thorlief and Gretha Hexum. His parents separated when Jon-Erik was nine, and his mother raised both Jon and his younger brother Gunnar by working two jobs. Although the family struggled, Gretha managed to support Jon-Erik's enthusiasm for the arts. She bought him a piano and took him to Broadway plays (due to limited funds, he would often go inside alone while she waited across the street, sipping a 25 cent cup of coffee).

Hexum excelled at Tenafly High School. He was extremely popular and participated in a wide range of extracurricular activities — everything from serving as class president to becoming the school's first male cheerleader. He then entered Case Western Reserve University in Cleveland to study pre-med but switched to Michigan State after becoming enamored of the college's Big-Ten football team. He made the roster but spent most of his three years there sitting on the bench, which frustrated him to no end. But it was at Michigan State that he discovered how much he truly loved acting. He made good use of the theater department

Actor Jon-Erik Hexum in full camouflage gear as Green Beret Mac Harper in a publicity photo for the CBS action series *Cover Up*. Hexum died from an accidentally self-inflicted gunshot wound during production of the program's seventh episode.

during his senior year (landing a lead role in *Pippin*), and after graduation headed immediately to New York.

There he took acting classes and began auditioning for Broadway plays. He did a little modeling but supported himself primarily with a series of odd jobs, such as cleaning people's apartments, including the home of talent manager Bob LeMond, who signed Hexum as a client.

LeMond, who also represented John Travolta, urged Hexum to move to Los Angeles to pursue his career. Hexum didn't need much convincing. In September 1981 he headed west.

In L.A., Hexum's life and career would move into high gear. Within four months he had landed the starring role in *Voyagers!*, a new NBC time-travel series aimed primarily at children. Recalls Hexum's cousin, newscaster Eric Paulsen:

> Jon-Erik grew up in New Jersey, I grew up in St. Louis. When his parents got divorced, they came to stay with us for a summer, and that's when I really got to know him. Then when I went off and got into broadcasting and Jack was in college, he would come to wherever I was and stay with me. He was pre-med at the time, but would tell me how he wanted to get into broadcasting or movies. And I kept telling him, "Jack, you gotta be nuts, the odds are so far against you, just stay with pre-med." Then he called me up one day and said he was moving to California, and again I told him he was crazy. Then a few months after that he called me up again and said, "Hey, I got a series." And I went, "Oh my God!"

There seemed to be no stopping Hexum at that point. He continued to be offered roles on both television and in motion pictures, and did a little modeling on the side. One of the perks of his success was that he was finally able to repay his mother for all of her sacrifices while Jon and Gunnar were growing up. Jon bought Gretha a home in Sylmar, California, and made sure she wanted for nothing.

Hexum himself may never quite have gotten over the economic conditions of his childhood. Despite happily dispensing a great deal of money to assure his mother's comfort, Hexum continued to exist quite simply. Instead of living the Hollywood high life, he bought a small home in Burbank that was sparsely furnished. He had two cars: a 1981 Pontiac valued at $3,500, and a vintage 1954 Chevy appraised at only $500. His only real item of luxury was a piano. Most of his money went into a savings account for the future, and indeed Hexum had grand plans for his future. He wanted to operate his own production company where he could develop the kind of thought-provoking motion pictures that he longed to be associated with.

That future was to be cut tragically short when in the fall of 1984 Hexum died in a senseless accident while filming his new series, *Cover Up*. His death shattered the lives of those closest to him, left his fans in a state of shock, and rattled the entertainment industry itself. Hollywood sets were supposed to be the place of make-believe, where the good guys prevailed and the bad guys were able to stand back up after the director yelled "Cut." But what occurred one afternoon on the set of *Cover Up* was frighteningly real and caused the industry to re-examine the issues of safety on its movie and TV soundstages. Of course, for Jon Erik-Hexum, the point was now moot.

Hexum's brief, meteoric rise to stardom began shortly after he arrived in Los Angeles in September 1981. He immediately drew the attention of Joel Thurm, then head of casting for NBC. Thurm felt Hexum was one of the most exciting new faces to come along in years, and hoped to find a role for the young man in one of the network's slate of upcoming pilots for the 1982-83 season.

In January a script came across Thurm's desk that he thought would be perfect for the young, inexperienced Hexum. NBC and Universal Television had a new fantasy series titled *Voyagers!* in development, and Thurm was determined to get Hexum an audition. He contacted producer James D. Parriott and pitched Hexum. Parriott, who had served as a writer-producer on *The Six Million Dollar Man*, *The Bionic Woman*, and *The Incredible Hulk* before creating *Voyagers!*, at first resisted.

Recalls Parriott:

I had always envisioned the part for someone older than Jon-Erik, someone in their mid-thirties. But Joel Thurm said, "I want you to see this guy." I said he was too young, but Joel replied, "I don't care, I want you to see him." So Jon-Erik came in and auditioned for us, and he walked out of the room with the part. I decided I'd do whatever I had to do to change the script to accommodate Jon-Erik. The guy just projected a tremendous amount of charisma. The star power was pretty blinding. He was nervous, but he really just blew us away.

The show was about a time cop, Phinneus Bogg, whose job was to patrol history with the aid of his "omni," a small, egg-shaped time travel device. He would drop in on certain historical events, at which point the omni would light up either green or red. If green, then time was progressing as it should. If red, then time had gone awry somewhere along the line, and Bogg had to fix it. In the field, Bogg would rely heavily on a historical guidebook in resetting history. Then, on one fateful visit to 1982, Bogg lost his guidebook but picked up a young companion, Jeffrey Jones, a recently orphaned 12-year-old whose parents had conveniently been history professors. Jeffrey knew his history cold, and together he and Bogg would leap through time fixing things that had once gone wrong.

The series was picked up and scheduled on Sunday evenings at 7 P.M., a timeslot set aside for either public affairs or family programming. *Voyagers!* was obviously meant for youngsters, and NBC hoped it would be a successful way of counter-programming CBS's *60 Minutes.* Hexum would have been too green to play the lead in a more heavyweight network drama; but *Voyagers!* provided a more likely proving ground for the young actor.

Says Parriott:

He was rough; I think we even bought him his SAG card. He had just started acting, but he grew quickly. I think he got better and better as we went along, more and more relaxed in front of the camera. Occasionally, we had to go a few extra takes than we wanted in order to get his performance up to par, but he was always very cooperative and anxious to do the very best that he could. He was always gung ho, one of those people you just feel privileged to have known. He was always upbeat and supportive of everyone around him, never a jerk. He always exhibited the very best behavior you could expect for anyone in his situation.

Playing Hexum's young sidekick was actor Meeno Peluce, who at age twelve was already a showbiz veteran, having appeared in the movie *The Amityville Horror,* as well as two short-lived series, *The Bad News Bears* and *Best of the West.* Hexum was the neophyte of the two and would often turn to Peluce for advice. Their chemistry onscreen was apparent, and the two became close friends off the set as well.

Peluce remembers:

There was this great spark between us. We built our friendship early on. When we went in for our wardrobe fittings, Jon-Erik brought a football and said, "Hey, why don't we just walk around the backlot throwing the football and get to know each other better." I said, "That sounds like a great idea." When you walk around the backlot of a studio, especially in the old days when studios were what they used to be, you'd be walking through time...you'd walk from New York City into Cairo or some other wonderful part of the world. My mom waited while we had this great afternoon of just walking through time together, which was so fitting because that is what we spent the next year doing, pretending we were in different worlds in different times and visiting different pieces of history.

Hexum was still relatively new to Los Angeles and was far away from his home and family, and perhaps a little lonely. Peluce's family took him in, and they all became very close.

Eventually Jon-Erik moved his mother out to California once he began to collect a regular paycheck from *Voyagers!* Says Peluce:

> He was essentially the kid from out of town. For most of the show he lived in his funny little apartment in Venice that he paid $350 a month for with his beat-up little car. Every morning before work, he would go running on the beach, and then go work out after filming ended. He was really a superhero.

Peluce also remembers Hexum as a fun-loving individual who liked to show off, but

> with total good-hearted mirth. He was always laughing, *we* were always laughing. In an era of hunks, he was such a genuine guy, warm-hearted, funny, outgoing, self-effacing, that you couldn't help but be won over by him. All the women who came on the show were instantly won over, and usually took him home. He and I had a crush on the same girl, a tour guide at Universal. We spent a lot of time filming on the back lot, and the tours would come by and watch us film a scene, and then go on. And a lot of times we would jump onto the trams and conduct the tour. We both chased her, but I don't think either of us won her heart.

Voyagers! debuted on October 2, 1982. It performed well during the '82-83 season, averaging a 17 share, which was not spectacular but still decent for the time. Initially, it appeared the show would be picked up for a second season. But when accusations surfaced about shoddy reporting practices on *60 Minutes,* NBC felt the news show might have a kink in its armor. They decided to cancel *Voyagers!* and replace it with a newsmagazine titled *Monitor,* a decision they'd soon regret. *Monitor* would average closer to a 7 share the following season, and NBC would never again manage the kind of numbers that *Voyagers!* had been pulling in.

Hexum took the cancellation of his first series in stride and anxiously moved forward. "He was disappointed, but he picked himself up and kept going," remembers Paulsen. "He was determined he was going to be a star, and nothing was going to stop him." Offers continued to pour in, but Hexum didn't want to accept just anything that came his way. He could afford to be choosy: he had collected $200,000 for his year on *Voyagers!* and had saved much of it. He purchased his house in Burbank but never did buy a new car.

Then a script arrived on Hexum's doorstep that he couldn't turn down. Producer Aaron Spelling (*Dynasty, The Love Boat*) offered Hexum a lead role opposite Joan Collins in his upcoming TV movie *The Making of a Male Model.* Collins played the owner of a renowned New York modeling agency seeking a new male superstar. Enter Hexum, a Nevada farmhand who takes the fashion world by storm. Broadcast October 9, 1983, the movie was filled with '80s flash and trash, and scored stellar ratings. Hexum spent most of the movie with his shirt off. It wasn't high drama and he knew it—but it was high profile, and he pocketed a quick $50,000 in the process.

Male Model had its intended effect on Hexum's career. No longer was he just a familiar face to those primarily young viewers who had tuned in to *Voyagers!* Now he had a legion of admirers the world over, primarily female, and could be marketed in a whole new light.

Hexum continued to read scripts through the fall of 1983 and into early 1984, anxious to move on to his next project. With pilot season quickly approaching, Hexum was being courted by every studio in town. At 20th Century-Fox Studios, producer Glen A. Larson was busy developing a new CBS pilot. Larson's idea, then titled *Harper's Bizarre,* was about the widow of a murdered government agent who decides to go after the man who killed her husband. To do so, she enlists the aid of a former Green Beret. The woman, Danielle Reynolds, happens to be a world famous fashion photographer. In order to establish a cover, she hires

Joan Collins and Jon-Erik Hexum co-starred in the 1983 ABC TV-movie *The Making of a Male Model.* The movie drew huge ratings, and a beefcake poster of Hexum became a best-seller (courtesy ABC/Photofest).

the ex-soldier as one of her models. After Hexum's success in *Male Model*, he seemed a natural for the role of the show's hero, Mac Harper.

Glen Larson was just coming off a decade as one of the most successful producers in Hollywood. In association with Universal Studios Television, he had created and/or produced such titles as *Switch, Quincy, M.E., The Hardy Boys/Nancy Drew Mysteries, Battlestar Galactica, BJ and the Bear, Magnum, P.I.,* and *Knight Rider*. Then, in 1981, on the advice of Stephen J. Cannell, another of television's elite class of super-producers, Larson left Universal and negotiated a huge, multi-series, multi-million-dollar deal with 20th Century-Fox Television. (Cannell had left Universal and formed his own independent production company.)

Larson's deal was one of the must lucrative in TV history. Remembers producer Brian Lane, whom Larson hired to produce *Harper's Bizarre*:

> When Glen left Universal to go over to Fox, it was a huge coup and a huge deal worth millions and millions of dollars. They built him his own building and put in a wet bar. You can't even imagine what was in there, it was so mind-boggling. He was living the high life; he had a jet plane, two houses in Hawaii, and this multimillion-dollar lifestyle. Fox wanted him to do for them what he'd done for Universal. They expected a lot out of him.

Larson certainly delivered on his first at bat, developing *The Fall Guy* for ABC. By the spring of 1983, Larson had become so successful that he could sell almost anything, and did. That spring he sold four new series to the networks: *Manimal* to NBC, and *Trauma Center, Automan,* and *Masquerade* to ABC. Along with his ongoing projects, Larson had seven series on the air that year. But the bubble was about to burst: all four of his new series failed, none running longer than 13 weeks. *Manimal,* in particular, a show which starred Simon MacCorkindale as an animal behaviorist who could transform himself into any species of animal at will, was universally panned by critics.

By the time pilot season rolled around for the 1984-85 season, Larson was eager to redeem himself with a hit. Recalls Larson:

> We'd had a really bad season the year before. We got a number of shows picked up, but they all kept getting put into the same timeslot on ABC against *The Cosby Show*. I used to quip that this timeslot had a radiation half-life of about a thousand years. It doesn't matter what you put in there, *Cosby* is going to kill it. I'd rather have one good series on than four that are all over the place and not quite finding their audience. So instead of getting four shows on the air, which I did the previous season, I got one the next year and it took right off. It was like restoring order.

Getting Hexum onboard wasn't a terribly difficult task. Sure, Hexum wanted to do great drama, but there was something about the premise of *Harper's Bizarre* that piqued his interest. Hexum's then girlfriend, actress/singer E.G. Daily, remembers how it brought out the little boy in him. "He was kind of like a big kid," she muses. "He loved living this rich fantasy life. He was a big strong man, looked kind of like a Viking bodybuilder, and he loved to show his strength. He also liked the whole idea of guns and soldiers." *Harper's Bizarre*, which cast him as a soldier of fortune who traveled the world under the guise of being a male model, provided an outlet for all of Hexum's yearnings.

To sell the idea to CBS, Larson shot his own music video starring Hexum. Recalls Brian Lane:

> Glen was clever in this respect. Glen literally just went out into his front yard, which had this sort of jungle look, with a film camera, and he shot a lot of handsome footage of Jon-Erik peeking through camouflage and palm tree fronds. And he put Bonnie Tyler's song "Holding Out for a Hero" to it. Glen was a good video music producer even before there was such a thing because he

came from a music background as part of the Four Preps. So Glen just shot this music video; there was nothing happening, but you saw a lot of pretty girls wearing cool clothes and Jon-Erik Hexum skulking around like a camouflaged uber agent. And that was it—Jon-Erik was the lock, he was the guy they wanted. The presentation was literally the length of the song.

For the role of fashion photographer Danielle "Dani" Reynolds, Larson turned to Jennifer O'Neill, the actress best known for her performance in the 1971 movie *The Summer of '42*. O'Neill's big break had come in 1970, when, after only a few small supporting parts, she was hand-picked by director Howard Hawks to play opposite John Wayne in the western *Rio Lobo*. Although her career got off to a promising start, O'Neill never matched the success of *Summer*. While she continued to act throughout the 1970s, she became most recognizable as a model for Cover Girl Cosmetics, which made her the perfect candidate to play opposite Hexum.

With Hexum and O'Neill now cast as the leads, Larson was ready to shoot the pilot. One obstacle that popped up was concern over the show's title. The magazine *Harper's Bazaar* complained about the series' play on their name, which had been trademarked. At the same time, with the addition of O'Neill, there was pressure on Larson to come up with a title that would complement both leads, not just Hexum. The show was temporarily re-christened *Under Covers*, then *Harper & Reynolds*, before O'Neill went to Larson and suggested *Cover Up*. She believed it would be an amusing nod to her Cover Girl days, and she assured him she would clear it with the company.

Then Hexum himself threw the producers an unexpected curve ball. That spring, he'd landed a role in a feature film called *The Bear*, a biopic of the life of legendary college football coach Paul "Bear" Bryant. Hexum played the role of University of Alabama quarterback Pat Trammell, who would later die of cancer. He had taken the role specifically to play Trammell's deathbed scene, but, unfortunately, it was never shot. (Many fans of Hexum complained when the scene was apparently edited from the movie, but director Richard C. Sarafian says it was dropped from the shooting schedule before it could be filmed.) Hexum's part was reduced to just a few minutes of fairly inconsequential screen time.

When Hexum showed up for work on the pilot episode of *Cover Up*, he had just completed *The Bear* and was still sporting a crew cut. Laughs Glen Larson:

> He walks into my office just a few days ahead of principle photography with his hair all cut off, not the most currently in-vogue look for a male model. So we had to go out and have a state-of-the-art hairpiece done for him. He was very rattled by it and kept asking us to trim it a little more; and if you left him alone with it, he was going to trim it himself right down to the roots. So we had to work our way through the first few episodes with that, and eventually his hair grew in.

Richard Anderson (*The Six Million Dollar Man*) was hired to play the government operative who sent Mac and Dani on their weekly assignments. Actor Mykelti Williamson (*Forrest Gump, Boomtown*) rounded out the cast as Rick, Dani's assistant. E.G. Daily, Hexum's real-life love interest, was brought in to sing a cover version of *Holding Out for a Hero* as the series' theme song. The show's impressive opening title sequence was similar to the presentation film that Larson had prepared, beginning with Hexum, in full military garb, fighting his way through the jungle, and proceeding to show him being discovered by O'Neill's camera, surrounded by a bevy of beautiful women.

CBS scheduled *Cover Up* on Saturday evenings at 10:00 P.M., following *Mickey Spillane's Mike Hammer* and *Airwolf.* The buzz on the show was tremendous, and insiders were predicting it would be a breakout hit. On the other hand, CBS's other new drama, *Murder,*

The original cast of the CBS espionage drama *Cover Up*. Pictured from left: Jon-Erik Hexum, Jennifer O'Neill, Richard Anderson (photo courtesy CBS/Photofest).

She Wrote, was being written off as doomed to failure. *Cover Up* premiered on the night of September 22, 1984, and in the following weeks delivered solid (though not outstanding) numbers. Hexum and O'Neill clicked onscreen, and CBS quickly ordered a full season's worth of episodes. Although he would sometimes complain (publicly) about the rigors of doing a weekly series, Hexum was having fun.

Behind the camera, however, there was some minor dissent occurring. Producer Brian Lane walked off the series after only a few episodes in a dispute with Larson over the direction the series should take. His duties were assumed by writer/producer Bob Shayne (*Simon & Simon, Whiz Kids*). As a result, all of the scripts that had been written under Lane's tenure were tossed out, and Shayne was left scurrying to prepare new ones.

To get one particular teleplay completed on deadline, Shayne turned to a story idea he had used previously. Recalls Shayne:

> It was actually based on a story that I had written into a script several times before. Originally, Glen Larson and Michael Sloan had written it for *Switch*, starring Robert Wagner and Eddie Albert. I saw that episode and loved the story, and it stuck in my head. I used it to save three different series after that which were in script trouble. I wrote it once for a show called *The Misadventures of Sheriff Lobo*, which got cancelled before it got shot there. I used it once for a show that I was story editor on called *The Sword of Justice*, and that one did get shot. And then I wrote it once as half of a two-part show that went from *Magnum, P.I.* to *Simon & Simon*, and it ended up being the episode that put *Simon & Simon* on the map.

Now he needed to revise it again in order to assure *Cover Up* would have a script ready to shoot the following week:

> I sent it to the network, and, unfortunately, the executive assigned to the show called up with a note saying there wasn't enough action in it, which I thought was totally untrue. But I was forced by that network note to try to come up with some more action. The script is all about Jon-Erik's character infiltrating the bad guys, going undercover. So I created a new sequence at the network's insistence where he shoots one of the good guys, Mykelti Williamson, to prove to the bad guys that he's one of them. He shoots him, of course, with a blank, and Mykelti, who's actually a colleague of Jon-Erik's, pretends to be dead. Then, in order to have that scene work, I wrote an earlier one where Jon-Erik is loading the blanks into the gun.

Once Shayne made those adjustments, CBS approved the script, subtitled "Golden Opportunity," and it was scheduled for production the week of October 7, 1984. It would be *Cover Up*'s seventh episode and, as fate would have it, Jon-Erik's final performance. The stage had been set for a senseless tragedy that would take the life of one of TV's most gifted young talents.

By Friday, October 12, production was winding down on the fateful episode. It had been a long day of shooting, and Hexum was in a bad mood already. He was tired and had to catch a plane later that evening for Las Vegas, where he'd be taping a segment for *Circus of the Stars*. Earlier he'd had lunch in the commissary with Larson, Shayne, and O'Neill, and afterwards was visited on the set by E.G. Daily. She recalls:

> I was supposed to go have lunch with a girlfriend, but I cancelled those plans to go see him because we were leaving that evening for *Circus of the Stars*. There was sort of an odd tension on the set. He was frustrated and seemed angry. He had been fighting with someone, but I didn't know what it was about. Just before I left he called me over to him. He was very tired and stressed out and just seemed overworked. He walked me over to his trailer, and he talked to me and held me very quietly and calmly and sweetly. And then I left the set to go home to pack for Las Vegas. It was the last time I'd ever talk to him.

The script pages to be filmed that afternoon on Stage 17 at 20th Century-Fox Studios included one of the scenes that CBS had insisted Bob Shayne add at the last minute. Actually, the scene was very basic. The stage had been dressed as the interior of a motel room. Hexum was to sit up on a bed, pull a .44 Magnum handgun from his handbag and load it with blank charges. The master shot had already been filmed once, but director Sidney

Hayers decided another take was necessary. Due to some technical problems, there was a long delay. While waiting, Hexum laid down on the bed and fell asleep.

Hexum awoke after about fifteen minutes and was told they still weren't ready to begin shooting. He became restless and began playing around with the revolver. To this day, it's still not clear why he had access to the gun at that particular moment. Routinely on movie and TV sets, weapons are only handed out immediately prior to a scene being shot, then collected immediately afterwards. But Hexum had retained possession of the gun throughout the long production delay. He began spinning it around on his trigger finger, then started loading and unloading the blank charges. Finally, with only one charge loaded, he spun the cylinder as if playing a game of Russian roulette. As it wound down and stopped, he raised the gun to his right temple and pulled the trigger. The blank charge fired only an inch from his head, expelling a wad of paper with such force that it shattered his skull, forcing a bone fragment about the size of a quarter into the center of his brain.

Hexum sat stunned for a second and then fell back onto the bed. He remained conscious but unable to speak for several moments as crewmembers rushed to his side. He was bleeding profusely from the wound to his head. The production staff was in a panic, some trying in vain to render whatever first aid they could. Others went for help. One young assistant stumbled onto the soundstage next door, in shock and crying uncontrollably, interrupting a scene being shot for *The Fall Guy*, another Glen Larson series.

A call was quickly placed for an ambulance, but anxious crewmembers decided Hexum's only chance would be to get to a hospital immediately. A station wagon was backed up to the stage doors, and Hexum was loaded into the back by several blood-soaked stagehands. By the time they reached Beverly Hills Medical Center, Hexum had lost four pints of blood. He underwent five hours of surgery and was then placed on life support.

Daily had been at home packing when her phone rang. It was someone from the studio who told her Jon-Erik had been hurt and that she should go to the hospital. Daily asked whether it was serious, but the voice at the other end of the phone either didn't know or didn't want to say. "When I walked in I saw a lot of the crew praying and asking for Bibles," she says. "The next thing you know they whisked me into the room where Jon was, and they were just beginning to cut his clothes off. The rest of it was just a nightmare. I slept on the floor at the hospital all week; I didn't want to go home."

Hexum's cousin, Eric Paulsen, learned of the accident while working as a news anchor at WWL-TV Channel 4 in New Orleans:

> I was anchoring the weekend news, and *Cover Up* would air just before I came on for the ten o'clock news. We had done a commercial together when he visited once that went, "Watch Jon-Erik Hexum and then his cousin Eric with the news on channel 4." Then, when he accidentally shot himself, I had to read the news story. That was tough. One of our people called me up in my office and said, "Eric, you better come down here, you need to see something." It came over the wire, so I got on the phone with his mother immediately, then spoke to his manager for awhile. I said, "Do you need me to come out?" They said, "No, there's nothing you can do." I said, joking nervously, "Well, if he wakes up, I want to kill him."

Co-stars Jennifer O'Neill and Richard Anderson had been working that afternoon but were in their trailers when the incident occurred. O'Neill rushed to the hospital; Anderson would visit Jon-Erik a few days later, slipping into the hospital early one morning to pay his respects after it was generally established that he would not recover. For O'Neill, it was a particularly frightening experience. Two years earlier, she had accidentally shot herself in the abdomen with a handgun. She was seriously injured but recovered. Ever since, she'd had a phobia towards guns. Hexum's fascination with them made her nervous, and she often asked him to be careful while handling weapons on the set.

Glen Larson had to deal with the tragedy on both a professional and personal level. Explains Larson:

> Jon had just been up to the house and had dinner two nights before. I had a teenage daughter, and he gave her one of those set chairs with her name on it. It was her first crush at thirteen, and then her first encounter with the stark reality of death. She visited the hospital, and it was tough to walk in and see this beautiful guy. It's like looking at a Clark Gable just lying there lifeless. The machines make noises. Harvey Shepherd from CBS was absolutely stunned. I had to turn and move him out the door because he just couldn't handle it. It was just unbelievable.

Larson's career had been built around doing action dramas that involved car chases and shoot-outs, so he was keenly aware of the adherent dangers involved in such productions:

> Jon specifically wanted to use the .44 Magnum, which is a massive handgun. It's a very ballsy gun, and one thing you don't want to do is put full loads in it for blanks. They do make a lot of nice noise, but that isn't necessary because we can put the noise in later. They were using half-loads. When you shoot any kind of a blank onstage you put protective glass in front of the cameras, you put goggles on all your cameramen and set people — everybody, from the director down to the script girl, and certainly all of the principles. These types of blanks pump out a pretty good wad of paper. And while it's paper, when Jon decided to goof around a little bit and held the thing to his head, he totally jarred his brainstem. There was no recovery from that.

Despite the work of trauma surgeons, and the prayers and goodwill of friends and family, Jon-Erik Hexum's life had ended that day at 20th Century–Fox Studios on the set of *Cover Up*. It wasn't until Thursday, October 18, 1984, that he was declared legally dead. The machines that had been artificially filling his lungs with air and keeping his heart beating were kept in place because Jon-Erik was an organ donor.

According to a letter sent to Jon-Erik's mother Gretha by the Northern California Transplant Bank at Pacific Medical Center on October 24, 1984, his organs were distributed to several recipients: His heart was transplanted into the body of a 37-year-old Las Vegas man; one kidney went to a five-year-old boy who would have lived for only a few months without the transplant; the other kidney to a 43-year-old mother and grandmother; his skin was grafted onto a 3½-year-old boy suffering from third degree burns; and his corneas restored sight to two others.

There was no funeral for Hexum. Remembers Daily:

> They didn't have a funeral because his mother was in a state of shock and it was such a traumatizing time because of the way he had died. His organs were being harvested and donated, and nobody was quite sure where his body was. His mother didn't know what to do, so we had a memorial for him. I was numb at first, then in shock, and traumatized. Jon-Erik was the significant love of my life.

Even as Hexum was being mourned, discussions were underway concerning the future of the show. Everyone was in agreement that *Cover Up* should continue. Even with the loss of Hexum, they still had O'Neill and Anderson as assets. CBS, 20th Century–Fox, and Glen Larson all felt the show could survive Hexum's loss. For Larson, the situation was déjà vu. He had created and produced the early '70s western *Alias Smith & Jones*. At the height of that series' popularity, its young star Peter Duel committed suicide. His part was recast and the show continued to run. Explains Larson:

I'd had that happen once before, and the circumstances were equally difficult. I don't know how you compare tragedies, but certainly the Peter Duel episode was a different sort of thing. I don't think Jon-Erik in his wildest imagination realized the possibilities of what could happen. He was just being reckless. He was young, lacking in maturity and trying to prove himself. It was a macho thing to do. He was trying to prove that he was deserving of being this traditional lead guy surrounded by beautiful women. It wasn't quite the way to do it. Pete Duel was an unhappy person who certainly entertained the thought.

The decision was made not to recast Hexum's role, but to introduce a new agent (or "outrider," as the series referred to its spies) who would then team up with O'Neill. There was very little time to find a replacement, as CBS did not want to put *Cover Up* on hiatus and lose any momentum. By using some creative editing, a body double, and a voice impersonator, the producers were able to salvage Hexum's final episode, "Golden Opportunity" (11/3/84). Even with that, there were only three completed episodes remaining. That didn't leave much time to find a new lead and get the show back up and running.

The role eventually went to actor Antony Hamilton, who was relatively unknown. He had appeared in a low-budget European horror film titled *Nocturna* in 1979 before being introduced to U.S. audiences in the coveted role of Samson in the 1984 mini-series *Samson and Delilah*. *Cover Up* was a big step in his efforts to build a career in Hollywood. Hamilton, with his chiseled good looks, certainly fit the criteria for the role.

Says Bob Murray, a Hamilton fan and biographer:

> For all intents and purposes, he was discovered playing Samson. Antony tested for *Cover Up* using the same scene that Jennifer and Jon-Erik shot in the pilot, where their characters are introduced to each other. He was pretty much cast on the spot. I think this was a time in his career when anyone who had a hand in Antony Hamilton's life decided they were going to push him. This was going to be his catalyst into the spotlight.

When Hexum's final episode aired on November 3, the master shot of the scene he was filming when he had his accident was included in the final print. Widely dissected in the press, the scene showed Hexum sitting up on the bed and loading the gun with the very blank he would only moments later fire into his head. Perhaps this was not the most sensitive move on the part of CBS, 20th Century-Fox, or Larson, but the shot was necessary in order to salvage Hexum's final performance.

Antony Hamilton joined the cast of CBS's *Cover Up* in mid-season after the death of original lead Jon-Erik Hexum. Above, Hamilton appears in character as secret agent Jack Stryker (courtesy Bob Murray).

Three weeks later, on the evening of November 24, Antony Hamilton was introduced as O'Neill's new partner, Jack Stryker, a mysterious agent used to working as a loner who is suddenly thrown into partnership with the equally independent-minded Dani Reynolds. Their relationship was a complete 180-degree turn from the chummy friendship enjoyed by Dani and Mac. She and Jack seemed to entertain an unending game of one-upmanship — reluctantly agreeing to work as partners, but both anxious to solve the case using their own methods. During Dani and Jack's initial adventure together, Hexum's character was noticeably absent, said to be off on another mission. Finally, at the end, Jack breaks the news to her that Mac has been killed on the other assignment and won't be coming back. Dani breaks down. O'Neill's tears were real. Then the camera panned back, and a touching memoriam, written by Glen Larson, appeared onscreen, narrated by Richard Anderson:

> They say when a star dies, its light continues to shine
> across the universe for millenniums.
> Jon-Erik Hexum died in October of this year, but his light will continue to
> brighten our lives forever...and ever.

The sentiment was somewhat sullied by the fact that, in the original network airing, Hexum's name was misspelled as "John Eric." Fans deluged CBS with phone calls and mail. When the episode was rerun the following spring, the name was again misspelled, this time as "John-Erik." Eventually, in syndication, it was corrected.

As the series continued to air throughout the winter of 1984–85, ratings held up. Remembers Richard Anderson:

> It was tough initially because of the circumstances of what had happened with Jon-Erik. There was a great deal of pressure on the crew, especially the unit who was responsible for supplying the weapons. Now, I've been involved in thirty-some westerns and been a regular on four series, and guns were all a part of them. But there was always importance attached to the use of them. So everybody was very upset that something like this happened. But once we got going the first week with Antony everything was fine. He was very fun and amenable and wanted to do a proper job. Jenny and he and all of us got along fine. We were so busy there was no time to do a lot of second-guessing. The best thing was just to get right to work. I think everything was going well, and it seemed as if we were well on our way to recovery.

But just when it seemed the series had a second lease on life, controversy again threatened to put an end to it. Word slowly began to circulate around the studio — and the Hollywood community — that Hamilton was gay. While more acceptable today, the idea of knowingly casting a gay man in the lead role of an action-adventure series in the 1980s was unheard of. Rock Hudson was a legend by the time he starred in *McMillian & Wife*, but Hamilton presented more of a problem. Despite the fact that he kept his sexual orientation quiet, CBS and 20th Century-Fox were still concerned about how viewers would react should his secret become public knowledge.

Hamilton's homosexuality never did become the issue many had feared. CBS cancelled *Cover Up* at the end of the season due to mediocre ratings. Part of the problem could certainly be attributed to *Cover Up*'s poor lead-in from *Mike Hammer*, which the network also dropped. A two-hour movie block replaced both series the following season, a less expensive and risky proposition for the network. CBS reran the Hamilton episodes of *Cover Up* throughout the summer of 1985, but opted not to rebroadcast the Hexum episodes. The series' 22 hours were then purchased by the Lifetime Cable Network, then in its infancy, and rerun from 1986 to 1987.

After the on-set death of her co-star Jon-Erik Hexum, Jennifer O'Neill was teamed with new regular Antony Hamilton (courtesy Bob Murray).

During the summer of 1985, Gretha Hexum filed a lawsuit against 20th Century-Fox, Glen Larson, and director Sidney Hayers. According to the papers, the producers had not properly supervised the use of weapons on the set, which led to Jon-Erik's death. In response, the studio and producers contended that Hexum acted irresponsibly and his actions were beyond their control. Eventually the suit was settled out of court.

In summation, we may never know the determining factors in Hexum's death. Although the stage was filled with crewmembers that day, no one claims to have actually witnessed Jon-Erik's shooting. Despite stringent safety measures established by all the major studios, rules have been known to be broken.

Richard Anderson worked on enough action-adventure series to know that sets can be inherently dangerous places:

> Once when I was doing *The Six Million Dollar Man,* I came in late for a location call. There was a scene just starting, and I saw Lee [Majors] standing on a platform. Then down comes this helicopter with a wire on it and a handlebar. Now, what Lee was supposed to do is jump up on the platform, then they'd cut and allow the double to come in and take the handlebars and fly away. Well, they're rolling and the double is waiting, and Lee jumps up on the platform and grabs the handlebars and off they go. My mouth just fell open. They didn't take the wire up for him to get into the helicopter or anything like that, they just flew him all over the valley. Finally they come back over and land, and Lee sees me and he starts to smile. I said something I won't repeat, basically asking him whether he was trying to shut us down. He just loved it.

Still, Anderson feels Hexum's death could have been the result of a careless moment due to exhaustion:

> I did both *The Six Million Dollar Man* and *The Bionic Woman,* two shows at once, and you have your days. With adventure shows there are explosions, action, jumping fences, fighting and the like, and although the parts I played in these shows did not warrant the kind of action that, say, Lee Majors or Jon-Erik were exposed to, I was aware of how tough it was. The first thing you have to realize is that these actors are tired all the time. They don't get to sleep like they should. You come in and you need some coffee or something to get going. But Jon-Erik, when he came in each morning, he'd come in fast and pick up a script and learn the lines right there. He had a wonderful intelligence. I'd never met a nicer guy in the business, full of ambition and very anxious for the show to work. That day, whether he was sleepy or hadn't gotten up to speed yet, or whether there might have been something bothering him...I don't know.

Eric Paulsen also offers an opinion on his cousin's death:

> I think it was just an accident, something really stupid. I mean, I would never have thought that a blank gun could kill you like that, and I don't think he did either. They probably should have schooled him about it if he was going to be around that sort of thing. I don't know why the gun was with him when he wasn't shooting it. There are a lot of questions, but I don't think it was planned or anything like that. Jon-Erik really loved acting. The only thing that frustrated him was all that waiting around the set, and that probably was his demise.

Decades after his death, Hexum's fans still remember him by establishing Internet sites and by trading episodes of *Cover Up* online. Leading the effort to keep Jon-Erik's memory alive is Alan J. Carell of Portland, Oregon, a Hexum archivist who runs an ongoing international fan club dedicated to Hexum's life and career.

After *Cover Up,* Jennifer O'Neill kept busy acting, writing, and serving as a chairperson for a number of charitable organizations, including the American Cancer Society and the March of Dimes. A born-again Christian, she now resides on a horse farm in Tennessee. Antony Hamilton also continued to act, most notably as another spy in ABC's revival of

Mission: Impossible from 1988 to 1990. Sadly, Hamilton died of AIDs-related pneumonia on March 29, 1995. Ironically, says Bob Murray, Hamilton's greatest fears in life were the disease that took his life and being forgotten after his death.

Cover Up never lived up to its early promise, nor did Jon-Erik Hexum ever have the opportunity to fully develop as an actor. Onscreen, Hexum got to play a larger-than-life hero, but in real life he was a human being — albeit a fiercely driven, extraordinarily handsome, and well-accomplished human being — who had to tackle life just like everyone else.

CHAPTER 7

Dallas
Jim Davis

Few television series in history were as successful as *Dallas*, and even fewer had the lasting impact of this long-running powerhouse. It premiered in the late 1970s while the United States was experiencing an oil shortage. Filling your gas tank was expensive and often meant waiting for hours in long lines. The country was also in the midst of a recession that meant couples had less money to pay a babysitter, dine in a nice restaurant, and take in a movie. Romantic evenings were being spent more economically at home where television was the main source of entertainment.

So perhaps it was fitting that a series about the oil-rich Ewings of Dallas, Texas, would become a weekly can't-miss for families feeling the financial pinch in their real lives. The Ewings were the ultimate dysfunctional family of the era — and had the money and power to act out in ways the average viewer couldn't resist tuning in for. *Dallas* would run for 13 years and forever change the face of television.

The Ewing clan all lived together under one roof on the sprawling Southfork ranch in Braddock, Texas, just outside of Dallas. There was the patriarch, Jock (played by veteran character actor Jim Davis), and his wife, Miss Ellie (long-time stage and screen star Barbara Bel Geddes). They shared Southfork with sons J.R. (Larry Hagman) and Bobby (Patrick Duffy), J.R.'s wife Sue Ellen (Linda Gray), and 16-year-old granddaughter Lucy (Charlene Tilton), who was having an affair with thirty-something ranch foreman Ray Krebbs (Steve Kanaly). Lucy's father was Jock and Miss Ellie's middle son, Gary, the black sheep of the family, who, suffering from alcoholism, had fled the ranch years earlier and was seldom seen on the series (when he did straggle back home, the character was portrayed first by actor David Ackroyd and later by Ted Shackelford).

As the series opened, youngest son Bobby took a bride, Pamela Barnes (Victoria Principal), the daughter of the Ewings' long-time enemy Willard "Digger" Barnes (David Wayne). Digger's son Cliff (Ken Kercheval) shared his father's hatred of the Ewings. Both the Ewing and Barnes families were appalled at the union of Bobby and Pam, but the newlyweds apologized to no one, and soon Pam was a resident of Southfork. The series touched on the seedy, often unprincipled private and professional lives of the two clans.

Seven of the thirteen seasons that *Dallas* was on the air were spent in the Nielsen ratings' top-ten, and the show would eventually become an international hit, playing in countries all

The Ewing clan of CBS's enormously popular prime-time soap *Dallas*. Pictured from left: Steve Kanaly, Patrick Duffy, Victoria Principal, Barbara Bel Geddes, Jim Davis, Charlene Tilton, Larry Hagman, Linda Gray.

over the world. It would also reinvigorate the idea of the prime-time soap opera, a concept that had been all but abandoned after *Peyton Place* had played out in the late 1960s. Continuing storylines were designed to assure that fans would tune in the following week, while season-ending cliffhangers would leave one or more of the Ewings in a life-or-death situation that would keep viewers in suspense until the new episodes began in the fall.

By the early '80s, *Dallas* had inspired at least a half-dozen imitations, including popular hits such as *Dynasty* (1981–89) and *Falcon Crest* (1981–90), a top-rated spin-off, *Knots Landing* (1979–93; featuring the character of Gary Ewing), and a number of less successful projects like *The Secrets of Midland Heights* (1980–81), *Flamingo Road* (1981–82), and *King's Crossing* (1982). While ABC's *Dynasty* gave *Dallas* the closest run for its money, *Dallas* still ultimately reigned as king of the nighttime soaps.

The series' history, however, is rooted in humble beginnings. Back when it premiered in April of 1978, CBS had committed to only five one-hour episodes. The series was added to the network's schedule as a replacement for the cancelled crime drama *Kojak*. *Dallas* surprised everyone by scoring a 37 share for its debut episode, "Digger's Daughter" (4/2/78). The show's second episode on April 9 went up against the TV-movie *A Family Upside Down*, starring Fred Astaire and Helen Hayes, and dropped to a 26 share. But by the time the fifth *Dallas* episode aired on April 30, subtitled "The Barbeque" and featuring what would be a seasonal event in which the Ewings held their annual Southfork rodeo, the audience returned and the program grabbed an incredible 39 share.

The show's impressive spring tryout earned it a spot on CBS's 1978-79 schedule. That fall, the network moved it to Saturday evenings at 10:00 P.M. against ABC's popular *Fantasy Island*. Not the most enviable time period on TV, but *Dallas* would endure and slowly build in popularity until reaching its zenith in the fall of 1980 with the "Who Shot J.R.?" craze.

For those involved in the making of *Dallas*, it was an incredible ride, with wild highs and lows. Many of those involved with the show found it to be the highlight of their careers — both professionally and financially. For relative newcomers Duffy, Gray, and Tilton, it was their big shot at stardom. For Hagman, it was a chance to put on a new face. Best known for his five-year stint as Major Anthony Nelson on *I Dream of Jeannie* (1965–70), Hagman saw *Dallas* as his chance to play drama — perhaps not heavy drama, but good old-fashioned melodrama. For aging veterans Bel Geddes and Wayne, it was an opportunity to get back into the spotlight late in their careers.

In retrospect, however, *Dallas* may have had the greatest meaning for actor Jim Davis. He had spent nearly thirty years playing supporting roles in B-movies, often as the heavy. He had an intense, rugged look that made him a natural in westerns. His credits ranged from the Kirk Douglas film *The Big Sky* (1952) to *Comes a Horseman* with James Caan and Jane Fonda (1978). But despite working steadily and becoming a familiar face to viewers, true fame had eluded him.

At age 63, it was *Dallas* that finally gave him the recognition his talent warranted. But the role of Jock Ewing would, unfortunately, be his last. His death at the end of the series' third year would shock viewers and test the show's resolution. The cast and crew would rally together, both onscreen and off, to keep the series going. Their efforts would not only save *Dallas* but also make it a genuine phenomenon. But the journey was not an easy one.

The man most directly responsible for *Dallas* is creator David Jacobs, who in 1978 was a relative newcomer to Los Angeles looking for his big break. "I moved to L.A. in 1976," he recalls. "I had been a freelance writer in New York, and then my ex-wife married an actor and moved to California with my eleven-year-old daughter, whom I had been very close to and instrumental in raising, so I followed them." It took him nine months to get his first Hollywood writing job. The producers of the Lorimar Productions/CBS police drama *The Blue Knight* needed a script rewrite, and in order to remain on schedule it had to be completed over Labor Day weekend. Few veteran writers wanted to spend the holiday laboring at a typewriter, so Jacobs got the assignment. He did such a good job that he was offered a position on the show's writing staff.

Unfortunately, *The Blue Knight* was cancelled four episodes into its second season, but Jacobs had accomplished the most difficult task facing most struggling newcomers — getting a foot in the door and making a first sale. Continues Jacobs:

> Once I broke that ice, it was easier to get in to see other people and make pitches. I did an episode of a show called *Family*, and then they hired me as story editor. So I got a good reputation pretty fast, because the people who ran *Family*, Nigel and Carol Evan McKeand, were wonderful but very demanding and very tough. And I'd been the only story editor to survive, so that alone gave me a good reputation.

Jacobs also had an ace up his sleeve:

> When I had left *The Blue Knight* at Lorimar, they had given me a development deal, $2,500 to come up with a show of my own. Even while I was doing *Family*, I still had this script to write elsewhere, so I continued to meet with Mike Filerman at Lorimar to discuss ideas. What I came up with first was an American version of *Scenes from a Marriage* [a 1973 Swedish TV series and

film by Ingmar Bergman], only times four. It was about four families living on a cul-de-sac in Southern California. The reason my partnership with Mike Filerman remained so good as the years went by was because I wanted to do art and he wanted to do trash, and between us we did television.

Doing *Scenes from a Marriage* was a very lofty aspiration; with Filerman's help, Jacobs managed to bring it down to a more realistic level and christened the project *Knots Landing*. They took it to CBS executives, who liked the idea, but said if they were going to do a continuing domestic drama they'd rather have something glitzier, more of a saga. The network also had Linda Evans under contract and was looking for something for her to do. Jacobs thought over what CBS had said and went to work on a new idea. "When they said 'saga,' I thought of Texas," he says. "I went home and conceived this female character, using *Romeo & Juliet* as my guide. She married the son of an oil magnate, but their fathers were enemies. And that was *Dallas*."

CBS was still a bit skeptical, but paid Jacobs his $2,500 and ordered five episodes. The pilot script for *Dallas* was dated December 10, 1977, and by February 1, 1978, the cast and crew were in Texas, filming the series' initial episodes. Linda Evans passed on the project, but *Dallas* would again influence her career when, in 1981, she landed a lead role in *Dynasty*, the most successful soap to wash ashore in *Dallas*'s wake.

Creating what would become perhaps the definitive series set in Texas was an odd accomplishment for Jacobs, who had no first-hand knowledge of life in the Lone Star State:

I did not base *Dallas* on any real-life family or individuals, although some people like to claim I did. [laughs] I didn't even have that much time to do research. In fact, I'd never been to Texas except to drive through it once. I was so busy at the time that I decided that I would just write the stereotypes, and then I would go to Dallas and pull it back. So I wrote the stereotypes. Then I went to Dallas and realized that I hadn't gone far enough in terms of the opulence and attitude.

Jacobs was able to take leave from his duties on *Family* and was on location while the first five episodes were being filmed. It was unusual for a series to be shot completely on location the way those early episodes of *Dallas* were. But CBS put the show into production so quickly that it would have been difficult to research, design, and build all the sets in time to get the program on the air as scheduled.

Ultimately, Jacobs believes the authentic locations became a key element to the show's appeal. "For the first five episodes we used a ranch owned by Cloyce Box of the Detroit Lions," Jacobs explains. "I think he enjoyed it for awhile, but when we got picked up I don't think he wanted his ranch subjected to a film crew continuously." Box probably made a wise decision.

Production that summer on *Dallas*'s first full season was moved to another ranch outside of Dallas owned by a man named Joe R. Duncan. Once the series became an international hit, the Duncan home and property began attracting thousands of tourists each year from all over the world. Eventually, the Duncans had to sell their home, after which it was turned into a museum dedicated to the show.

Although Jacobs appreciated the look the locations provided, shooting in Texas did have its share of drawbacks:

The pilot was originally written to take place during a very hot time of the year, but it was freezing when we got down there. That's one of the obstacles you face when shooting on real locations outside of Los Angeles. We did a scene where Victoria Principal was thrown into a lake, and, of course, the scene had been written to take place on a sweltering day. But it was literally freezing the day we shot it. We tried to come up with something comparable to throwing her into the water, but couldn't come up with anything. So we had to throw her in the lake in 30-degree temperature. We had snow in the second episode. So it was very odd, but I still think the episodes looked good.

The final, crucial element to making *Dallas* work was the casting. Jacobs was grateful that CBS and Lorimar gave him a say in the process. Explains Jacobs:

> I was involved to the extent that I could be. Again, I was very new. Robert Foxworth was originally offered the role of J.R., but he really wanted to make the character more sympathetic. I was new so I didn't push my weight around, but I didn't think J.R. should be made more sympathetic. I thought we should understand why he was the way he was. Foxworth said, "Why is this guy so mean, why is he like that?" And I said, "For his father. He could be twenty times more powerful, a hundred times richer, and his father still likes his kid brother the best." I wanted to keep J.R. a guy who was unapologetically bad although understandable, and wanted to have fun with him.

When Larry Hagman's name was first brought up in connection with J.R., Jacobs was initially against casting him. "I thought of him as Major Nelson from *I Dream of Jeannie*, a much softer actor than he proved to be," explains Jacobs. "But he came into our first meeting wearing cowboy boots and a Stetson, and as soon as I saw him standing in the doorway, I thought, 'There he is, there's J.R.' There was never any question he would dominate the show."

After *I Dream of Jeannie*, Hagman had been pegged as a comedic leading man. Since *Jeannie* left the air in 1970, he had starred in two failed sitcoms, *The Good Life* (1971) and *Here We Go Again* (1973). In 1978 he was offered the role of a high school basketball coach in the NBC sitcom *The Waverly Wonders*. He was given the option of doing the lead role in that comedy or becoming a part of the large ensemble that would become *Dallas*. Wisely, he chose to give drama a try and accepted the role of eldest son J.R. Ewing. *The Waverly Wonders*, with Joe Namath in the lead, ran for a mere three episodes in the fall of 1978.

Hagman's J.R. character soon became the linchpin that held *Dallas* together. Although viewers in the '70s may have been shocked at J.R.'s total lack of ethics, Hagman insists that J.R. was not that uncommon a figure in the business world. Decades later, to audiences that have witnessed the many scandals that have rocked U.S. corporations, J.R. would not seem nearly as ruthless. Insists Hagman:

> He was just a regular Texas businessman. I mean, this guy is not unusual down there, or anywhere for that matter. We have the mindset now, and the political regime that reflects the Texas way of doing business, which is "fuck your buddy." In the real world, you have to do business with that kind of guy.

It was important that J.R. not become a one-dimensional villain. One way of doing that, recalls story editor Camille Marchetta, was to make it clear that greed alone was not the overwhelming driving force in J.R.'s underhanded dealings:

> One of my favorite scenes was at the breakfast table with J.R. and Jock. J.R. is just going on and on about some deal that he pulled off, and he's just exuberant and happy and waiting for Jock to say, "Well done." Jock's just eating his breakfast and going, "uh huh," "uh huh," "yes, good, good." And then Bobby comes down the stairs and comes into the dining room and says, "Good morning, Daddy," and Jock turns around and his face lights up, and he says, "Good morning, Bobby." And then the camera cuts to JR, and his face falls because nothing he does is ever, ever going to equal Bobby's walking into a room as far as his father's approval and appreciation. And in that moment, you got the dynamic, the family dynamic, which I think is what made the audience respond.

By the spring of 1980, CBS was so pleased with the show's performance that it placed a last-minute order for additional episodes that season. Remembers Hagman:

CBS made an offer to pick up four more shows, and the producers quickly needed some story ideas. They thought, "What are we going to do," and somebody said of J.R., "Let's shoot the son-of-a-bitch, and then worry about it later," which is what they did. I remember growing up in the days of the serials. You'd go to the movies and see two westerns and three or four serialized things, and you'd go every Saturday to see how things turned out. So we have always had cliffhangers, just not on TV.

In the season finale, subtitled "A House Divided" (3/21/80), J.R.'s devious antics finally catch up with him. Throughout the episode, his enemies swear vengeance against him. In the final moments, J.R. is working late in the Ewing Oil offices when an unidentified assailant enters and shoots him. Viewers were left stunned, not so much by the gunplay as by the fact that they'd have to wait six months to find out whether J.R. was going to live or die — and who had pulled the trigger.

The question of "Who Shot J.R.?" would inspire an international craze over the summer of 1980. T-shirts were made up, songs were written, and bets were placed. "It became ridiculous, but it was warranted," says Hagman. According to supervising producer David Paulsen, "What people didn't know is that we didn't know who'd done it. Any one of a number of people could have. We started figuring out whom we could afford to lose on the show. It was extraordinary because all over the world people were speculating on who might have done it."

The writers and producers huddled that summer to answer the question everyone was asking. Says Marchetta:

We decided that it would be a terrible cheat dramatically if a character of no great importance was the one who had shot him. So we went through our list of important characters and tried to decide who we could sacrifice, and the list got smaller and smaller. Kristin Shephard was an important character who could have gone on to be integrated more into the fabric of the show, but she was also expendable in that she wouldn't have affected the basic dynamic. We couldn't have given up Bobby; we couldn't have given up Pam; and certainly Jock and Miss Ellie were out of it. These were the people who created the dynamic that made the show work.

It was finally revealed, after months of worldwide speculation, that Kristin (played by Mary Crosby) had shot J.R. The episode, subtitled "Who Done It?" aired on November 21, 1980, and drew an amazing 76 share in the ratings, which translated to approximately 41.5 million viewers. It remains to this day one of the highest rated series episodes in television history. It all paved the way for the cliffhanger season finales that are commonplace in series television today.

Dallas would become the number one series on television that season. Everyone involved with the show was on top of the world. Recalls Marchetta:

It was an extremely happy set. People got on very well. Larry, who could have turned it into a nightmare if he'd been J.R., was not. He's an enormously generous actor, good humored and intelligent and great fun to be around. The set was a delight to visit, and I always had a good time when I went down. The actors were happy, and the show was doing well.

Unfortunately, the good times were not to last. Just as *Dallas* was hitting its stride and celebrating its greatest success, tragedy was waiting to strike.

Back when David Jacobs was working with CBS and Lorimar to cast *Dallas*, one of the most pressing concerns was finding just the right patriarch to hold court over the Ewings. They realized that as strong as the other characters were going to be, the character of Jock

Ewing would have to be a figure imposing enough to keep the others in line. It would require an actor with a demanding presence.

Ironically, it became one of the easier parts to cast. Jim Davis didn't even have to come in and read for the part. CBS and Lorimar offered it to him based on his reputation and strong physical stature. Ironically, only Jacobs had reservations. "I thought he was too obvious," explains Jacobs. "That's how much I knew about casting."

Jim Davis was born Marlin Davis on August 26, 1909, in Edgerton, Missouri. He spent his early years working a number of odd jobs, including a stint as a tent-rigger for a circus. He first arrived in Los Angeles in the early 1940s while working as a traveling salesman, and decided to give acting a try. He spent many years as a contract player at Republic Studios, where he became adept at playing both heroes and villains. One of his first major roles was in the 1948 Bette Davis film *Winter Meeting,* but he was never able to establish himself as a leading man. He would go on to appear in over one hundred movies.

Davis also began working in television in the 1950s, co-starring in three series before *Dallas.* In the western *Stories of the Century* (1954), Davis played a railroad detective in the Old West who crossed paths with everyone from Billy the Kid to Tom Horn. His next series, *Rescue 8* (1958–59), was an early version of the '70s hit *Emergency!* in which Davis played a member of the Los Angeles Fire Department's rescue team. He returned to the western genre in 1974 in a short-lived TV version of the John Wayne film *The Cowboys.* He was also a frequent episodic guest star in everything from *The Time Tunnel* to *Gunsmoke.*

Davis married his wife Blanche in 1945, and their daughter Tara Diane was born in 1953. Sadly, Tara died in a car crash in 1970 at age sixteen. The event left her father devastated. Davis never fully recovered emotionally from the trauma. Initially, it caused him to withdraw from his work, and he was fairly inactive in the business for a number of years, working only enough to support his wife. In time, however, he began to find solace in his acting.

Davis's *Dallas* co-star Steve Kanaly greatly admired Davis and became close friends with him during production of the series. Says Kanaly:

> Jim was a great guy that everybody admired and thought highly of. He contributed greatly to the look and authenticity of the show simply by his bearing. I think over the years people have said they could not imagine another actor being Jock Ewing. He just fit the part so well physically. He'd been around in the business for thirty years before he was finally on a show that really developed

Jim Davis (pictured) was a long-time veteran Hollywood character actor by the time he landed the role of patriarch Jock Ewing on the CBS drama series *Dallas* (courtesy CBS/Photofest).

into a huge hit. He used to call himself "the poor man's John Wayne." He had been in many, many B-westerns as the bad guy, and that was OK. He had a nice, long career, but it was full of ups and downs. It only took him thirty years to become a hit. Jim used to think it was kind of fun to say that.

Davis particularly enjoyed it when the cast would travel to Texas each summer to shoot the new season's first batch of episodes on location. Kanaly remembers:

He was definitely in his element when we were in Texas. He had made numerous other films and shows there, and had business relations with the Justin Boot Company, for which he had done print ads. He had a lot of cronies there he played golf with all the time. So he was very happy when we went on location. He thought it was a good idea, and Larry Hagman, of course, also did because he grew up in Fort Worth.

The character of Jock Ewing was often the family peacekeeper. Jock had founded Ewing Oil, or stolen it from the Barnes family, depending on whose story you believe. As the series opened, Jock had just retired from Ewing Oil, although he still kept an office there and consulted. He had hoped sons J.R. and Bobby would bond together and continue to run the company, but it became obvious from the beginning that J.R. did not intend to share the presidency of Ewing Oil with his brother, despite his father's wishes. It was only Jock's presence that kept the peace.

Davis impressed his co-workers, but privately harbored doubts about his abilities. Reveals Hagman:

He was a wonderful guy, but he didn't think he was much of an actor, to tell you the truth. He'd always say, "Well, I just sit there and do my lines." And that's really what he did, but he came over as a very strong character. I think he always felt privileged to work with all the people he did. He was always surprised that everybody thought he was so good. He was much more western than anybody else on the show, except Steve Kanaly. Steve's character turned out to be Jim's bastard son, and he was much more like Jock than anybody in the family.

By the spring of 1981 everyone involved with *Dallas* was still basking in the afterglow of that season's "Who Shot J.R.?" mania. But as the year wore on, the happy climate began to erode as it became clear that Jim Davis's health was failing. "He used to have serious migraine headaches that were debilitating," remembers Kanaly. "He had a history of those. So we were sort of semi-used to the idea that Jim had some bad days."

Midway through the season, Davis's headaches became so bad that he sought medical treatment. Tests revealed that he had an inoperable brain tumor. His only course of action was to undergo chemotherapy and radiation treatments. Throughout it all, Davis was determined to work. Little was said on-set about Davis's illness, but it was no secret. Says Kanaly:

He was a wonderful example to anyone, and especially to us, of how to face this terrible thing. He was determined that it was not going to stop him, that he was going to get through it, and that he was not going to let it hurt the show. He came to work every day that they needed him. He was very brave about it, and had a pretty good sense of humor through the whole thing, even though it was just horrible for him. There was sort of a general deterioration that goes with that treatment — loss of vision and balance, hair loss, weight loss, and these sorts of things. But they kept sort of putting him back together again, and he got through that season — every episode except for the very last one.

The cast and crew were there to support Davis throughout his ordeal, which included an effort to keep word of his illness from leaking to the press. Kanaly remembers:

At the time, everyone was very guarded about the subject. Both Jim and the studio really didn't discuss that there even was a cancer going on. I don't think it was known at all in the business, and none of us talked about it publicly. The whole cast and crew was united on this. It was difficult, because here's our guy, and he's walking in with two guys holding him at the elbows. Memory is another thing that goes, and you can't remember the lines anymore, so he had to work with a teleprompter. It was very obvious to those close to Jim, but we protected him from the press.

Davis made his final appearance in the episode subtitled "New Beginnings" (4/10/81). In the storyline, Jock and Miss Ellie had just reunited after a very public feud that almost tore Ewing Oil apart. They then decide to take a trip for their second honeymoon. In the final scene, we see the two ride away from South Fork in a limousine. This may have been a move on the part of the producers to explain Davis's absence should he not be able to return in the fall. Kanaly felt positive about Davis's prospects: "We really thought that he had this thing pretty well beat, and I expected to see him the following season."

Jim Davis, however, passed away due to complications from his illness on April 26, 1981, at the age of 71. Davis's coworkers had spent months witnessing his declining health. When word finally came that he'd died, they weren't surprised, but were still devastated by the news. States Hagman:

> He had a very long and painful illness, so we were all ready for it. But, of course, when it comes, when you're informed, it's a different matter. I was at a hotel in Scotland, way up in the mountains, and I came down for breakfast and there was a reporter there with a photographer. And as I was coming down the stairs he said, "What's your reaction to Jim Davis dying?" And I thought, "Well, this is a hell of a nice way of getting the news." He wanted some surprised expression on my face or something; and, of course, I didn't give it to him. But I thought it was a rather callous way of getting a reaction; but it was the Hollywood way of finding out what had happened.

Davis was laid to rest at Forest Lawn Memorial Park in Glendale alongside his daughter Tara Diane. He left behind his wife Blanche and half-a-century's worth of performances. *Dallas* is the role he would be most remembered for. Davis was nominated posthumously in 1981 for an Emmy as Outstanding Lead Actor in a Drama Series for his portrayal of Jock Ewing (Daniel J. Travanti took home the award that September for his lead role on *Hill Street Blues*).

"My initial feeling was that I was really glad he did *Dallas,* because *Dallas* gave him that credibility," says Jacobs. "It was a great way to finish his life. My first thought was sadness because we'd lost him, but I was also glad that Jim Davis became an icon before he died. He was terrific, and I saw how the cast was so affected because he was such a great guy."

After Jim Davis's death, the pressure was on the *Dallas* production team (lead by executive producer Philip Capice and supervising producer Leonard Katzman) to find an acceptable way of dealing with Davis's absence. The show had such a loyal legion of fans that Lorimar realized that they risked angering and possibly even alienating viewers if they mishandled the situation.

Even though *Dallas* was a large ensemble, and J.R. had become the central figure, there was still no serious thought given to the idea of bringing in another actor to play Jock. Insists Kanaly:

> I really believe that we were united in our thinking that that was not going to happen. Leonard Katzman respected Jim a lot. Leonard was really the heartbeat of the show for so many years. I mean, there were many people that had their fingers in the pot and were a part of the success of the show, but Leonard was the day-to-day guy to go through — the writer, the producer, the director — the guy we all trusted, who cared about us the most, and I don't think that he would have let that happen. He had a good feeling for what made the show successful, and I'm fairly certain that he felt that to replace the actor would not be accepted.

Eventually, the decision was made not to deal with Davis's death, at least not immediately. When *Dallas* returned for its fourth season in the fall of 1981, it was explained that Jock and Miss Ellie had extended their second honeymoon and would be gone for several more months. Says Paulsen:

That was how we kept him alive. They would call in, and we would do little things like having one of the characters, like J.R. or Bobby, talking to Momma over the phone. And she would say, "Daddy's in the next room and can't talk to you," or "Your Daddy sends his love, but he's taking a walk," or something like that. So we did things like that to keep the character alive, even though the audience knew the actor was dead.

Everyone realized that the trip was only a temporary solution, but it was considered necessary in order to develop an appropriate final farewell for Jock. As Paulsen explains:

It kept our options open. We always knew we would never replace him, we would never replace the actor. It was a question as to how Jock would die. It would not be the way that Jim had died in real life. He had to have a more theatrical death, so to speak.

Miss Ellie returned to Southfork alone early in the season, and it was explained that Jock had flown directly to South America on urgent business for the State Department. Finally, on the January 1, 1982, episode, "Barbecue Two," Jock's fate began to take shape. Miss Ellie had planned a large barbecue to celebrate Jock's homecoming. At the last minute, she received

Jim Davis and Barbara Bel Geddes exuded wonderful chemistry as Jock and Miss Ellie Ewing on the CBS drama series *Dallas* (courtesy CBS/Photofest).

a phone call informing the family that Jock's helicopter had crashed into a lake in South America and sank. In the following episode, "The Search" (1/8/82), J.R., Bobby, and Ray flew down to the crash site to join the search, but nothing was ever found except for a medallion that Jock had worn. They returned to Southfork, and in an emotional finale confronted Miss Ellie with the sad news. The screen then faded to an onscreen tribute to Davis.

It would take until the end of the season for Miss Ellie to finally accept Jock's death. Many felt that the producers should have wrapped up the storyline more quickly. "They got a lot of shows out of that one," admits Hagman. "It might have gone on a little too long."

Observes Marchetta:

> I think they kept him alive for two reasons. One was that the character of Jock was extremely important to the show, and it was very difficult to assess how to move on without him; and the second thing was that he was much loved, and no one wanted to let him go. I think it was personal on the part of Leonard Katzman and everyone doing the show. They were just heartbroken and didn't want to let Jim go.

Despite Jim Davis's death, *Dallas* would continue on for ten more seasons. J.R. and Bobby would repeatedly fight for control of the company their father had founded. J.R.'s scheming would later get him into legal trouble with the U.S. government. As a consequence, the company was ordered to close its doors. The brothers eventually reconciled and started a new company from the ground up. Throughout it all, Davis was never forgotten. A large portrait of Jock continued to hang prominently in the Ewing living room for many years. In troubled times, family members, particularly J.R., would talk to the painting as if Jock himself were in the room. The portrait today hangs prominently in Larry Hagman's home.

Miss Ellie eventually found love again with wealthy Clayton Farlow (played by stage and film star Howard Keel), and the two married at the end of the 1983-84 season ("End Game," 5/18/84). "We realized we had to give her some kind of love interest at that point," offers Paulsen. Howard Keel first appeared on *Dallas* in late 1981 as Clayton, the father of Sue Ellen's lover Dusty Farlow. The producers also considered a romance between Bel Geddes and Morgan Woodward, who had been a recurring character for many years as Punk Anderson, an old friend of Jock's. "We also thought about bringing in someone new, but Howard was such a powerful figure, and he came in and did very well," says Paulsen.

Howard Keel was a one-time automobile mechanic who went on to star in several of MGM's most celebrated musicals: *Annie Get Your Gun* (1950), *Show Boat* (1951), *Calamity Jane* (1953), *Kiss Me Kate* (1953), and

After the death of series regular Jim Davis, the producers of CBS's *Dallas* invited another long-time Hollywood veteran, actor Howard Keel, to join the cast (courtesy CBS/Photofest).

Seven Brides for Seven Brothers (1954). He also performed the same roles on stage, as well as appearing in productions of *Camelot, South Pacific,* and *Man of La Mancha.* By the early '70s, however, he was finding it difficult to land good film roles, and was working mostly in episodic television. Whereas *Dallas* had provided Jim Davis the recognition he'd never achieved, the show served to help Keel regain some of his past glory.

Says Kanaly:

> Howard came in as another character, rather than someone assuming the role of Jock, and that was acceptable. That was the compromise. Everybody was thrilled to have someone like Howard, who was a great guy with a very long and prestigious MGM film career, including some fabulous old musicals that we all loved when we were growing up. He was very fun to be around, he used to sing on the set, and he fit right in. We all immediately loved Howard, and he did a fine job with Clayton. He became an important part of the show. Keel remained with *Dallas* for the remainder of the series' run, although both Clayton and Miss Ellie were absent for most of the program's final season after actress Barbara Bel Geddes decided to retire.

After *Dallas*, Keel continued to make occasional guest appearances on programs like *Murder, She Wrote* and *Walker, Texas Ranger.* He passed away on November 7, 2004, of colon cancer at age 85.

Dallas ended its remarkable run in 1991 after 357 hours had been produced. There was also a 1986 TV-movie titled *Dallas: The Early Years,* a period drama that recounted the story of how Jock Ewing and Digger Barnes first struck it rich back in the 1930s and fought for the love of Ellie. Two sub-par reunion movies also aired in later years: *Dallas: J.R. Returns* (1996) and *Dallas: War of the Ewings* (1998). Reruns remain incredibly popular around the world. With its emphasis on power, lust, and greed among the Texas elite, *Dallas* has truly earned its place as an American classic.

CHAPTER 8

Eight Is Enough
Diana Hyland

On the evening of Tuesday, March 15, 1977, American television viewers witnessed the beginning of one of TV's most fondly remembered family programs. That night from 8:30 to 9:30, ABC aired the pilot episode of *Eight Is Enough*. Audiences were introduced to the Bradford family — father Tom, mother Joan, and their brood of eight offspring. The show came from Lorimar Productions, headed by Hollywood moguls Lee Rich and Merv Adelson.

Like *The Waltons,* another Lorimar series, the Bradford clan was based on a real-life family, that of *Washington Post* columnist Tom Braden, his wife Joan, and their eight children. Braden had written a humorous account of he and his wife's efforts to raise such a large family. The book, published in 1975, captured the attention of producer Rich, who purchased the rights in hopes of developing it into a TV series. Unlike *The Waltons*, about a Depression-era family struggling through financial hardships and eventually World War II, *Eight Is Enough* tackled issues of sex, drugs, rebellion, and racism in a style befitting the 1970s — with humor, just like Braden's book. The series even employed a laugh track, practically unheard of for an hour-long filmed program.

Familiar character actor Dick Van Patten had been cast as Tom Bradford, a columnist for the *Sacramento Register*. Playing Joan, his bride of 25 years, was Diana Hyland, who had viewed *Eight Is Enough* as a vehicle to kick-start her acting career. After getting off to a promising start with roles in two popular soap operas, *Young Doctor Malone* (1958, alongside Van Patten) and *Peyton Place* (1964), followed by a handful of supporting feature film roles, Hyland put her acting on hold after marrying in 1969 and giving birth to son Zachary in 1973. But by 1975 her marriage to Joseph Goodson was over, and Hyland, at age forty, was looking to rekindle her relationship with Hollywood.

Things had been looking up in recent months for Hyland. She'd landed a role as young superstar John Travolta's mother in the critically acclaimed 1976 TV-movie *The Boy in the Plastic Bubble*. As a bonus, she and Travolta, some 18 years her junior, had fallen in love and become one of Tinseltown's most intriguing couples. Then along came *Eight Is Enough*. The pilot was shot in April of 1976, but ABC had passed on it for their fall schedule. But Hyland continued to lobby for the project and was delighted when it was finally given a mid-season order for eight episodes. By the spring of 1977 a spot had finally opened up on ABC's schedule after the network's drama *Rich Man, Poor Man — Book II* concluded its season early.

Diana Hyland played the original matriarch of the large Bradford clan of ABC's family drama *Eight Is Enough*. Hyland had already been diagnosed with breast cancer when production began on the series but had hoped to beat the disease (courtesy ABC/Photofest).

Therefore, the evening of March 15 should have been a joyous occasion for the cast of *Eight Is Enough*—an exciting time filled with hope for the future. But life had taken a fateful twist that had shattered the cast of *Eight Is Enough* and their onscreen family. Instead of viewing the show's debut from the comfort of his home, Dick Van Patten instead watched the premiere broadcast lying in a hospital bed at Los Angeles's Cedars-Sinai Medical Center next to his TV wife Diana Hyland. She'd been diagnosed with cancer after filming had begun and was dying. Van Patten's real-life spouse, Pat, sat close by.

Together they watched the saga of the Bradford family unfold, laughing along at the poignant humor that was to become a trademark of the show. It was a bittersweet evening, everyone trying so desperately to enjoy what they hoped would be the beginning of a long run for *Eight Is Enough*. Yet in the backs of their minds was the ever-present awareness that Diana was dying. She had struggled to complete only a handful of episodes before her disease had become too debilitating for her to continue. They were all keenly aware that whatever the future held for *Eight Is Enough*, Diana Hyland would not be a part of it.

Earlier that evening, Hyland, having grown tired of the hospital food, had asked Van Patten to run down to Chasen's, a popular L.A. eatery, and bring back a takeout order. He returned with three orders of salt steak, which they dined on shortly before the show began. Her spirits never wavered. She continued to vigorously support the ambitions of her castmates even after her own hopes and dreams had been cruelly trampled upon, a testament to what an extraordinary human being Hyland was.

Eight Is Enough had been planned as a series about a nuclear family in an era when two-parent households were becoming less common, a throwback to the days of *Ozzie & Harriett*. Now it, too, was to become an example of a splintered family trying to pick up the pieces of their lives.

When Lee Rich purchased the book *Eight Is Enough*, he immediately turned to veteran writer/producer William Blinn to adapt it for television. Blinn had spent the '60s writing primarily for westerns, including *Rawhide, Bonanza, Gunsmoke, The Big Valley,* and *The High Chaparral.* In the early '70s he'd created two of the decade's most popular police dramas, *The Rookies* and *Starsky & Hutch.* He also wrote the 1971 TV-movie *Brian's Song,* and would receive an Emmy for adapting Alex Haley's *Roots* in 1977. He was one of television's most bankable writers when he sat down to adapt Tom Braden's book. Lee Rich, pleased with the results, then hired Blinn to produce the series as well.

Blinn immediately began casting the Bradford family.

Van Patten and Hyland had worked together during the early 1960s on *Young Doctor Malone,* a soap opera shot in New York. In 1966 Van Patten moved to Los Angeles; Hyland followed suit a short time later, but by then the two had lost touch. It wasn't until the casting sessions for *Eight Is Enough* that they were finally reunited.

Recalls Van Patten:

> When I first had to test for *Eight Is Enough*, I went in and there were about five other couples reading. I tested with Mariette Hartley, and when we were through I was coming out and Diana was waiting to test with some other guy. She said, "Dick, how are you? I love this script, I hope I get it. I really want to get this. Wouldn't it be wonderful if you got it, too. We could play opposite each other." About three days later I got a call saying that I'd gotten the part. And, of course, Diana got it, too. So we were working opposite each other and she was so happy.

Rounding out the cast for the *Eight Is Enough* pilot were eight young performers with varying degrees of experience in the industry: Mark Hamill as oldest son David (age 23), Lani

O'Grady as Mary (21), Susan Richardson as Susan (19), Laurie Walters as Joannie (20), Kimberly Beck as Nancy (18), Connie Needham as Elizabeth (15), Chris English as Tommy (14), and Adam Rich as Nicholas (6). Production on the pilot began in the spring of 1976 and went as well as could be expected. Shooting a show with so many primary characters proved to be a tough introduction to the world of series television for the young actors. The entire cast of ten would appear in many scenes together, which required them to first shoot a master shot, followed by numerous close-ups, while sitting for hours under the hot lights on the soundstage.

Once the pilot was finished, everyone waited while ABC considered its options for fall. When the network finally announced its 1976-77 schedule, *Eight Is Enough* hadn't made the cut. Lee Rich had enough faith in the project that he believed ABC eventually would find a place for the series on its mid-season schedule. But for the time being, all the cast could do was wait. ABC had until January 1977 to make a decision, which put the actors in a tough position. They had to be sure any work they found in the interim would not prevent them from returning to work on *Eight Is Enough* should ABC order it into production.

This arrangement didn't sit well with some of the cast members. Actress Kimberly Beck had been offered a prominent role in *Rich Man, Poor Man — Book II*, a continuation of the award-winning mini-series that had aired on ABC the season before. Since the show was also for ABC, Beck was allowed out of her contract for *Eight Is Enough*.

Mark Hamill also had reservations. After ABC rejected the pilot in May 1976, Hamill headed to England to film the movie *Star Wars*. He'd already completed a starring role in another film, *Corvette Summer,* and returned from England that fall with ambitions to become a presence on the big screen. Unlike the situation with Beck, ABC would not accommodate him.

William Blinn recalls:

> I liked Mark a lot, we got along well. I remember at the end of the pilot I said, "Where are you off to now, what's next?" and he said, "I'm going to England to do some science-fiction thing, and I'm getting a chance to work with Alex Guiness." Then when he came back, he'd done *Star Wars*, which was going to be huge. Then ABC picked up the series. And here he is, *Star Wars* is about to come out, with all that word of mouth, and Mark was committed to this series that no one believed was going to rival Eugene O'Neill in terms of American drama. Mark asked for his release, but Lorimar said no, and I was the one who had to tell him. I said, "They're in a profit business and you're hot commercially, so they're not going to let you out. You'll just have to make the best of it." He stormed out of my office, pissed off, not at me but at the situation, and he went off and got in a car crash and put his face through the windshield. Now I don't know what the power of the unconscious mind is, but at that point we couldn't use him. He needed a year or more of cosmetic, reconstructive surgery. So we replaced him.

When ABC finally did greenlight *Eight Is Enough* as a series early in 1977, actor Grant Goodeve was hired to portray eldest son David; Dianne Kay was signed to replace Beck in the role of Nancy; and Willie Aames assumed the character of middle son Tommy. Such recasting is typical with many series during early development. But other factors were going on behind the scenes that few were aware of, factors that would alter the course of *Eight Is Enough*.

The previous summer, shortly after the pilot had wrapped production, Diana Hyland had been diagnosed with breast cancer. She believed the cancer had been caused by breast implants she'd gotten in the 1960s, which at one point had ruptured and been replaced.

Blinn remembers Hyland's courage throughout the entire ordeal:

The Bradford family of ABC's ensemble drama *Eight Is Enough*. Pictured from left: (top row) Lani O'Grady, Susan Richardson, Grant Goodeve, Dick Van Patten, Diana Hyland, Dianne Kay, Willie Aames, Adam Rich, (front row, seated) Laurie Walters, Connie Needham (Newton) (courtesy Dick Van Patten).

I became friends with her during shooting of the *Eight Is Enough* pilot. She was just a sweet, funny lady. She was diagnosed with breast cancer a month or so after the pilot was out of production. Either she or her doctor found a lump in her breast. It was suspicious. Her mother and father flew out from Shaker Heights, Ohio, where Diana had grown up. I know they were out here when she got the final diagnosis because I was at the hospital with them while they were waiting for the doctor to come out of Diana's room. I can remember the doctor going into the room and asking us to leave. We did and stood there in the hallway for a couple of minutes, and I began thinking it doesn't take this long to deliver good news. And it didn't. He was in there for five or ten minutes, and when we went in, Diana had received the bad news. It was dire in terms of what her therapy was to be. She had a mastectomy, and it seemed to be a successful procedure. Obviously, the emotional and physical toll was horrific.

Hyland underwent a radical mastectomy, followed by several weeks of chemotherapy at Cedars-Sinai. By early July, 1976, she had completed the treatments, and her doctors were optimistic about her recovery. So was Diana, who had managed to avoid many of the more severe side effects of the radiation. She then opted for breast reconstruction surgery in order to rebuild as much of the affected areas as possible.

Afterward, she felt well enough to accept a role in *The Boy in the Plastic Bubble.* Hyland played Mickey Lubitch, a mother whose son had been born with an impaired immune system, forcing him to grow up isolated from direct human contact inside a specially designed germ-proof environment. Robert Reed co-starred as her husband, while rising superstar John Travolta was signed to play her son. Travolta had just finished his first season as Vinny Barbarino on TV's *Welcome Back, Kotter,* and that fall would sign a million-dollar deal with producer Robert Stigwood to star in two upcoming films: *Saturday Night Fever* and *Grease.* By the time production on *The Boy in the Plastic Bubble* had wrapped in early September, 1977, Hyland and Travolta were deeply in love. Travolta was fully aware of Hyland's health problems and was totally committed to remaining by her side regardless of what was to come.

Hyland managed to conceal both her health crisis and her budding romance with Travolta from the cast and crew of *The Boy in the Plastic Bubble.* Recalls director Randal Kleiser:

Diana was very professional throughout the shoot. I had no idea that she had any medical problems. The one observation that I remember was the last night of shooting, she had a scene where she was in the bedroom with her husband, played by Robert Reed. She was dressed in a white slip, and I noticed she was acting very seductive on the set, flirting with the crew. This did not seem in character with her behavior on the rest of the shoot. It occurred to me that she may have been motivated by wanting to appear attractive to the male crew members, knowing she was facing medical problems.

It wasn't until later that fall that Hyland and Travolta would unveil their relationship to the world. On November 17, 1976, they attended as a couple the premiere of the horror movie *Carrie* (in which Travolta had a supporting role). Kleiser was at the Avco Cinema Center in Westwood that evening and admits to being caught off guard. "I was surprised to see Diana and John sitting together," he says. "I asked what they were doing. They told me they were dating, and I was amazed. The idea that I cast them as mother and son and now they were lovers seemed surreal."

Unfortunately, Hyland and Travolta's love story was about to take another turn for the worse.

Production on the first batch of *Eight Is Enough* episodes began in late January 1977. But before she could return to the set, Hyland's cancer returned. She had begun experiencing severe back pain and fatigue earlier in the month, but told everyone it was the result of a back injury.

In truth, her cancer had spread to her spine and into her brain. Only William Blinn knew the truth, but he was determined not to replace Hyland. They kept her condition from the rest of the cast and crew in hopes that, once again, her cancer would go into remission. She continued to work each day in a great deal of pain while simultaneously returning to Cedars-Sinai for a second round of chemotherapy.

Dick Van Patten recalls those early days on the set. "When we did the second show, she seemed fine," he says. Then one day while shooting the series' third episode, subtitled "Pieces of Eight" (3/29/77), Hyland began to feel the strain. Early one afternoon when the cast broke for lunch, Van Patten caught up to Hyland outside the soundstage on the Warner Bros. lot.

"Let's walk to lunch," he said.

"No, Dick, I don't think I'm going to walk there. I think I'll just have them bring it to me."

"No, no, it's better for you to walk."

"You go, I'll eat in the dressing room."

"Come on, don't be lazy," Van Patten teased.

Van Patten had no idea how much pain Hyland was actually in. "I didn't know that she was sick," he says. "The reason she didn't want to walk was because she had no energy, she was saving it all up for the show. She wanted that part so badly that she didn't want anyone to know that she was sick. But she passed the physical, that's the part that I'll never understand."

Hyland had managed to pass the physical exam that a studio requires of each actor to determine whether he or she is healthy enough to meet the demanding physical requirements of doing a weekly series. It usually involves a physician coming to the performer's dressing room, giving him or her a physical examination, and drawing blood. Despite her deteriorating health, Hyland got through the exam without raising any red flags.

There had been other signs, as well, that Hyland was having difficulty. Actress Dianne Kay remembers first auditioning for the role of Nancy after Kimberly Beck left the project. "I was supposed to audition opposite Diana, because the role was for someone to play her daughter," remembers Kay. "But when I got there, John Travolta's sister Ellen performed the screen test with me because Diana wasn't feeling well at the time."

Kay finally got to know Hyland during production of the "Pieces of Eight" episode:

I didn't know at the time that she was so ill. But that episode featured Diana and myself in several key scenes together. Diana's hobby on the show was photography, and my character wanted to model, so the episode was about her trying to encourage me to go into modeling and she would take pictures of me. I remember working with her, and she was always very, very tired, but she kept it to herself. She didn't ever complain, despite being in so much pain. I do remember that she had a stand-in who was a very close friend of hers, and what I learned is that she had incredible back pain and she was also going blind, so she couldn't hit her mark. But she never told anybody these things. Every time we would break on the set, she'd go into her trailer, and this woman who was her stand-in would give her back massages. The cancer had gotten into her spine, and she was just in incredible pain. She was so sweet to me because I was so new to the business.

Hyland was able to continue working through *Eight Is Enough*'s fourth episode before her condition deteriorated and she could not report for work. "We got to a point where we couldn't put Diana in front of the camera anymore," explains Blinn. "So we manufactured a storyline whereby her character went off to visit a relative who was having a baby."

Even then, Blinn refused to discuss the prospect of replacing her. Hyland was at a critical point in her fight for life, and Blinn wanted her to know that he was behind her. Diana's parents, Mary and Ted Gentner, had moved out from Ohio to help care for her. John Travolta, who was busy shooting *Saturday Night Fever* in New York, would call nightly and fly home often to be with her. Says Blinn:

There have been books written about the vacuous nature of some performers, but John Travolta never wavered. He was as stand-up a human being as one could possibly be. Once he left for New York, he was in touch all the time, and when the cancer reoccurred, he was there for her as much as one human being could possibly be. You don't give out grades for life, but he certainly got an A+ from me.

Although Hyland couldn't physically be on the set of *Eight Is Enough*, Blinn worked out a way to keep her a part of the ensemble. He explains:

I went over to her house a number of times with a tape recorder and would record her side of a phone conversation with Dick Van Patten. Later, we'd shoot Dick on the other end of the call; he would be on camera, and we would just hear Diana. And to her everlasting credit, Diana's energy and her intelligence and her performance in those off-camera telephone conversations was terrific. It was kind of hard to do because she'd been drained in just about every possible way from cancer. She'd lost most of her hair to the radiation. She was a beautiful woman and proud of her beauty — properly so, not vain. Obviously, something like that, especially to a beautiful woman, has got to be really awful.

It became impossible to keep the rest of the cast and crew in the dark about Hyland's illness at this point, so Blinn called everyone into his office one afternoon and explained the situation, told them that Hyland was dying and would not be returning to the show. They were understandably devastated:

I let the cast and the crew know, only because there were so many rumors flying around. In this town, maybe in any town, if someone doesn't show up for awhile, they're in rehab or they've been in a car crash or they're having plastic surgery. So there are all these conspiracy theories going all the time. I didn't want that to happen with Diana.

Blinn also credits Lorimar and ABC for backing his decisions about how to handle Hyland's illness. In particular, however, he felt it important to make a statement to the young cast members, many of whom were getting their first real taste of the business:

I don't think it was ever talked about, but implicit was the fact that it was wrong for the kids, the young performers, to see Diana being viewed as just a piece of a machine that could get replaced. You can replace a character, but not a human being. I wanted the kids to understand the difference.

Blinn would face eerily similar circumstances when he was hired to develop and produce the television version of the hit movie *Fame* in the early 1980s. Actor Michael Thoma was a recurring character on *Eight Is Enough*, playing Tom Bradford's best friend and physician, Dr. Greg Maxwell. Blinn also hired him to portray drama instructor Mr. Crandall on *Fame* in 1982. Just as the second season of *Fame* was about to commence production, Thoma came to Blinn and told him that he had cancer. Says Blinn:

Michael was a good friend of mine. He had actually been a teacher of mine back in New York at the drama school I had gone to, and he was also heading up the American Academy of Dramatic Arts out here. The hardest day I ever put in was when Michael came to me at the beginning of that season and said to me, "I have cancer, they think it's bad; they don't know if it's terminal, but if you don't want to use me, I'll understand." He was perhaps the most professional man I have ever known. I said, "I wouldn't do that." Then three or four months later, he came to me and said, "I'm terminal." So I had an episode written that was our effort to say goodbye to Michael. The fictional springboard of the episode was that there were budget cuts and they had to let some people go, and they let the drama teacher go, and he was going to be out in the cold. There was a party at the end of the episode where all the students said goodbye to him. Word got out to the other actors, and when they were saying goodbye to him, they knew they were really saying goodbye. It was both awful and wonderful, but I'm glad Michael realized how much we cared about him.

But with Diana Hyland, circumstances were just the opposite. She would not admit the disease had beaten her, even after landing back in the hospital in mid–March. She insisted on returning home later in the month, perhaps sensing the end was near, but refusing to outwardly concede to it. Her son Zachary was staying with his father. Recalls Blinn:

> At that time, there was a lot of groundless optimism. People were saying, "You're going to be fine, they can do wonders, you'll get by all this." Whistling past the graveyard. How much Diana bought into all that, I don't know. I suspect she had more reality in her soul than to be swept up in all that. But I think, knowing Diana, that she would have gone along with that for the kids' sakes.

On the morning of March 27, 1977, Dick and Pat Van Patten had just attended church services at St. Paul's in Westwood. As they were leaving the church, Dick began to think about Diana. Memories of that evening at Cedars-Sinai, nearly two weeks earlier, during which he and Pat had watched the premiere of *Eight Is Enough* with Diana, were still fresh in his mind. He states:

> I still hoped she would come back. I said to Pat, "Diana is at home, why don't we go and see her?" Her home was only a few blocks from the church. So we went to her house and rang the doorbell, and John Travolta answered. He was wearing a white suit. He said, "Come on in, it's almost over. She's going to die today. She only has a few hours." I don't know what made us go by that day, but we did. We went in, and there was a nurse, John Travolta, and Diana's mother and father.

When it had become clear that the end was near, production on *Saturday Night Fever* in New York City was shut down so Travolta could jet back to Los Angeles and be by Hyland's side. Earlier that morning he'd stopped and bought the white suit he'd been wearing because Diana had suggested he pick one up for a trip they'd been planning, one they'd never now be able to take.

The Van Pattens did their best to make things easier for Travolta and Mary and Ted Gentner. Diana was in a coma, but everyone took turns at her bedside. Recalls Van Patten:

> We were talking, and I said to John, "Did you talk to a priest or a minister?" He was at a loss, in a daze, he didn't know what he was doing. He said, "No, no, what should I do?" I said, "Well, I can go back to St. Paul's, we've got a good friend there, Father Curtis. I'll get him to come right over." So I went over to the church, which was just a few blocks away, and told Father Curtis, and he came over immediately with me and gave her the last rites.

Father Robert Curtis had been a movie producer before joining the priesthood. Just two months earlier he'd been called in to help eulogize the late actor Freddie Prinze, who'd committed suicide during production of his hit series *Chico and the Man*. Explains Van Patten:

> Father Curtis told us, "She can hear you. I've seen people like this before, and even though she's not responding, tell her what you want to tell her because she can hear you." We then took turns talking to her, John was talking to her, her parents talked to her, and I talked to her. And she did respond the best she could. That was a wonderful thing for John because there were so many things he wanted to say to her, and now he knew she could hear him.

Dick Van Patten and Diana Hyland portrayed Tom and Joan Bradford, parents of eight rambunc-tious siblings on the ABC family series *Eight Is Enough*. Hyland lost her courageous battle with breast cancer after completing only four episodes (courtesy ABC/Photofest).

An hour and a half after Father Curtis administered the last rites, Diana Hyland died in the arms of John Travolta. She was only 42 years old. There was a tremendous amount of sadness mixed with relief that her suffering was at last over. Although her life had been cut so tragically short, she'd made the most of every moment and accomplished her goals. Through hard work, she'd made her way from a small town in Ohio to Hollywood, where she achieved fame not once but twice. She was a loving and caring mother to son Zachary, whom she'd done her best to shield from her pain over the past year. She wanted him to remember her as being happy and vibrant.

After Hyland had passed away, the nurse on duty didn't know who to call. Van Patten again stepped in and called the funeral parlor that had taken care of arrangements for his mother. There was a bit of controversy when the county coroner arrived. Because of a loophole in California divorce law, Hyland and her husband, Joseph Goodson, had failed to properly finalize their divorce proceedings, and therefore were still legally married at the time of her death. The coroner required the signature of her next-of-kin before the body could be released to the undertaker, so Van Patten had to go with them to Goodson's home and inform him of the situation in order to get his authorization. Goodson then retained full custody of their son.

Diana Hyland was cremated. Travolta spread the ashes on her favorite stretch of beach a few days after her death. Plans for a memorial service had to be scrapped when the press learned of the pending arrangements and showed up in droves.

Travolta could not escape the onslaught of media attention that resulted from Hyland's passing. He re-teamed with director Randal Kleiser that summer on the big-screen musical *Grease*. Travolta arrived on the movie's set mourning for Hyland. His co-workers tried their best to shield Travolta from the press. "The day we were shooting the 'Greased Lightning' musical number, *People* magazine had a cover story on Diana's death and how it affected John," recalls Kleiser. "He was angry and depressed because the journalist promised not to talk about Diana. He felt frustrated because there was nothing he could do about it."

The cast of *Eight Is Enough* also had to return to work. They were just completing work on the series' initial order of eight episodes, and although ratings for the show were good, no one knew whether ABC would ask for a second season. If they did, there was still the question of what direction the show would take. Without Hyland, the program seemed to lose its way.

A meeting was held early in May between Blinn, executives at Lorimar, and Brandon Stoddard, head of prime-time programming at ABC. Stoddard wanted to know how the show would handle Hyland's death before making a final decision whether to put *Eight Is Enough* on the fall slate. Before going in, Blinn and Lorimar began discussing their options: how do they replace Hyland's character, and should they? One school of thought was to just bring in another actress to play Joan Bradford. The other was to have the mother pass away, let Tom Bradford deal with that and then maybe start to date, providing storylines for a man with eight kids attempting to re-enter the dating pool.

Blinn felt the latter option provided the opportunity for some interesting and humorous storylines. "How many woman are going to say, 'Oh, great, you have eight kids...' and all that stuff," he laughs. "My vote, and I campaigned heavily at Lorimar, was to portray him as a widower, and then if in the dating storylines we found some actress with whom Dick Van Patten had some really funny, attractive, appealing chemistry, then we would consider making that woman the stepmom."

That was Lorimar's stance, and that was the storyline that Blinn and the studio decided they would pitch to Stoddard. Recalls Blinn:

Then we walked into the ABC meeting, and the first sentence out of Brandon Stoddard's mouth was, "I certainly hope we're agreed that we're not going to play him as a widower." And the Lorimar executives said, "Oh, we'd never do that. Of course not." I just looked around the room; I felt like John Dean when he saw the tape recorder. I was absolutely dumbstruck. But eventually we compromised. We just set up a timetable — for the first six episodes we would play him as a widower just starting to date. We would pick him up at the start of the season at a period where he was missing his wife, but he'd already progressed through that stage of intense grieving. Then, by the fourth episode, he would meet a woman and we'd take things from there.

Based on their agreement, and the fact that *Eight Is Enough* had placed 23rd in the yearly ratings for the 1976-77 season, ABC renewed the show for a second season. The cast, still shaken by Hyland's loss, was happy they'd be remaining together. Van Patten had assumed the show would be cancelled, and "was surprised and thrilled when I heard the news," he says. Dianne Kay felt likewise:

Everyone was very sad, there was a sadness on the set because everyone really loved Diana. We were wondering how the show was going to do and what direction they were going to go in right after she died. But they made good decisions and obviously the right choices because the ratings continued to climb. The show moved in a whole new direction and took on a life of its own, and America related to it.

According to Kay, dealing with Tom Bradford as a single parent probably added a greater realism to the series in terms of the drama:

It was an interesting dynamic because it changed the format of the show in that now we were dealing with a widower with eight children, whereas before it was a family show with a mom and a dad. It was like *Ozzie & Harriett* in its own way, only with eight kids. Then that changed. I got a lot of fan mail from children who were in a similar situation in their home and watched our show regularly because it made them feel comfortable seeing how other families dealt with death, especially a mother. I liked the show before he got married again, to tell you the truth, because the kids were more involved in what dad was doing, and that was interesting.

When *Eight Is Enough* opened its second season on September 14, 1977, it was explained that Joan Bradford had been dead for about three months, the approximate time of the program's summer hiatus. In the opener, subtitled "Is There a Doctor in the House?" Tom's friend, Dr. Maxwell (Thoma), moves in with the Bradfords after a fight with his wife. He and Tom soon find themselves contemplating the single life again. By the end of the episode, Maxwell was reunited with his wife, and Tom has successfully re-entered the dating scene.

He wouldn't remain single for long, however. In the second episode of the season ("Trial Marriage," 9/21/77), far earlier than originally anticipated, Tom met the woman who was to become the next Mrs. Bradford. The storyline centered on middle son Tommy breaking his ankle while playing football and missing five weeks of school. To ensure that he would keep up with his schoolwork, Tom hires a tutor to come to the house, Sandra Sue "Abby" Abbott. Several actresses had tested for the role, including Mariette Hartley (who had tested for the role of Joan Bradford) and Ellen Travolta. Eventually the part was given to Betty Buckley, an actress whose background was primarily on the stage. Her one feature film credit was 1976's *Carrie,* alongside Sissy Spacek and John Travolta.

Tom and Abby's relationship continued to develop throughout the fall, and by November

Shortly after the loss of co-star Diana Hyland, actress Betty Buckley was added to the cast of ABC's family ensemble *Eight Is Enough* as a new romantic interest for father Tom Bradford. Pictured, clockwise from top left: Susan Richardson, Connie Needham (Newton), Grant Goodeve, Willie Aames, Lani O'Grady, Dianne Kay, Buckley, Adam Rich, Dick Van Patten, Laurie Walters (courtesy ABC/Photofest).

sweeps they were ready to walk down the aisle. In a special two-hour telecast subtitled "Children of the Groom" (11/9/77) they exchanged vows, and Abby became stepmother to the eight Bradford children.

Audience reaction to Betty Buckley and the remarriage of Tom Bradford was positive. Ratings began to rise, and soon the show was placing regularly in the top ten. Buckley was initially a little concerned about whether she'd be welcomed by the cast or seen as the person trying to take Diana Hyland's place in their family. But her concerns were unfounded. "Yes, she was welcome," insists Blinn. "They knew they had to have a mom and did everything in their power to make it as un-awkward as possible. There was no animosity; everybody understood the reality of Betty coming in." Buckley soon started to feel at home. An accomplished singer, she would often lobby the producers to develop scripts where she could put her impressive vocal talents to use.

Eight Is Enough had clearly become a bona-fide hit. Many TV producers in William Blinn's place would have opted to move forward and leave the tragic memories of the first season and the late Mrs. Joan Bradford behind. But Blinn opted instead to offer frequent reminders of the series' darker period. He didn't want Diana Hyland's memory, or her contributions to the program, to be forgotten. Says Blinn:

It would be unbelievable to think they could just move on. Anyone who's lost a parent at a young age knows what I mean. My dad died when I was sixteen. That's not a kid, a child, but neither is it quite an all-put-together human being. And it's always going to leave a little scar. Looking back from a writer's standpoint, I didn't know how to do it any other way. I just couldn't see us believably getting through the first Christmas without the mother and not referencing her and not having her mean so much to them.

The series' Christmas episode that year was a special two-hour telecast subtitled "Yes, Nicholas, There Is a Santa Claus" (12/14/77). The episode opened with a thief breaking into the Bradford home shortly before the holiday. Young Nicholas catches him in the act, but assumes the stranger standing beside the Christmas tree with a sack over his shoulder has to be Santa Claus and allows the intruder to walk out the door with the family's gifts. Upon learning the truth, Nicholas runs away, leaving his family frantically trying to locate him. By the time Christmas Eve arrives, Nicholas is safely back home, but there are still no Christmas presents, save for one — a gift that their mother Joan had purchased for Tommy earlier in the year, before her death, and hid away. In a tear-filled finale, Tom produces the single gift, bearing a note to Tommy from his mom. The episode ranks as a favorite among cast members and fans alike. "As we were doing that scene where Tommy read that note from our mom," says Kay, "the tears were all real. I'll always remember that show."

Producer William Blinn left *Eight Is Enough* after the second season but looks back on the show as one of his proudest accomplishments. He also remembers it because it allowed him to cross paths with Diana Hyland, whose courage will always live with him. He's also proud of the way in which others handled her illness as well: John Travolta, the cast of *Eight Is Enough*, ABC, and Lorimar. In a business often known for being cold and ruthless, Diana Hyland brought out the best in everyone. He says:

Obviously, something like this in never anything but tragic, especially for a woman Diana's age who was just getting into a series that would have been a hit and could have provided her with a nice income that she could have used for her son. One thing that a lot of people don't know is that Lee Rich had Lorimar set up a trust fund for Zachary, Diana's son, which ended up paying for Zachary's college education. I think it goes largely to Lee being an extraordinarily decent human being. He's a salesman and a hustler, but his word is very good.

Eight Is Enough had a successful five-year run, ending in 1981 after 112 episodes. The Bradford clan was reunited for two TV-movies in later years: *Eight Is Enough: A Family Reunion* (1987) and *An Eight Is Enough Wedding* (1989). The entire cast returned for the specials, with the exception of Betty Buckley, who had stage commitments. Mary Frann replaced her in the first telefilm; Sandy Faison in the follow-up.

Eight Is Enough is fondly remembered as one of TV's most popular family programs, and although Diana Hyland was with the series for only a brief time, she managed to instill in her co-stars and fans an unending inspiration for the brave approach she took towards both her life and death.

CHAPTER 9

Gimme a Break!
Dolph Sweet

In the spring of 1979, CBS began developing *Featherstone's Nest*, a sitcom pilot starring Ken Berry as Dr. Charlie Featherstone, a busy physician and single father who hires a black housekeeper to help raise his two young children. African-American actress Virginia Capers was cast as nanny Bella Beauchamp. The gimmick was that Bella would talk to God in moments of crisis or indecision, and He would tell her what to say or do. The pilot came from producers Danny Thomas and Ronald Jacobs *(Make Room for Daddy, The Andy Griffith Show)*, and was helmed by director Jim Drake *(Alice, Mary Hartman, SCTV)*. Although the pilot appeared promising, CBS President William Paley killed the project as soon as he viewed it. Remembers Jim Drake:

> Paley said, "I don't want to do a show about a black maid. Not because of racism so much as I don't want a white man telling a black woman what to do." The whole thing got scrapped over his attitude that this wasn't the sort of thing we should be doing in the early '80s. He said, "As long as I'm on this network, I will not have that."

In the fall of 1981, NBC President Brandon Tartikoff must have felt differently. He decided to give a similar pilot from producer Alan Landsburg *(Barney Miller)* a place on the network's schedule. *Gimme a Break!* was co-created by writer/producers Mort Lachman *(All in the Family)* and Sy Rosen *(Rhoda, Taxi)*. Gone was the idea of having the housekeeper receive messages from God, but beyond that, *Gimme a Break!* very closely resembled *Featherstone's Nest*.

Actress Nell Carter was hired to play Nellie Ruth "Nell" Harper, surrogate mother to the three spirited young daughters of Glenlawn Chief of Police Carl Kanisky. Nell had been the Kanisky's longtime housekeeper and was very close to the Chief's wife Margaret. When she learned she was dying, Margaret asked Nell to stay on and help Carl raise the children after her death. Carl knew he couldn't raise the girls alone but didn't want to admit it. The conflict and the comedy emerged primarily from the relationship between Nell and Carl. She was strong and opinionated and determined to keep her promise to Margaret, while Carl felt Nell often overstepped her bounds and violated his role as head of household.

Star Nell Carter was a native of Birmingham, Alabama, whose acting ambitions led her to New York. She first earned notice for a dazzling performance in the Tony Award-winning play *Ain't Misbehavin'* in 1977. On film, she sang and danced in director Milos Forman's movie version of the stage play *Hair*. She also appeared on television in the soap opera *Ryan's Hope*

A first-season photo of the Kanisky family of NBC's domestic sitcom *Gimme a Break!* Pictured clockwise from left: Nell Carter, Lauri Hendler, Kari Michaelsen, Dolph Sweet, Lara Jill Miller (courtesy NBC/Photofest).

from 1978 to 1979. Her work quickly garnered the attention of Joel Thurm, head of casting for NBC, who put her under exclusive contract to the network in 1980. Carter, who'd been rehearsing the role of Effie in a workshop for the play *Dreamgirls*, packed up her belongings and made the move from New York to Los Angeles.

Immediately upon her arrival, Thurm and Tartikoff found a regular role for Carter on *Lobo* (the second-season title for the network's comedy *The Misadventures of Sheriff Lobo*). Carter played Sgt. Hildy Jones, the sassy aide to Atlanta's grumpy Chief of Police. The future of the low-rated series was already in doubt, but it was a way of keeping Carter busy until something more suiting her talents could be found. By the time *Lobo* was cancelled in the spring of 1981, the pilot for *Gimme a Break!* was in development and beckoning to Carter.

Cast as *Gimme a Break*'s Chief Carl Kanisky was character actor Dolph Sweet. The New York-born Sweet got his start in acting under the most bizarre of circumstances. While fighting in World War II, Sweet was taken prisoner and sent to a German POW camp. It was there that he began to act in plays staged by prisoners for the benefit of both their compatriots and the enemy. When Sweet returned to the U.S. after the war, he continued to pursue acting as a career. Pudgy and stone-faced, he was often cast in roles that presented him as slow of wit, which bothered him greatly. He worked hard, studied his craft, and eventually made it to Broadway. He also directed some two-dozen plays during his stage career.

In the early 1960s Sweet relocated to Los Angeles to pursue work in films and television. He landed his first movie role in the 1961 film *The Young Doctors*, and was later cast by novice filmmaker Francis Ford Coppola in the director's feature debut, *I'm a Big Boy Now* (1966, as a police officer), and then in Coppola's *Finian's Rainbow* (1968, as the sheriff).

He continued to work steadily throughout the '60s and '70s, playing grouchy police officers in films such as *The Out-of-Towners* (1970), *The New Centurions* (1972), *The Migrants* (1974), and *An Act of Violence* (1979). On TV he appeared opposite Peter Falk in the series *The Trials of O'Brien* (1965–66), and as Police Chief Gil McGowan on the daytime drama *Another World* (from 1972 to 1977). His resume also included a number of big-screen comedies, including *The Bad News Bears in Breaking Training* (1977) and *Heaven Can Wait* (1978), and the short-lived ABC TV-series *When the Whistle Blows* (1980–81). Then, in 1981, Sweet won his role on *Gimme a Break!* Joel Thurm had remembered Sweet from the play *The Penny Wars* and suggested him to Tartikoff.

Rounding out the *Gimme a Break!* cast as the Kanisky daughters were a trio of talented young actresses. Kari Michaelson beat out actress Helen Hunt for the role of oldest daughter Katie (age 16), the "bad girl"; Lauri Hendler was hired to play middle daughter Julie (14), the bookworm; and Lara Jill Miller was cast as Samantha (11), the baby of the family. Character actor and director Howard Morton rounded out the cast as hair-brained Officer Ralph Simpson, who worked closely with Carl Kanisky at the Glenlawn Police Department.

NBC introduced the Kanisky family to TV audiences on the evening of Thursday, October 29, 1981. *Gimme a Break!* was certainly a product of the conservative early '80s. The idea of a black housekeeper working for a white man would have been fodder for an unending string of racially-charged storylines just a few years earlier. But arriving in the fall of 1981, the series was incredibly tame. Little was made of the domestic situation onscreen. Critics, too, had few words to offer up in regards to the arrangement; they were, however, brutal in the critique of the series in general, branding it one of the fall's least amusing new shows.

The series' initial ratings were nothing to laugh at. *Gimme a Break!* would probably have faced an early cancellation were it not for two overwhelming factors in its favor. First,

Brandon Tartikoff had a great deal of faith in Nell Carter and her potential to become a break-out star. The other, more ominous, reason, was that the network simply didn't have another series to replace it with. NBC was still trying to live down the trouncing it had experienced with *Supertrain* two years earlier, and its fall 1981 schedule included such dubious titles as *Here's Boomer, Bret Maverick, Harper Valley, Lewis & Clark,* and *Fitz and Bones.* The few hits that NBC had, like *CHiPs, Little House on the Prairie,* and *Quincy, M.E.,* were aging, and *Hill Street Blues* (which had just debuted), while a critical favorite, was at least a year away from attracting a sizeable audience.

Despite being ratings challenged, several exceptional episodes emerged during *Gimme a Break!*'s first season. Among them was "Mom's Birthday" (11/19/81), in which the family struggled to get through Margaret's birthday six months after her death. Just as touching was "Sam's Affair" (3/18/82), in which young Samantha kisses a boy for the first time. Her concerned father warns her that kissing boys can lead to pregnancy, and soon Samantha is convinced she's expecting. Rather than simply playing the situation for laughs, the episode realistically portrays the horror a young girl in such a situation would be experiencing. A bit of real-life controversy did arise with "The Emergency" (2/4/82), in which Carl learns that Katie is using birth control.

But as things were coming together onscreen, backstage problems were beginning to mount. The source of the tensions centered primarily on Nell Carter. As a child, Carter had been physically abused. She became pregnant at seventeen; after the birth, she gave up daughter Tracey for adoption, which would haunt her in later years. As a young adult, Carter suffered from feelings of anger, guilt, insecurity, and loneliness. She developed an addictive personality that led to abuse of drugs, alcohol, and food. Now that she was receiving a large weekly paycheck as the star of her own sitcom, Carter could afford to indulge in her self-destructive behavior as never before. By the end of the first season, she had a cocaine habit that was costing her $1,000 a week. Her weight ballooned to 200 pounds.

Featherstone's Nest director Jim Drake, who also frequently helmed episodes of *Gimme a Break!*, recalls Carter's erratic behavior on the set:

The Director's Guild used to sponsor gatherings of teachers and educators, and I would always open my set to them. On one occasion, Nell had gone out at lunch time and gotten pretty drunk, and had come back and for twenty minutes was just kind of badgering everybody on the set, yelling at the kids and so on. It was obviously out of character. If she hadn't been drinking she wouldn't have behaved that way. Then she turns around and sees twenty adults looking at her from the bleachers, and she says, "Where the hell did they come from?" Well, later I called the Guild to apologize, but they said the teachers loved that they'd finally gotten a real first-hand look behind the scenes at a TV show. By that afternoon, when it wore off, Nell was fine again. You had to kind of weather those storms.

Carter's weight gain also became reason for alarm. Besides being overweight, Carter had developed high blood pressure and diabetes. Claims Drake:

On one occasion we were going to shut down. The cast got physicals at the beginning of the year to confirm they didn't have any health problems. Normally, when you go in for the physical, if you walk in and breathe and follow a light with your eyes, they'll say you're ready to go. With Nell, they found that her blood pressure and diabetes were so advanced that the doctor said if she didn't start on medication and cut down on some of her eating and other bad habits that he wasn't going to give her insurance, and that would mean the show couldn't be shot. They were deadly serious; they weren't going to be responsible if she had a heart attack. So they got her onto a program. She seemed to get on track, so they lifted the ban and we didn't shut down.

Nell Carter helped Dolph Sweet raise three feisty young girls in the NBC family comedy *Gimme a Break!* Sweet's death from cancer after four seasons irreparably damaged the show (courtesy NBC/Photofest).

Dolph Sweet also provided his share of problems, especially when paired with Carter. Their vastly different backgrounds, both in life and in show business, contributed to clashes on the set. Continues Drake:

> The run-ins that Dolph had with Nell came primarily from the fact that he was painted as somewhat of an *In the Heat of the Night*–sort of guy. Not a racist, but a guy who, to be honest, in real life had some of that attitude. Dolph was concerned more with the reality of the situation than the comedy. He was concerned that Nell combated him too much, and this would not stand if you were in the South. It wasn't that she was black or a woman, but rather that she was a "servant," and he called her that one time and she really got upset. She saw herself as more of a surrogate nanny. But Dolph felt that she was a hired hand and she should not be so "uppity." All those words were the wrong words to use, and she took offense. He didn't mean it the way that she thought he meant it. But that was kind of thrashed out in the first couple of seasons, and then I think they made peace and became good working partners.

While Carter and Sweet managed to work out their differences and become friends, their individual problems continued to hamper the series. By the end of the first season, Nell Carter's drug use had escalated, along with her weight. NBC was leery of Carter's behavior, but her double Emmy nomination that spring (both for *Gimme a Break!* and a TV broadcast of her hit play *Ain't Misbehavin'*, for which she'd won a Tony) led to their decision to renew the show for a second season.

Yet an eventful summer hiatus still lay ahead.

Shortly after the season ended, on May 26, 1982, Nell Carter surprised everyone by marrying Dr. Georg Krynicki. No one involved with the series knew much about Krynicki, except that he was of Austrian decent and spent much of his time in Europe on business. Carter's commitment to the show kept her at home. If she had intended the marriage to end her feelings of loneliness, the long-distance relationship had little chance of working.

One day early that summer, NBC casting executive Joel Thurm made several attempts to contact Carter by phone but failed to reach her. With Krynicki away, Thurm became concerned and went to Carter's home to check on her. "I found her passed out and nude on the living room floor with an empty bottle of Jim Beam nearby," recalls Thurm. "I called her doctor, who came to the house and decided the best thing was just to let her sleep it off. I later learned she had used alcohol to come down from the coke." The ordeal was enough to scare Carter into rehab, delaying production on the series. She spent several weeks fighting to gain control of her many addictions. Eventually, she made enough progress that she felt ready to return to work.

To take some of the workload off of Carter and Sweet, executive producers Mort Lachman and Sy Rosen made several additions to the cast that fall. First, they beefed up co-star Howard Morton's role as dimwitted Officer Simpson in order to compensate for Sweet's reluctance to himself play an absent-minded character. Veteran actors John Hoyt and Jane Dulo were then added as Carl's parents, Stanley and Mildred Kanisky, while Pete Schrum appeared occasionally as Carl's portly brother Ed.

On September 19, 1982, Carter lost her bid for Outstanding Lead Actress in a Comedy Series to Carol Kane for her role in ABC's *Taxi*. Carter did, however, win a special category Emmy for the TV airing of *Ain't Misbehavin'*.

The second season of *Gimme a Break!* kicked off on October 2, 1982, in a new timeslot, Saturday nights at 9 P.M. Unfortunately, Carter's behavior continued to be unpredictable that

Gimme a Break! co-stars Nell Carter and Dolph Sweet had their run-ins, both onscreen and off, during production of the NBC series. But Carter was at Sweet's bedside, holding his hand and singing to him, when he died of cancer in the spring of 1985 (courtesy NBC/Photofest)

year. No one could be sure whether her addictions had again gotten the better of her or if she was simply suffering from the effects of being overweight.

Two events that season would cause them great concern. The first occurred during production of the episode "The Return of the Doo-Wop Girls" (2/17/83), guest-starring the Pointer Sisters. Remembers Jim Drake:

> Nell had been binging on something and wound up sleeping through the first two days of rehearsals. One day, Mort [Lachman] took a strong stand and said, "Let's all go home," so we left her sleeping on a couch. The Pointer Sisters weren't happy because they had flown all night from Florida and wound up feeling a little cheated. Nell was so humiliated that she came in the next day and apologized to everybody, but didn't understand why we had left her sleeping there. We said, "Because you were unable to work. We kept getting you up, and then you'd doze back off to sleep again." It turned out to be one of the strongest episodes we ever did, but she was furious that we had treated her that way. She did a wonderful gospel number with the Pointer Sisters. I think we got all this energy out of her because she was so mad at us.

Several weeks later production began on "Nell and the Kid" (4/28/83). The episode was a back-door pilot for a new Don Rickles series. Rickles played a delicatessen owner named Max who takes in a young homeless girl. Recalls Drake:

> Don and Nell did not get on well together. I wasn't directing it, but I was asked to come by and offer my input, and Nell and Don were just clashing all over the place. Don Rickles can be a sweetheart, but if something rankles him the wrong way he has as sharp a tongue as anybody. He referred to her as "the mud slide" once. He said to an entire room of executives, "Is the mud slide ready to work?" because she was in the corner dozing. Don was looking at it as an opportunity to do another TV show, and he felt Nell was just slumming through it. She then got up and gave the performance of her life, but it took that kind of goading from him to get her going.

The pilot never went to series.

Gimme a Break!'s ratings plummeted on Saturdays, and in January 1983 it was moved to Thursday nights at 9:00 P.M., where those numbers improved slightly. Ironically, the show was at that time a lead-in to *Cheers*. Despite her recurring health problems, Nell Carter's performance earned her a second Emmy nomination. She again lost, this time to Shelley Long for *Cheers*. But NBC's faith in Nell Carter remained strong, and the network picked up *Gimme a Break!* for a third season. By this time, it was more than mere admiration that was keeping Carter at NBC. She had three Emmy nominations and one win to her credit. Brandon Tartikoff's admiration for Carter's talent had turned into genuine concern that if he cancelled *Gimme a Break!*, Carter could very well turn up in a hit series for another network, which he'd then be in the dubious position of counter-programming against for years to come.

A number of changes were in store for the show in the fall of 1983. Actress Jane Dulo was dropped from the cast; it was explained that Grandma Kanisky had passed away. Young actor Joey Lawrence was added as a homeless seven-year-old con artist taken in by the family. Lara Jill Miller was fourteen and growing up, so Lawrence had been hired in an effort to maintain the show's cuteness factor. Telma Hopkins was also brought onboard full-time as Nell's best friend, Addy Wilson. The idea was that Nell would now have a contemporary to get into scrapes with, rather than just becoming involved in the kids' problems. Carter and Hopkins had a great deal of chemistry, and their antics would often resemble that of Lucille Ball and Vivian Vance. Says Hopkins:

We had it going for two people who were so different. I learned a lot from her; she and I were comedically very well-matched. I was up for anything, and she liked that about me. I'm not sure that she loved me, or anything like that, but I think she really did come to like me. I came into the job with the full realization that if it had been left up to her, I probably wouldn't have been there. I was hired without her knowledge. There were times when she'd piss me off and I'd stop talking to her, and she hated that. I'd talk to her as long as it was scripted, but other than that I'd just ignore her. It would just drive her nuts; it was so easy to get her back. But in time we developed a good working relationship and managed to bond.

Another big change also occurred behind the scenes. The relationship between Carter and producers Lachman and Rosen had become so volatile that Carter had demanded they be replaced or she would not return. Lachman and Rosen resigned from the show and were replaced by veteran showrunners Rod Parker and Hal Cooper (*All in the Family, Maude*). NBC hoped the duo would have better luck relating to Carter. Remarks Parker:

> Nell was naturally very funny and could sing up a storm. When we took over the show, the first thing we did was get Nell to sing more. We would stretch her talent and allow her to do different things. You can write broader when you have an actor with that kind of talent. On the other hand, privately, there was a little paranoia there. Hal and I played good cop/bad cop, and I was the bad cop. So anytime she would be really upset, they would say, "Well, go see Rod." I had a large office with a table and chairs for meetings, but whenever Nell would come in I would sit behind my desk so she always knew she was talking to authority. I was usually able to calm her down. I was good at that. But Hal and I worked it out so I was the one she had to come to, because Hal couldn't be arguing with people he had to work with five days a week on the floor as a director.

Privately, Carter was again fighting a losing battle against her demons. By 1984, her weight reached nearly 300 pounds, and her cocaine habit, which before her stint in rehab was running $1,000 a week, was now costing her $2,000 a day. The level of her excess seemed to increase with her earnings, which had reached $50,000 a week. She had grown increasingly depressed because of her troubled marriage. In early 1984 Carter traveled to London to see her friend Liza Minnelli on stage. While there, she attempted suicide by overdosing on sleeping pills and champagne. With Minnelli's help, Carter was flown to the Hazelden Clinic in Minnesota, where she kicked her habit for a second time. She also managed to lose 91 pounds.

Carter returned to the series healthier than she'd been in years. Her weight loss was written into the script, but, unfortunately, she would end up gaining it back and then some.

Darker days were still ahead for the series. Toward the end of the fourth season, events began to unfold which would adversely affect the future of *Gimme a Break!* While everyone's concerns had been tightly focused on Nell Carter and whether she would overcome her life-threatening addictions, ironically, it would be another member of the cast whose death they would soon be mourning.

In the spring of 1984, as the show was close to wrapping its fourth season, Dolph Sweet began to experience health problems of his own. He was fatigued, experiencing stomach pains, and was losing weight. The fiercely independent Sweet eventually had to turn to the producers for help. He asked if someone could drive him to see his doctor. Associate producer Brigit Jensen-Drake, wife of director Jim Drake and an eight-season veteran of *All in the Family,* picked Sweet up at his home and drove him to his physician's office. "He was so thankful and appreciative of me for doing it," says Jensen-Drake. "He wouldn't say much in the car. He would talk a little bit about the show, but he was not an open guy. We mostly exchanged small talk about what was going on at work, and that was about it."

Sweet ended up in the hospital for stomach surgery in August 1984. Shortly afterwards he went to executive producers Parker and Cooper with the news that he was suffering from pancreatic cancer. The prognosis wasn't good. Says Cooper:

It was shocking. Dolph asked us, "What would you like to do about it?" and we said, "It's up to you, do you want to continue working?" He replied, "I would love to continue to work." He really needed the show at the time. So Rod and I went to Brandon Tartikoff and had a private meeting where we told him about Dolph and how we wanted to proceed with him as long as he felt well enough to work and wanted to work. Brandon was saddened by it. What we didn't know at the time was that Brandon had cancer as well, which was in remission at that point. He didn't say anything, but years later after we lost Brandon, we realized what a tough face he had to put on.

By the time Sweet returned to work in the fall of 1984, his weight loss had been drastic and he tired easily. Many times he was unable to rehearse or had to retire to his dressing room early to rest. As Rod Parker explains:

He'd lost a lot of weight and hair, which we covered as best we could with makeup and hairpieces. We used him lightly, effectively but lightly, so it wouldn't wear him out too much. I don't want to sound like one of these people who, just because someone dies, is saying all these wonderful things, but Dolph was a very sweet man, a very nice man. That's why it hit everybody when he got sick.

No official announcement was ever made to the cast and crew about Sweet's condition. Word spread privately from person to person that he was sick. The severity of his weight loss and exhaustion were evidence of just how serious it was. Says Lauri Hendler:

I knew that he was sick, but I didn't know with what and I didn't know how serious. He was a very quiet and private man, and it wasn't the sort of thing you wanted to just go up and ask about. I guess I was also in a little bit of denial because you don't want to believe that somebody is as sick as he clearly was. So his illness was a tremendous shock, despite the evidence in front of me for a year that he was wasting away.

Eventually, Hendler and everyone else had to accept the inevitable. "Despite my denial, I did have a year to get used to the fact that he was dying," says Hendler.

Co-star Telma Hopkins saw subtle changes in Sweet's personality as his health continued to falter throughout the fall and winter of 1984:

Dolph was always pretty scary to me. He had that military background, and it really wasn't until he got sick that I personally saw a different side of him. But I remember during the same season we found out he was ill, my uncle died and then my stepfather died, like thirty days apart; it was just horrendous. The first person who came to me was Dolph, and it really floored me because he was so kind to me and so understanding and supportive, and it wasn't what I expected from him. He also gave us all Christmas presents that year, which he'd never done before. I think definitely we got to see a softer side of him once he was diagnosed.

The series continued on as usual during the 1984-85 season, despite Sweet's deteriorating condition. No reason was given onscreen for Sweet's appearance. Sweet continued to fight, and had to be written out of four or five episodes. The characters of Grandpa Kanisky and Addy Wilson were given increasingly more to do to make up for Sweet's absences. On February 23, 1985, *Gimme a Break!* aired a special live broadcast. Initially, NBC's entire Saturday night schedule was supposed to air live, but one by one each series dropped out except for *Break!* Sweet was anxious to participate, and the episode went off without a hitch.

During the season, Parker and Cooper realized Sweet was unlikely to beat his cancer and began to plan for the inevitable. "Dolph was very important to the show, but the show really belonged to Nell Carter," insists Cooper. "It was her show. If you lost Nell, you wouldn't have had a show, but you could lose anyone else and continue." Replacing Sweet, however, was never an option. "We never thought for a moment about recasting the part," maintains Cooper.

Sweet continued to be in high spirits, at least in the presence of others. The season's final episode, "Julie's Birthday" (5/11/85), strangely enough ended with a cliffhanger. Julie and her boyfriend Jonathan (new series regular Jonathan Silverman) eloped and returned home in the final scene. The newlyweds were seated in the kitchen with Nell, having just broken the news to her, and now had to face the music with her father. From off-screen we then heard Sweet call out, "Is that Julie in there, Nell?" The confrontation was evidently meant to play out in the fall, an odd tactic considering the severity of Sweet's health. That episode, the show's 88th, would indeed be Sweet's last. He would not even live to see it air. He was readmitted to the hospital and died on May 8, 1985. Ironically, Nell Carter was at his bedside. When Sweet began to slip away, his wife Iris Braun called Carter, who rushed to the hospital. She held Sweet's hand and sang to him as he died. She then gave the eulogy at his funeral. Sweet was also survived by a son, Jonathan, from his previous marriage to Reba Gillespie which ended in divorce in 1973.

Although Sweet's death did not come suddenly, it was still painful to those who knew him. Says Hendler:

> He died during the hiatus between the fourth and fifth season, and it certainly left a gap. He was the grounded center of the show. Nell was the emotional part of the show, and Dolph was kind of the thinking part of the show. Because he died during hiatus, they had several months to figure out what they were doing, and they basically approached it head on by coming back at the beginning of the fifth season with his character, Carl, having died about three months ago, which would have been in the show's timeline right after the last episode we filmed in the spring.

Going back into production that summer was difficult for the cast. Continues Hendler:

> The first week that we worked after that hiatus was very weepy for everyone, except for me. I somehow wasn't ready to let go until we finished shooting that first episode. But as soon as we finished it, I burst into tears. As for the other actors, I can't put words into their mouths, but I do know that he was sorely missed.

For Lara Jill Miller, Sweet's death was a little difficult to comprehend at her young age. She explains:

> I don't think it was a shock. He died during the hiatus, and I was back home in Pennsylvania. So I didn't attend his funeral or anything like that. But he was one of the first people I knew who died. My grandparents hadn't even died yet, so it was just kind of weird. But I certainly didn't look at it like it was my real father dying. I wasn't that close to him. It was sad, and it felt very different on the set when I came back, but after knowing he was sick and then being away from him for a few months and him dying over hiatus, as a little kid it didn't seem to affect my life as much as the others.

Although they did their best to support Sweet during his illness, executive producers Rod Parker and Hal Cooper had nonetheless spent the previous season considering the direction the show would take once Carl Kanisky was no longer present in the family setting. "We had a full season to think it through, so we knew exactly what we were going to do," says Cooper. "Nell was going to adopt the kids and get approval to be head of the household." There had been many episodes before Sweet's death in which he'd had only a small part. Those shows had revolved around Nell and the girls and their friends, so the show didn't really need to be reinvented to deal with Sweet's loss. The difference was the knowledge that he was no longer there and wouldn't be returning, and that the girls were now orphaned and in Nell's custody.

The decision was made not to have the family dwell on Carl's death. Recalls Hendler:

We had a few episodes where we dealt with missing him and moving on. We lived in a crowded house, and one episode was about whether somebody should take over his room or not. And then, fairly quickly, because it's a comedy, his character was sort of left behind and referred to infrequently because you want to keep it light, and if you keep referring to him and his death, it ceases to be light.

The series' fifth season saw *Gimme a Break!* moved to yet another timeslot, Saturdays at 8:00 P.M., where, despite less than formidable competition (*Hollywood Beat* on ABC and *Airwolf* on CBS), the ratings-challenged program continued to suffer from a decline in viewership. Initially, that year's storylines dealt with Nell attempting to serve as adoptive mother to the girls and Joey. Many episodes also dealt with Julie's and Jonathan's first year of marriage. As the season played out, though, the emphasis shifted more and more towards Nell and Addy and their increasingly Lucy and Ethel-type misadventures. Whenever Nell and Addy weren't being featured, the spotlight seemed to fall on the relationship between Joey and Grandpa Kanisky. The girls were featured less and less as the season progressed. Perhaps the person whose character was most stranded that year was Howard Morton's Officer Simpson, because he had been a fellow cop, and now, with Sweet gone, he didn't have a reason to visit the Kanisky home on a regular basis anymore.

By the end of the season, with ratings falling (and a scheduling move to the show's ninth timeslot in five years), NBC demanded a major overhaul of the series for the following year. Explains Parker:

Without the father figure there, and the girls growing up, we were manufacturing everything. The girls were pretty much grown up, and there was no voice in the house that could control Nell. The marriage thing with Julie and Jonathan obviously did not click with viewers. So we had made Nell and Telma a little like Laurel and Hardy anyway, and they were very good at it, very funny. So that helped us make a decision.

That decision would be harsh. The following season Nell, Addy, Grandpa Kanisky, and Joey would pull up roots and leave Glenlawn for New York City. Daughters Katie and Julie, Julie's husband Jonathan, and Officer Simpson would be dropped from the cast entirely. Samantha would continue to appear on a semi-regular basis as she had begun attending college in New Jersey. The decision to eliminate half the cast was drastic but necessary if the show was to continue.

"It was very difficult to let the girls go," insists Parker:

They were not only talented, but they were very nice young girls who really cared about people and about each other, which is a little unusual for teenage girls all wondering who's going to get the better part this week. But I never had any complaints from any of the girls. As a matter of fact, they were thrilled with some of the stuff we were giving them.

Recalls Lauri Hendler:

I wasn't privy to the thought process on that. I was simply told that they felt they'd explored enough storyline with the girls, and they were going to change the focus of the show. I thought that a lot of the stuff we did the fifth season was fairly strong. But nobody asked me.

Gimme a Break! began its sixth and final season on September 24, 1986, with a one-hour special, "Sam Goes to College." It marked the final appearances of Kari Michaelson, Lauri

A sixth-season cast photo taken from the NBC comedy *Gimme a Break!* Pictured clockwise from top left: Nell Carter, Telma Hopkins, Joseph Lawrence, John Hoyt, Matthew Lawrence (courtesy NBC/Photofest).

Hendler, Jonathan Silverman, and Howard Morton. The following week, Nell, Addy, Grandpa and Joey began life anew in New York. Lara Jill Miller would appear in four more episodes that season. No sooner had the group settled into their new home than they received a visit from Joey's father ("Below Sea Level," 10/1/86). Joey learns his father has a surprise for him, which turns out to be his little brother Matthew (played by Matthew Lawrence, Joey Lawrence's real-life younger brother). The boy's father was soon out of the picture, and Nell took custody of Matthew. What goes around had come around, and Joey Lawrence, like Lara Jill Miller before him, was growing up. NBC had insisted on adding Matthew in order to preserve that cuteness factor once again.

Matthew wasn't the only addition to the cast that season. The show needed a New York character that could also go toe-to-toe with Carter. Rod Parker received a tip about a talented stand-up comic named Rosie O'Donnell. Parker caught one of her shows and signed her to play Nell's new neighbor, Maggie O'Brien. "She was wonderful, you could tell she was going to be a huge star," says Parker. Paul Sand also joined the cast, as did actress Rosetta LeNoire (*Family Matters*) as Nell's mother, Maybelle Harper.

Despite the new faces, the show continued to struggle. The changes may have come too late for some, and may have been too sweeping for others. Says Parker:

> We'd been on for six years, and you have to have a really strong show to keep going at that point. You're asking yourself, "How do we do this now..." or "How do we do this again..." I was on *Maude*, one of the funniest shows in the world as far as I'm concerned, which I thought went one year too long. I spun that off from *All in the Family*. The sixth year of *Maude*, we just got tired, so they were going to take her to Washington. I didn't want to do it, and Bea [Arthur] didn't want to do it, either. She didn't want to start out with new characters. It would have been just her and Bill Macy and all new characters. Instead, she left the series, which I think was a smart idea.

Hopkins felt the show was losing ground quickly. "Once that original formula was broken, it just didn't feel the same," she insists. "And as much as we tried to make it work, there were just a lot of things missing. When we went to New York, it just wasn't the same show anymore."

Nell Carter's personal problems also continued to plague the production. Relates Parker:

> Her weight went up and down. It depended on how happy or unhappy she was. She had a very strange marriage. First of all, the guy was in Paris, and she'd go to Paris to see him. Then, when she was successful, they decided to get divorced and he sued her for money. So that didn't work out very well. She could be volatile — not with me, because she was kind of scared of me. But she could also be very nice to everyone, and had fun at Christmas giving presents. When I got married again, she gave me a bachelor party at the office. Basically, there was a very nice person there who could get very mixed up.

What concerned Parker the most was the effect that Carter's mood swings could have on the kids:

> Nell had a little falling out with Joey [Lawrence] because she thought he was getting too much screen time. She spoiled him for two years and then turned on him; don't ask me why. She just wasn't very nice to him, didn't want to do too much with him. That's why I had a lot of talks with him, because I loved the kid, he was a real pro. Nell could be volatile, but basically she was a nice person. Mort had a lot of trouble with her the first couple of years; that's because I think Nell was on coke. Nell was a party girl; she loved parties and loved to have a good time. Everybody on the show liked Nell. It's just that you never knew if something was going to happen.

The changes made to *Gimme a Break!* for its sixth season didn't work. In the spring of 1987 the series was moved to its tenth timeslot, but again it failed to ignite ratings. Plans were hastily concocted to revamp the show yet again for the following year. The idea was to make Nell housemother at Samantha's college dorm, reminiscent of the early days of NBC's *The Facts of Life.* But in May the network decided enough was enough and pulled the plug on *Gimme a Break!* The series' final original telecast aired on the evening of Tuesday, May 12, 1987. The cast and crew received word at that season's wrap party that the show was over.

Gimme a Break!'s 137 episodes were sold into syndication for a reported $70 million and enjoyed a healthy life in reruns for many years.

After the show ended, Telma Hopkins and Rosetta LeNoire both graduated to the long-running ABC family sitcom *Family Matters.* Kari Michaelson has married, become a mother, and distanced herself from the business. Lauri Hendler continues to act, guesting on such programs as *Charmed, The West Wing,* and *Without a Trace.* Lara Jill Miller attended New York University in the early '80s before earning a law degree from Fordham. She later chose to quit practicing law in favor of returning to her first love — the entertainment world. She's become much in demand for her work as a skilled voiceover artist, having contributed to such popular projects as *Clifford's Puppy Days, Digimon,* and *The Life and Times of Juniper Lee.* Joey Lawrence followed *Gimme a Break!* with a five-season run on NBC's popular teen series *Blossom* (1991–95), followed by the short-lived series *Brotherly Love* (1995–97) and *Run of the House* (2003). He's also appeared in a number of TV movies. John Hoyt died of lung cancer in 1991, and Howard Morton passed away in 1997 after suffering a stroke.

For Nell Carter, life after *Gimme a Break!* had its ups and downs. She appeared in the short-lived series *You Take the Kids* (1990), did a stint on *Hangin' with Mr. Cooper* (1992), and appeared in a string of TV movies. She adopted two sons, four-week-old Joshua and newborn Daniel, in 1992, just before divorcing Georg Krynicki. A second marriage in 1992 lasted only one year. Then in July 1992 she suffered a double brain aneurysm and barely survived. With the help of her friend, director/choreographer Debbie Allen, she recovered and was able to perform at the 65th Annual Academy Awards in 1993. She followed that with a successful return to the stage in 1997 as Miss Hannigan in the 20th Anniversary revival of *Annie.*

But over the next few years her career went into a tailspin. In January 2003 she was in Long Beach rehearsing for the play *Raisin',* which she hoped would serve as her comeback vehicle. Unfortunately, it was not to be. On January 23 her son Joshua, then 13, found her dead in their Beverly Hills home. The cause of death was ruled heart disease complicated by diabetes. She passed away with only $200 in the bank.

"That was really hard, especially since I heard about it from *Entertainment Tonight* calling me up," says Lara Jill Miller:

> I went to her funeral. That was a very weird time for me because she was the biggest part of my childhood. And now she won't be able to see me as a grown-up. We kept in touch, and I'd go see her in plays like *Annie.* When she was doing *The Vagina Monologues,* she wrote to me and said, "I'm doing this play, but I can't tell you the name because your baby ears shouldn't hear this word." It's weird knowing that I'm never going to see her again.

Says Telma Hopkins:

> It's hard to lose anyone when you feel they died before their time. In many ways, it was not a surprise. I knew that she was not healthy, that she'd lost and gained back a lot of weight and had two aneurysms, but I did not realize that she was as ill as she was. The last time I had seen her was at Roscoe's Chicken and Waffle, probably the last place either of us needed to be. She was with one of her sons, and we were like a couple of eleven-year-olds.

Adds Lauri Hendler:

She was an incredible talent. She had the most amazing singing voice, with such a unique turn on how she'd sing a song. She was a huge force of nature. Toward the end of her life she had gotten to a point where she was very content and happy, so it was very sad. Nell had amazing comic timing — oddly enough, a very different school of comic timing than Dolph. They were both very funny. I was delighted to have two masters of the genre to learn from. It was a great experience for me.

It wasn't until after Carter's death that her bi-sexuality became public knowledge. In accordance with Carter's last wishes, custody of her adopted sons Joshua and Daniel was awarded to her domestic partner Ann Kaser.

Gimme a Break! remains one of TV's most revered family sitcoms. It also serves as a testament to the talent of its cast, and a lasting legacy for its late stars.

CHAPTER 10

Lime Street
Samantha Smith

Robert Wagner was perhaps the closest TV ever got to finding a Cary Grant. He arrived in Hollywood in 1950 where his natural good looks allowed him to advance from bit parts to notable supporting roles in major motion pictures such as *The Mountain*, with Spencer Tracy (in 1956), and *The Longest Day*, with Richard Burton (in 1962). But it was television that would make him a leading man.

Professionally, Robert Wagner seemed to soar higher and higher as the years passed; personally, his life was shaken by the unbearable tragedy of his wife Natalie Wood's death in 1981. At the time, Wagner was starring in the ABC mystery series *Hart to Hart* alongside Stefanie Powers, and he immersed himself in the show in order to fend off some of the pain of Wood's passing. Four years later, tragedy would strike again while filming his 1985 TV series *Lime Street*. Whereas Wagner had used his work to help manage the anguish of Natalie's death, it could not serve as a refuge this time. Each day spent on the set of *Lime Street* was to become a heart-breaking reminder of a young life that ended much too soon.

It was a far cry from the early days of Wagner's bright career.

In his first series, ABC's *It Takes a Thief*, Wagner played Alexander Mundy, a master thief paroled into the custody of the U.S. government, which put his talents to use as an unofficial espionage agent. Mundy was suave, sophisticated, and could have any woman he wanted. *It Takes a Thief* had a relatively short two-and-a-half-season run, from January 1968 until September 1970, but Wagner would go on to become a staple of series television, never steering far from the debonair persona that was his trademark. In 1975 he began a three-year run on CBS's *Switch* as Pete Ryan, a con artist who teams with a retired cop (played by Eddie Albert) in a detective agency that specialized in running elaborate cons to aid their clients.

But Wagner's most definitive role would come with ABC's light-hearted murder mystery *Hart to Hart* in 1979. From producer Aaron Spelling, the show teamed Wagner and Powers as husband and wife socialites Jonathan and Jennifer Hart, whose "hobby was murder," or, more specifically, solving murders. The series was basically an updated version of *The Thin Man*. For five seasons the Harts were TV's most glamorous team of crime-fighters. The series ended its run in September 1984, a victim not of declining ratings but of ABC's desire to appeal to a younger demographic.

Despite its move to cancel *Hart to Hart*, ABC eagerly signed Wagner to do another series

Director Raymond Austin and actor Robert Wagner first worked together on *Hart to Hart* and would later re-team for ABC's ill-fated crime drama, *Lime Street* (courtesy Raymond Austin).

for the 1985-86 season. Wagner was game, and also eager to add a new dimension to his performances. He wasn't about to exorcise the urbane nature of his characters, but wanted to add another layer to his trademark style.

Under a deal with Columbia Pictures Television, he hung out his own production shingle, RJ Productions, and began calling the shots. He realized that, as a lead actor who'd be appearing in almost every scene of any new series, his time would be limited, and it would be in his best interest to find a production partner. He found that partner in Mozark Productions, the film company run by the husband-and-wife producing team of Harry and Linda Bloodworth-Thomason. Harry Thomason was a veteran producer on *The Fall Guy* and had directed several independent features. Linda Bloodworth-Thomason was a former English teacher who had written for *M*A*S*H* and *Rhoda* before creating her own short-lived sitcom, *Filthy Rich*, a take-off on prime-time soaps like *Dallas* and *Dynasty*. Although *Filthy Rich* lasted only 13 episodes, Bloodworth-Thomason had proven herself a capable showrunner.

The premise devised by Bloodworth-Thomason in a two-hour pilot script titled *Lloyds of London* cast Wagner as James Greyson Culver, a globetrotting insurance investigator for the world's most noted insurance company. His job required Culver to depart at a moment's notice for exotic locations around the globe, where he would then have the task of solving high-profile crimes in an effort to save the company from paying out millions in insurance settlements.

The twist was that Culver was also the divorced father of two young daughters, ages thirteen and seven. The family lived together on a working horse farm in Virginia, operated by Culver's father. The farm came complete with a landing strip for Culver's Cessna airplane, which he would use to fly to his office in Washington, D.C. There he would receive his assignments from the company's headquarters in London.

The network was a little leery at the mixture of international intrigue and family drama presented in Bloodworth-Thomason's script. Culver's home life in Virginia and his investigations abroad were separated geographically by thousands of miles and creatively by two different genres. On the one hand, the show was a crime drama where people were often murdered. On the other, it was a family drama where Culver would have to deal with the growing pains of his young daughters. The pilot, in particular, dealt with an overseas plot to kill a Mediterranean Princess, while at home Culver's oldest daughter had just had her first period.

ABC was concerned, but Wagner loved the idea of combining the two elements. It enabled him to be the world traveler he envisioned while at the same time being a caring single parent. This really was not the stretch it might have initially appeared. Wagner did love to travel, and his work as an actor often required him to leave his family for long periods of time. He had also been a single father raising three daughters after Wood's death.

Wagner's and Wood's lives together were one of Hollywood's most tragic tales. Wood was a highly respected child actress who grabbed national attention in the 1947 holiday classic *Miracle on 34th Street*. She successfully made the transition to adult roles in films such as *Rebel Without a Cause* (1955) and *West Side Story* (1961), both of which earned her Oscar nominations. She and Wagner first married in 1957, but the union lasted only until 1962.

Wagner then married actress Marion Marshall, and they had a daughter, Kate. Wood married screenwriter Richard Gregson and gave birth to Natasha. Then, in 1971, Wagner and Wood ran into one another in a restaurant and their romance blossomed anew. Wagner had already divorced; Wood was soon to follow suit. In 1972 they remarried and two years later had a daughter together, Courtney Brooke. Tragically, Natalie slipped off the couple's yacht in 1981 and drowned. Wagner never recovered, and spent the following decade raising their three daughters as a single father. In 1991 Wagner married actress Jill St. John, but Wood's drowning continued to haunt him.

Filming of the pilot episode of *Lloyds of London* was scheduled for April 1985 and was to take place on locations in Virginia, Washington, D.C., London, and the Bahamas. One afternoon the legal department from Columbia Pictures called to say that Lloyds of London had decided not to play ball. They didn't want the lives of their investigators dramatized in a weekly TV series. The show was briefly re-titled *J.G. Culver* before British director Raymond Austin, who had been hired to helm the pilot, suggested the moniker *Lime Street*. Besides being immortalized in a Beatles song, London's Lime Street was home to many of the worlds most prestigious insurance companies and banks.

The next step was to cast *Lime Street*. British actor John Standing was hired to play Wagner's partner and sidekick, Edward Wingate; veteran thespian Lew Ayres was chosen to fill the role of the family patriarch, Henry Wade Culver; and Anne Haney stepped in as the family caretaker, Evelyn Camp. The role of Celia Wesphal, Culver's personal assistant in the Washington, D.C., office, went to Julie Fulton, a recent graduate of Yale's School of Drama who was in Los Angeles for her first pilot season.

That left the two young daughters to cast. Seven-year-old Maia Brewton, who appeared briefly that summer in the film *Back to the Future*, was signed to play Margaret Ann, the youngest girl. Attention then turned to older daughter Elizabeth. Little was anyone aware of the impact the casting of this part would have on the future of *Lime Street*.

Although the script called for a girl in her early teens to play the part, Wagner claims he never considered fifteen-year-old daughter Natasha for the role, despite her desire to follow in the footsteps of her mother and stepfather. Wagner told *Ladies' Home Journal* in the September 1985 issue:

> It's in her genes. Natasha is exposed enough just by being a daughter of mine and Natalie's. She's studying a little drama in school, but what if the show goes on for five years? I don't want her hanging around a soundstage all that time. And she's too young to be left vulnerable to criticism. You can imagine what they'd say if I put my daughter in the show.

Wagner instead felt the need to find a young actress who'd already been thrust into the limelight and experienced the scrutiny of public exposure and the vulnerability that accompanies it.

In December of 1982, Samantha Smith was a typical 10-year-old girl growing up in the small, quiet town of Manchester, Maine. She enjoyed reading, spending time with friends, playing with her dog, and was beginning to notice boys. Her father, Arthur, was a college English professor; her mother, Jane, a social worker. By all outward appearances they were living the American dream. But that all changed one early winter afternoon when the inquisitive girl read an article in *Time* magazine about new Russian leader Yuri Andropov and the threat of nuclear war between the United States and the Soviet Union. Her concerns and curiosity led Samantha to write an innocent letter that invoked a remarkable response that would change the Smiths' lives:

> Dear Mr. Andropov,
> My name is Samantha Smith. I am ten years old. Congratulations on your new job. I have been worrying about Russia and the United States getting into a nuclear war. Are you going to vote to have a war or not? If you aren't please tell me how you are going to help to not have a war. This question you do not have to answer, but I would like to know why you want to conquer the world or at least our country. God made the world for us to live together in peace and not to fight.
> Sincerely,
> Samantha Smith

Those were the words that Samantha mailed to Andropov, addressed simply to the Kremlin. The letter was dropped into the mail and then mostly forgotten until several months later when Samantha was called out of her elementary school classroom and told to report to the principal's office. Concerned she had done something wrong, she meekly made her way as instructed. Upon arrival, she was ushered into a chair and told that a journalist was on the phone and wanted to interview her. It seemed her letter had somehow made its way from the small Manchester Post Office to the Communist newspaper *Pravda* in the Soviet Union, which had printed a photo of the correspondence. The UPI news service then picked up on the story and was able to track Samantha down to her elementary school.

Despite the worldwide media frenzy that followed, Samantha failed to receive a reply from Andropov. Determined, she wrote him once again to inquire as to why. Samantha's second letter succeeded in eliciting a response from Andropov. In the spring of 1983, the Soviet Embassy in Washington, D.C., called the Smith home to inform them that a letter from the Soviet leader was on its way. The Smiths began to make daily trips to the post office anticipating its arrival, which took only a few days. Their front lawn soon became the grounds of a media circus, with camera crews from all over the globe setting up camp to catch a glimpse of Samantha.

In his response to Samantha's inquiry, Andropov told her that the people of the Soviet Union only wanted peace. He called Samantha courageous and honest, comparing her to Becky Thatcher in Mark Twain's book *Tom Sawyer*, a favorite, he maintained, of young girls and boys in his country. Andropov then proceeded to invite Samantha and her parents to visit the Soviet Union that summer.

The family discussed the pros and cons of the trip. They were already experiencing the invasion of privacy that accompanies any sort of celebrity status. But Arthur and Jane Smith, who had always encouraged their daughter to expand her horizons, felt that the trip would be a positive one for Samantha. So they announced they would take Andropov up on his offer that summer. Remembers Jane Smith:

> We were worried about whether this was good for Samantha or for the country. We made the trip to the Soviet Union because we thought it was probably good for the two countries to see each other as more human and family oriented. We actually did get a visit from the State Department before we went. We had asked for their guidance, and they had quietly sent a person to spend a day with us, which was very helpful because we weren't professional diplomats. They didn't want to advertise that they had done that, because they were not publicly supporting us, but they were helpful. We were concerned about what we would do over there, whether we would be used or how careful we should be not to look foolish. As parents, we were concerned about the ramifications, although Samantha didn't have enough knowledge to be concerned really.

The Smiths' two week foray into Communist Russia began July 7, 1983. Arthur, Jane, and Samantha visited Leningrad and Moscow, strolled through Red Square and also spent some time at Camp Artek, a Soviet youth camp located on the shores of the Black Sea. They were accompanied every step of the way by a caravan of media representing every major outlet in the world. The only drawback to the trip was that the Smiths never did get to meet with Andropov. The official reason was that he was too busy with matters of the state; the truth was that he was too ill to receive visitors.

The Smiths returned home to Maine on July 22, where Samantha was greeted as a hometown hero. She spent the next few weeks doing interviews about her trip. While the public branded Samantha "Our Littlest Ambassador," many of the hard-line news organizations had a different take on the matter. Some believed the Soviets were using Samantha as a pawn in their public relations efforts. The Ronald Reagan White House refused to officially comment on Samantha or her trip.

After returning from the Soviet Union, Samantha was invited to travel to Japan to speak at an international symposium for children; while there, she met with Japanese Prime Minister Yasuhiro Nakasone. She also wrote a book about her visit to Russia titled *Journey to the Soviet Union*. Even Hollywood was taken with Samantha. In the fall of 1984 she was invited to appear in an episode of CBS's *Charles in Charge*, then preceded to make a round of appearances on national talk shows. That year she also hosted a Disney Channel special in which she interviewed presidential candidates, including George McGovern and Jesse Jackson, from a child's perspective.

Eleven-year-old Samantha Smith made worldwide headlines when she and her parents, Jane and Arthur Smith, were invited by Russian leader Yuri Andropov to visit the Soviet Union in July of 1983 (courtesy Photofest).

Meanwhile, with production on the pilot of *Lime Street* scheduled to begin in April of 1985, the producers were desperately looking for the right actress to play daughter Elizabeth. Then one evening executive producer Harry Thomason answered his phone, and the search ended. Recalls Thomason:

My brother Danny is an optometrist who lives in Little Rock, Arkansas. He saw Samantha on the central time-zone airing of *The Tonight Show* and knew we were casting. He called us in California and said, "Here's a little girl you should look at." So we watched her that night on *The Tonight Show* and were very impressed. We then flew Samantha out and auditioned her. We thought she was wonderful, and ABC agreed, so we put her in the show. She was a very good actress. There was no doubt about it — this girl was going to be a star.

As they had done before their trip to the Soviet Union, Jane and Arthur Smith carefully considered whether the experience would be in Samantha's best interests. Jane Smith remembers:

We were concerned, but it seemed like it was going to be a positive move and could lead to a possible career for Samantha. What more could a child ask for than to have a chance at that? And to Samantha, that proved to be a lot more fun than the political stuff. It was fun for all of us after the seriousness of the whole Soviet business.

The pilot episode of *Lime Street* involved an attempt to assassinate members of the royal family of a small Mediterranean principality after an enormous untapped oil reserve is located off the country's coastline. Unable to negotiate drilling rights, the head of an oil company turns to an assassin to eliminate the line of ascension so he can acquire the rights from a distant relative who stands to inherit the throne.

Production of the pilot went smoothly, and, as expected, *Lime Street* was added to ABC's fall 1985 schedule, slated on Saturday nights at 9:00 P.M. between two Aaron Spelling vehicles, a new cop drama called *Hollywood Beat* at 8:00, and the ninth and final season of *The Love Boat* at 10:00. More notably, *Lime Street* was scheduled opposite the NBC freshman sitcom *The Golden Girls*, which wasn't expected to generate much heat. Ad buyers were predicting *Lime Street* would be the season's breakout hit.

According to playwright and friend Mart Crowley (*The Boys in the Band*), Wagner was very excited about the new show. Crowley had served as the producer and showrunner of *Hart to Hart*, which included supervising all the writing, before joining the staff of *Lime Street*. Says Crowley:

> RJ was always very excited about the things that he chose to do. I think this property gave him opportunities that he looked forward to inasmuch as he was going to have a family and he could relate to children and be sort of an ordinary man. I certainly think it allowed him to draw on his own life to relate to the characters, himself being the father of three girls who at that time were about the same ages as the characters in the series. But I think the conclusion that the network people jumped to may have been, "Oh, the public doesn't want to see him in this kind of a part." ABC felt that people liked to see him as the slick, debonair guy in the tuxedo solving a crime. This was more folksy, although it certainly wasn't Hicksville.

Samantha Smith and Robert Wagner enjoy a relaxing moment between scenes while filming the pilot episode of ABC's adventure series *Lime Street* in April, 1985 (courtesy ABC/Photofest).

Julie Fulton shared Wagner's enthusiasm for *Lime Street* and felt that ABC was behind the show, despite their concerns about whether it could work as both an action adventure and a family drama. Recalls Fulton:

> There was always a tug of war. But everybody felt that it would be a hit because of the show's pedigree, Robert Wagner and Linda Bloodworth and Harry Thomason. They were finding their way script-wise, but we were all aware there was that difference of opinion over where the concentration of the show should be, how much the family would play, and how risqué the adventures could be.

Nowhere on the series was the issue more apparent than in Bloodworth-Thomason's script for the episode subtitled "The Mystery of Flight 401" (9/28/85). The teleplay centered on the cockpit crew of a 747-passenger jet who stage a hijacking in order to collect four million dollars in ransom from the airline. The hijacking story was considered the episode's primary storyline. The B story involved Culver's daughter, Elizabeth, preparing for her first date. Culver's attention throughout the episode diverts back and forth between his efforts to expose the flight crew's deception and his own preoccupation with his daughter's blossoming love life.

Eventually, Culver uncovers the evidence he needs against the flight crew, who then try to make a last-minute escape utilizing a seaplane docked on the Potomac River. Culver and Wingate manage to chase them down in a pilfered speedboat. During filming of the chase scene, the seaplane capsized and sank. No one was injured, but producer E. Jack Kaplan saw it as a sign. "After that plane nosed over and sank, I remember saying, 'Oh, God, this show is doomed,' just sort of joking about it. Because that was only the second episode."

While an exciting climax to the primary storyline, the seaplane chase was hardly a finale, occurring early in the fourth act. The final eight minutes of the episode are then dedicated to wrapping up the B-story. Elizabeth's date calls to cancel at the last minute, sending the young girl running to her room in tears. Culver follows her to her bedroom and consoles her, then insists on the dance that she had promised him. The episode plays out with father and daughter dancing to a cover of Englebert Humperdink's "This Moment in Time." It was a wonderfully scripted scene that was equally well executed. Bloodworth-Thomason had demonstrated that the show could indeed work on both levels, so long as the writing could maintain that level of excellence.

In a scene from the *Lime Street* episode "The Mystery of Flight 401," co-star Samantha Smith tries on a new dress for her character's first date. Robert Wagner, in character as her on-screen dad, offers his input (courtesy ABC/Raymond Austin).

The cast and crew of *Lime Street* returned to the east coast in July of 1985 to begin shooting the first couple of episodes, utilizing locations in and around Virginia, Maryland, and Washington, D.C. Unlike a series being filmed in Los Angeles, where everyone can return to their homes at night, the cast and crew of *Lime Street* were thousands of miles from their families.

Director Raymond Austin remembers enjoying that summer immensely, despite the high humidity. It was tough enough on the adults, but he was impressed by how professionally both of the show's young co-stars, Samantha Smith and Maia Brewton, presented themselves, particularly when the crew was sequestered on the farm in Virginia. Laughs Austin:

> Samantha and Maia were always playing around and having a lot of fun. If you were shooting a scene and there was a bang somewhere in that house, you could bet your life it was one of those two. Samantha was so dedicated because it was her first acting experience, and she always wanted to be prepared. Everyone was very busy, but she used to read lines with Maia or whoever had time. Then she used to break away from that every so often, and you'd see the little girl come out in her, especially out in the riding paddock. You'd see her and Maia out there enjoying themselves.

While everyone else was busy shooting the first two episodes on location, Bloodworth-Thomason was busy back in Los Angeles writing and preparing the next three episodes, which were going to be shot overseas. The schedule called for the crew to travel first to London, then Switzerland, and finally Amsterdam before once again returning to the United States. It

The Culver family of ABC's adventure series *Lime Street* enjoy a happy moment together on their horse farm in Virginia. Real-life tragedy would shatter the close-knit cast just weeks later. Pictured from left: Samantha Smith, Robert Wagner, Maia Brewton, Lew Ayres.

was to be a monumental effort on behalf of the entire crew, but it was also the reason Wagner had pursued the series to begin with.

In early August 1985 the crew traveled to England for two weeks to film an episode subtitled "The Wayward Train" (10/5/85). The segment was about an antique train that vanishes on its final run before being placed into a rail museum. One British location used prominently in the episode was the historic 13th century Brocket Hall in Hertfordshire, which was leased by the producers for use as the ancestral home of Culver's partner, Edward Wingate. The storyline had the visiting Culver family staying at Wingate's castle, which delighted Elizabeth to no end. A scene in the episode called for a long "walk and talk" sequence between Wagner and Smith that Kaplan recalls vividly:

RJ was quite taken with this girl. He really liked her a lot, and she had a girlhood crush on him. RJ sort of protected her. During this scene, she kept blowing her lines and getting more and more nervous. Then RJ started blowing his lines. We figured out he was doing that to make Samantha feel more comfortable about blowing her lines, which is a pretty generous thing for an actor to do.

Production on "The Wayward Train" was completed on August 24, 1985. Austin and his assistant immediately left for Switzerland to begin preparing the next episode, subtitled "The Swiss Watch and Wait," written by Kaplan and scheduled to be shot on location at the luxurious Gstaad Palace Hotel. Wagner, Standing, Thomason and Kaplan remained in London for another day while Samantha, Maia, and their parents headed back to the United States. Arthur Smith had chaperoned Samantha on the trip, while Jane had remained back home.

The first leg of the European shoot had gone smoothly, and everyone was feeling really good about the show. With four episodes securely in the can and good word of mouth, the show seemed to be well on its way to becoming yet another feather in Wagner's cap. The Smiths, who'd begun preparations to relocate from their small town in Maine to Los Angeles, shared that optimism. Then, one day later, their world fell apart. It was August 25, 1985. "It was heartbreaking ... just heartbreaking when it happened. It was the worst catastrophe. Nobody saw it coming," utters Fulton emotionally.

Back in the United States, Samantha and her father landed in Boston on Sunday afternoon, August 25, and then made arrangements to board a commuter flight that would carry them the rest of the way back home to Maine. They were last-minute additions to the passenger list. The flight was originally scheduled to go directly to Augusta, Maine, but a stop at Auburn-Lewiston Airport was hastily added to accommodate another passenger.

Their plane, Bar Harbor Airlines Flight 1808, departed from Boston's Logan Airport at 10:30 P.M. that evening. Besides Arthur and Samantha Smith, four other passengers and two pilots were aboard the Beechcraft 99. It was a rainy evening, with patches of dense fog and low visibility. Bar Harbor was a small commuter outfit that had recently experienced a turnover in personnel. It's likely that the crew was, therefore, not intimately acquainted with the route.

Practically from the time of departure, records show that the aircraft followed an erratic flight path, fluctuating in air speed and altitude. Because of the poor visibility and their unfamiliarity with the area, the pilots were relying heavily on the plane's computer system to maintain their course. At some point during the flight they should have picked up a transponder signal from Auburn-Lewiston that would have led the plane safely into the airport. For some reason, the aircraft flew through the signal without detecting it. When air traffic controllers contacted the pilot at approximately 9:40 P.M. to inform him he was off course, the pilot changed direction to re-intercept the signal. But records indicate the plane flew back through the transponder signal again without picking it up. The pilot then took over the controls himself for a visual landing.

At 10:04 P.M. the plane approached Auburn-Lewiston Airport. But something went terribly wrong. Local residents reported seeing the plane flying too low, sheering the tops off scores of trees, its engine revving heavily in a desperate attempt to regain altitude. Unable to do so, the plane crashed into a hillside and erupted into flames approximately 1,300 yards short of the runway.

Earlier that evening, Jane Smith had driven from the family's home in Manchester to Augusta Airport to await the arrival of her husband and daughter. Augusta was a small facility equipped only with a reception counter and a waiting area for passengers and their families. The airport was nearly deserted that evening, save for Jane Smith, an employee stationed at the reception desk, and a taxi driver who worked out of the terminal and was hoping to find a fare among the passengers scheduled to arrive shortly. Smith grew impatient as the plane's scheduled arrival time came and went, with still no word.

It wasn't until the flight was nearly an hour late that she began to notice signs that something might be wrong. Recalls Smith:

> I noticed the guy behind the counter kept going back into his office, then coming back out to the counter ... back and forth. He looked distressed. Finally, he came over to me and said, "I'm sorry, it's down." I didn't know what that meant at first. I asked him, and he explained that the plane had crashed. The poor guy, I felt really sorry for him. He was there by himself and had to deal with this. Once it became clear to me, I was stunned and confused. I went over to the taxi driver and asked if I could use his phone to call a neighbor. At that time, I didn't know if Samantha and Arthur were alive or not, or whether I should drive to Auburn myself.

A neighbor arrived shortly and drove Smith to the accident scene, which by then was besieged by emergency crews and the media. The area around the downed aircraft had been cordoned off to keep unauthorized persons away. Continues Smith:

> There were police and ambulances all around, and my friend helped me talk my way through them. They weren't supposed to let anybody in, but we were allowed through. We stood on top of this hill and looked down into this ravine where the plane was. It was covered in foam that the fire crews had sprayed to put out the flames. There didn't look like there were any survivors, and there weren't. I was weeping the whole time, but I was trying to do what I thought might be useful if they were there and alive.

The two women then drove back to the Smith home in Manchester, where Jane's mother-in-law had been staying with her while Arthur and Samantha had been away. Smith had to break the news to her that her son and granddaughter had been killed. The rest of the evening remains a bit of a blur to her. She recalls others arriving at the house, and at some point trying to lie down and sleep:

> I'm not sure if I actually slept or not. But I do remember the next morning thinking the press was going to be here, and I ought to have a statement, and I couldn't think of what to say. So I actually went to the gym to work out because I had all this energy. I think it was a sort of fight-or-flight syndrome. I thought if I got to the gym early enough, nobody would know, and if I could get rid of some of that energy maybe I'll feel better, and I could go home and deal with it. I was in the gym and working out, and somebody had a radio on, and they announced it. And I was caught. I don't even remember what I did after that; I must have left. But I just thought I was making everybody uncomfortable. I think I just sort of walked out. Nobody knew what to do with me. I really made it uncomfortable for people, I suppose.

A continent away, Raymond Austin had just touched down in Switzerland and learned that a large contingent of media had gathered at the airport and were waiting for him. Austin recalls:

We got into Gstaad International Airport and the press wanted to talk to me. I didn't know what it was about, and I was very nervous, so I avoided them. Then I got a call from someone in Los Angeles saying, "Terrible news. Watch Robert Wagner, because they're going to mob him with it. Samantha has been killed." I said, "What do you mean?" She said, "Well, Sam and her father completed most of their trip home, they were on the last leg of the journey when their plane crashed."

Austin was deeply wounded by the news but realized he had to notify Wagner quickly, so he began making calls to London. Wagner and Standing were already on their way to the airport and were preparing to board a plane for Gstaad. Austin remembers:

I couldn't find RJ, then I remembered we had friends at Heathrow International Airport. I called them and said, "As soon as you see RJ, take him aside and tell him to call me before he talks to anyone else." A little while later he called me from a phone in an office somewhere near the runway, and I broke the news to him. He was absolutely devastated. We then had to tell the crew before it broke in the news the next day. It was a terrible shock. When we finished shooting at Brocket Hall on the front lawn and Samantha was ready to leave with her father, she had a script for the episode that she got us all to sign. That night, when they showed the newsreel footage of the crash site, the camera panned over the wreckage and came to settle on the script for *Lime Street* with all our signatures on it, which upset RJ very badly.

Back at the Athenaeum Hotel in London, Harry Thomason recalls first hearing the news:

I was going to leave for Switzerland that morning. I remember I was up very early packing, and the BBC News said, "Little Samantha Smith..." and I remember thinking, "Oh great, they're going to plug the show." Then they said that she'd been killed in a plane crash, and I dropped to my knees.

Shortly thereafter, E. Jack Kaplan answered a knock at his door. "Harry Thomason pounded on my door and said, 'Something terrible has happened,'" recalls Kaplan. "It was really awful. Then he had to go across the street to Queens Park and do an interview with all the press. It was tough on him." And on Wagner: "It really took a lot out of him. He was nearly inconsolable. He said, 'Everybody around me dies.' I think he associated it with Natalie Wood. It made him think of her, which is always a sad thing for him."

Wagner also had to console young daughters Natasha and Courtney, 11, who'd become fast friends with Samantha. Wagner explained the impact of Samantha's death on his daughters in *People Magazine*'s November 1985 issue: "When kids are that young and they lose someone who is a contemporary, they have no way of understanding." Courtney asked her father difficult questions. "She was concerned about how Sam was when they found her," continued Wagner. "She wanted to know, 'Was she together? Was she in her seat? Where was she in the airplane? Was she cold? [Samantha's mother] told me later that Arthur must have grabbed Sam and held her because she was pretty much together."

Wagner and Thomason flew back to the United States for Samantha's and Arthur Smith's funeral in Maine. The service was difficult enough without some of the allegations that had recently been waged against the production crew. Earlier that week a Russian newspaper had reported that members of the *Lime Street* crew were spies for the U.S. government and may have had Samantha killed.

As a result, the Russian delegation on hand at the funeral was extremely cold to any member of the show's staff. As absurd as it may sound today, Thomason believes "at that time and place at the height of the Cold War, it was possible they believed it." Nobody from the United States government showed up, in keeping with the opinion that Samantha had been used as a propaganda tool by the Soviets.

While funeral services were taking place in Maine, the rest of the crew, who were now on location in Switzerland, held a memorial service in a small chapel in Gstaad, with Austin officiating. "We gave Samantha a last round of applause, which is a custom when actors die," he says. "You give them their last round of applause. I said the actor's prayer for her, and that was it."

With everyone still in mourning, Wagner and Thomason returned to Switzerland to continue production on "The Swiss Watch and Wait." Explains Kaplan:

> At this point we were just trying to keep the damn thing going. Here's the problem, when you've got all these shows written for Europe, you can't just shut down and then come back. You've got to finish them. We had to shoot all that stuff and then figure out how to handle Samantha's passing later.

Returning to the set wasn't easy for anyone. "There's no doubt about it," adds Thomason, "one of the hardest things we ever did was gather back in Switzerland once Samantha had been killed. It was tough, and it never got any easier. It just took the heart right out of it." Adds Kaplan, "I know it was a somber trip. RJ's a trouper and a real pro, but that Swiss show was hard because that was right on the heels of her death. He was not in good shape. Everybody was shaken."

Completing the episode served two purposes. The first was to preserve Samantha's performance. She had already filmed a few scenes for the episode back in the U.S. before the crew departed for Europe. The other reason was to reassure ABC that the show would remain on schedule, and, therefore, would be ready to premiere as part of the network's fall lineup. *Lime Street* was set to debut in less than one month, on September 21.

After wrapping "The Swiss Watch and Wait," the crew then moved on to Amsterdam for the final stop in their European tour. Samantha was completely written out of that episode, "Diamonds Aren't Forever" (10/12/85), a light-hearted piece about two hick sisters from Poplar Bluff, Arkansas (Linda Bloodworth-Thomason's hometown), who manage a daring diamond heist. The episode guest-starred Annie Potts and Jean Smart, who just a year later would be starring together in Bloodworth-Thomason's hit sitcom *Designing Women*. Although the episode is credited to writer Mark Redmond, Bloodworth-Thomason may well have had a hand in rewriting it.

At the time, "we were just concentrating on getting through the Amsterdam shoot and getting back home," concedes Thomason. After the episode wrapped, the crew returned to the United States, where important decisions would have to be made about the future of the series, particularly about how to deal with Samantha's death. The homecoming was bittersweet.

The cast was invited to the Thomasons' home for lunch. Recalls Fulton:

> We were seriously discussing the series going on or not. It felt like a family reunion after a wake. We all talked about what we'd been doing since we'd last seen one another, and how we felt about things that had happened. I realized they were sounding people out about how we felt, but at that time Linda told me they had made no decision and they were really perplexed, that they were going to try to struggle through and figure things out.

Lime Street premiered as scheduled on September 21, 1985. The pilot episode had been trimmed to 90 minutes, and shared the evening with the 90-minute premiere of Aaron

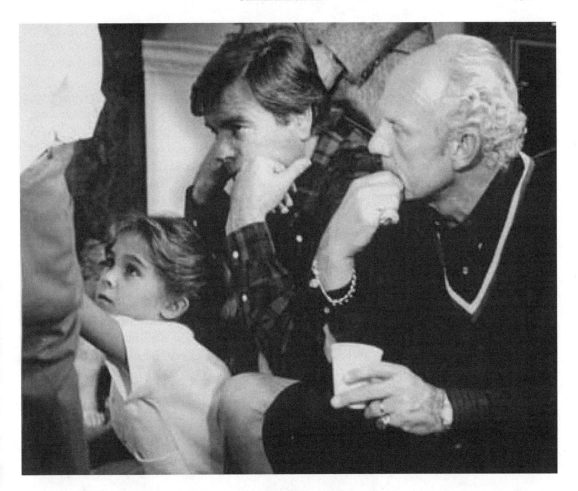

After the tragic death of co-star Samantha Smith in August 1985, the cast and crew of ABC's *Lime Street* reassembled and attempted to move forward. Pictured on set in an October 1985 photograph are actors Maia Brewton (left) and Robert Wagner (center). Director Raymond Austin (right) looks on (courtesy Raymond Austin).

Spelling's *Hollywood Beat*, which went on first at 8:00 P.M. The series opened with a scene in which a Mediterranean prince boards a small private jet that has been sabotaged by an assassin. Moments after takeoff, it plunges to the ground and explodes into a fireball. ABC was immediately deluged by angry phone calls from viewers who felt another scene should have been substituted in its place.

Three more episodes of *Lime Street* aired in the following weeks ("The Mystery of Flight 401," "The Wayward Train," and "Diamonds Aren't Forever") as the producers worked to regroup. During this period, yet another problem threatened the future of the series. Recalls Thomason:

> We were on against this half-hour that was driving them crazy called *The Golden Girls*. ABC just didn't understand why our show wasn't doing better than this show about these four old women. But it was just the time and the fate of the slot that we drew. Looking back on the numbers of *Lime Street*, they were actually very good, even after all that we had been through. It was just that ABC was struggling, and it needed something to hit big numbers out of the park. *Lime Street* was doing very well, but it was just good enough for second place in its timeslot.

ABC still had enough faith in the show that it allocated a large sum of money to duplicate the interior of the Virginia farmhouse on a soundstage in Los Angeles. Additional scripts were also prepared, but it was agreed they'd be shot at the Burbank Studios rather than on location, as the first batch of episodes had been.

By then, Wagner and the Thomasons were feeling the pressure — the loss of Samantha, too little time to prepare new episodes, and a staggering ratings punch from *The Golden Girls*. They felt if the show was going to have a chance to succeed, they needed some time. That's when they made the decision to go to ABC and ask to be taken off the air. ABC, realizing how far behind production had fallen, agreed. The plan was to put *Lime Street* on hiatus, get the show up and running again, and then bring it back in a new timeslot in January. This was also an acknowledgment that NBC's *Golden Girls* had proven to be tougher competition than originally expected. ABC's entire Saturday night schedule was collapsing. *Hollywood Beat* was also being badly beaten in the ratings and would be cancelled in November; *The Love Boat* would manage to finish the season before being cancelled (although ABC did order a series of specials for the following year).

The hiatus should have allowed time for Wagner and the Thomasons to breathe. But the pressing and emotional issue of how to deal with Samantha's death continued to complicate matters. Under normal conditions, replacing a character billed fifth in the opening titles would have been a fairly uncomplicated matter. But emotions were running high and overruling common-sense business decisions. Whereas Wagner and Standing were meant to be the show's

After the real-life death of young co-star Samantha Smith in a plane crash, the focus of ABC's international adventure series *Lime Street* began to center increasingly on the investigations of leads John Standing (left) and Robert Wagner (right) and less on the family aspects of the show.

primary leads, it was the relationship between Wagner and Smith that had taken center stage. In the beginning, the question was: could the show survive as both an action adventure and a family drama? Now the question was: could it survive as anything else?

Fulton agrees, and feared that Wagner felt responsible for what had happened to Smith. "Samantha was so close to Robert," Fulton says. "And I guess there was some guilt at having put her in harm's way, inadvertently, because she was on her way home with her dad when she was killed. So more than anything else, it was his inability to conceive of the idea of replacing her."

Wagner wasn't the only one feeling the loss. Kaplan believes Bloodworth-Thomason had her own personal reasons for mourning Samantha's loss. States Kaplan:

> Linda fell in love with this little girl. The series was created for Robert Wagner as an action series, but Linda is very interested in women's issues. And here was a girl, a young girl, and Linda could show her development. Just look at the pilot and the storyline involving Elizabeth having her first period. Linda wasn't all that interested in the mystery/action/adventure part of the show. The part of the show with RJ and Samantha and RJ's father (Lew Ayres) was the part that interested her. Linda's father was a very prominent lawyer in Poplar Bluff, and I think that, intentionally or not, Greyson Culver was sort of an idealized version of her own father. I think she loved her father very much, and I think she liked the girl-father relationship, she related to that. Without it, I don't know if the show meant as much to her.

The decision was so difficult for the producers that when production finally resumed in early November, no decision had yet been made. The primary reason was Wagner's inability to let go of Samantha. To Wagner, writing the character off the show would have meant losing what little bit of Samantha he had left, and he couldn't bring himself to lose her all over again.

Raymond Austin sympathized with Wagner's dilemma, but felt that it was a mistake:

> We were in a panic not knowing what to do. And then I think the producers, including RJ, made a big mistake. They decided to keep Elizabeth alive, and I think that was a mistake because the whole world knew that Samantha was dead. We would do things like calling upstairs, "Elizabeth, are you coming down?" but, of course, there was no Elizabeth. I think we should have taken her out of the show or used an episode to deal with her absence, which her mother would have let happen. I thought it was a mistake, and so did many other people on the crew. Everybody just sort of shuddered when we did scenes and pretended that she was in the next room or had just left the house. It was especially difficult for Maia. She went through a very hard time.

But explaining the character's absence by saying that Elizabeth had passed away was never an option. She and Culver had been so close that such a move would have changed the direction of the show. It would have been impossible to do a show where she died and then have Culver off on an adventure the next week.

The series resurrection was to be short-lived. After only two more episodes had been filmed, production was halted again. By then, says Harry Thomason:

> We were thinking, "can we survive this, do we want to survive this, and how would we survive it?" We thought it would be good for the show to go on, and we had enough shows banked by then that we could have just hired a replacement and continued forward. Now, by hiring a replacement, I don't mean a new actress to play Elizabeth. All of us were against recasting.

Finally, in January of 1986, it was officially announced that *Lime Street* would not be returning to ABC's schedule. Insists Thomason:

> The show was never officially cancelled. It just never came back on the air. I think that was ABC's decision, because I know we would have tried if they said that they really wanted to go forward.

But they could tell that we were disheartened. The show just sort of dissipated its energy and went away. I think the reason was because we just never knew quite how to deal with Samantha's loss.

Mart Crowley recalls Wagner's sadness over the show's failure. "He was disappointed that it didn't go," Crowley explains. "One is always disappointed to work so hard on something to get it up and running, and then to see it fail. It was the first failure in his attempts with series television. He'd had three very successful shows prior to that."

By this time, back in Maine, Jane Smith had begun laying the groundwork to keep her daughter's memory alive. Immediately after the plane crash she had taken a leave of absence from her job as a social worker. As she contemplated the future, she began to receive mail from all over the world.

"People started sending me money and telling me I should continue on with what Samantha had started," she recalls. "So I was dealing with all this mail and all these ideas and suggestions, and that's when I started the foundation." The mission of the Samantha Smith Foundation was to sponsor exchange programs amongst American and Soviet children between the ages of eleven and sixteen in an effort to foster understanding and peace. (Robert Wagner served on the board of trustees.) In the summer of 1986, Jane accompanied twenty of Samantha's former classmates to the first Goodwill Games in Moscow, which were dedicated to Samantha. The following summer, the foundation arranged for a group of Russian youngsters to visit a youth camp in Maine. The foundation continued to operate until the fall of the Soviet Union over a decade later.

The Soviets themselves were also very active in remembering Samantha. Besides dedicating those first Goodwill Games in Moscow to her, a Russian commemorative stamp was issued with Samantha's picture on it, a priceless diamond was named after her, and even a mountain was christened as St. Samantha.

In the United States, a school in Sammamish, Washington, was named Samantha Smith Elementary. In Augusta, Maine, a statue of Samantha was erected in front of the State Library, depicting the young girl releasing a dove, as a bear cub rests at her feet. Her home state also enacted a law officially declaring the first Monday in June as Samantha Smith Day.

Jane Smith sued Bar Harbor Airlines and eventually accepted an out-of-court settlement that she is still barred from discussing publicly. After investigating the crash of Flight 1808, the NTSB ruled pilot error as the cause. Today, Jane still lives in Maine and continues to speak occasionally about issues of international peace at schools and other organizations. She made a return trip to the Crimea, the site of Samantha's visit, in June of 2005, and was pleased that so many in Russia still recall and continue to be inspired by her daughter's efforts of two decades ago.

The three unaired episodes of *Lime Street* were eventually broadcast in 1987 when the fledgling Lifetime Cable Network purchased the rights to the series' 90-minute pilot and seven one-hour episodes. A tag at the end of each episode of *Lime Street* carries a tribute to its fallen young star: "This series is dedicated to Samantha Smith and her dream of peace in the world."

CHAPTER 11

NewsRadio
Phil Hartman

NBC's situation comedy *NewsRadio* had beaten the odds. Despite being constantly uprooted by the network and moved into ten different timeslots in three years, the series had managed to hold onto a loyal, if not huge, audience. In May 1998, NBC announced the show's cancellation, only to reverse itself a day later and order a fifth season of 22 episodes for that fall. The cast was ecstatic. The set of *NewsRadio*, an ensemble workplace comedy, was by all accounts a happy environment where creativity was welcome. Cast members were encouraged to offer their input; new ideas were often introduced right on the stage floor, incorporated at the last minute, long after scripts had been finalized. "We were all thrilled to have a diamond job, a smart and funny show that you could actually have input on," offers costar Stephen Root. "Opportunities like that don't come around often. We were a big happy family."

But when the cast broke for hiatus in the spring of 1998, no one could have predicted the tragedy that would forever alter the future of *NewsRadio* and bring a premature end to the life of one of the series' brightest stars.

Much of the success of *NewsRadio* was due to the wonderful chemistry enjoyed by the series' cast — a mixed bag of young, up-and-coming talent working alongside industry vets. The series starred Dave Foley, who'd immigrated to the United States after making a name for himself in his native Canada as part of the cult-hit series *Kids in the Hall*. Foley landed the starring role in *NewsRadio* early in 1995. NBC had ordered seven episodes of the sitcom and scheduled it for a tryout that spring. Foley was hired to play Dave Nelson, the young, incoming programming director at WNYX, a New York radio station with an all-news format. Dave was from Wisconsin and a bit green, but was determined to use his new job at the station to make a name for himself. His boss was WNYX owner Jimmy James (Stephen Root), an overbearing, somewhat eccentric billionaire who'd dropped the boom rather quickly on Dave's predecessors. Jimmy was always on the lookout for a new Mrs. James, and was well known for his penchant for placing odd bets on a whim.

Dave's first hurdle was to earn the trust of his staff. Although a talented bunch, they were all a bit insecure, due to the lack of leadership at the station. Lisa Miller (Maura Tierney) was a gifted writer who thought she should have gotten a shot at Dave's job. Her bitterness, though, was offset by her attraction to Dave, and they were soon engaged in a hot-and-cold-running romance. Beth (Vicki Lewis) was Dave's secretary and gal Friday, who kept him abreast of office gossip by eavesdropping on the other employees. She would show up for work wearing a plethora of strange outfits. Matthew Brock (Andy Dick) was an offbeat news reporter who was the perpetual black sheep due to his bizarre antics both at work and in his personal life. Joe Garelli (Joe Rogan) was the station's mechanical engineer (and all-around fix-it guy), who fancied himself a self-styled MacGyver, preferring to repair things with his own home-made inventions rather than purchasing the correct tools. Joe was also a bit of a conspiracy theorist, adding his own twists to the news stories that came through WNYX.

The station's most bizarre characters, however, were its two on-air personalities, Bill McNeal (Phil Hartman) and Catherine Duke (Khandi Alexander). Bill was ego-driven and usually told it like he saw it, which could lead to extremely colorful exchanges, considering his skewed point-of-view. Matthew idolized Bill, who reciprocated by referring to the station outcast as "Spaz" and using him as the punch line for many cruel jokes. Catherine turned a blind eye to Bill's antics, as well as to all of the other shenanigans that occurred at the station.

Despite the over-the-top characters and constant hijinks that ensued, *NewsRadio* proved to be a very smart, highbrow comedy. Paul Simms, a former writer for *The Larry Sanders Show* and *Late Night with David Letterman*, created the series. On the television evolutionary chart, *NewsRadio* fell somewhere between the '70s classic *WKRP in Cincinnati* and NBC's acclaimed 2000s take on the British hit *The Office*. The series debuted on the evening of Tuesday, March 21, 1995, and although it didn't exactly ignite a ratings firestorm, it performed well on a night that had included, over the course of the season, such low-rated fare as *The Martin Short Show* and *John Larroquette*. NBC quickly found a spot for it on their fall schedule.

Phil Hartman as newscaster Bill McNeal in the NBC workplace sitcom *NewsRadio* (courtesy of NBC/ Photofest).

The cast of *NewsRadio* hit it off immediately, both on-camera and off. The show clearly worked as an ensemble, much as *WKRP* had before it. The workplace scenario worked exceptionally well, despite the fact that some of the cast clearly had more experience and were more recognizable to viewers than others. Leading the pack was the multi-talented Phil Hartman, who was just coming off an eight-season run on NBC's *Saturday Night Live*. Perhaps it was because of his time spent on *SNL*, or due to his earlier work as part of the popular comedy troupe *The Groundlings*, that Hartman preferred being part of a team. Had he wished, Hartman could certainly have headlined his own NBC series. Instead, he chose to become part of the mix at *NewsRadio*, where he would add Bill

McNeal to his portfolio of unforgettable characters. It was also as a member of *NewsRadio* that Hartman's life and career would end abruptly and tragically.

Philip Edward Hartmann was born on September 24, 1948, in Brantford, Ontario, Canada. He was one of eight children born to Rupert and Doris Hartmann, who relocated their large brood from Canada to the United States in the 1950s. They first lived in Connecticut and later Southern California. (Phil would eventually change the spelling of his last name, dropping an "n," although it's not known precisely when or why.) Hartman was a quiet yet gifted child. As a youngster, he and his brothers shared a room. They had a tiny record player on which they would play over and over again comedy albums by the legendary Jonathan Winters. At night, when they were ready to go to sleep, Phil would entertain the others by doing verbatim the monologues he'd heard Winters doing, including all the different voices. After high school he attended California State University, Northridge, where he studied graphic design. Upon graduation, Hartman decided to pursue a career in art that eventually led to his being hired to design a number of memorable album covers for the bands Crosby, Stills, & Nash and Poco.

In 1975, while still working as a design artist, Hartman joined the California comedy group the Groundlings, where he got an opportunity to write, direct, and appear on stage. Actress and comedian Edie McClurg remembers meeting and working with Hartman back in the '70s:

When I first met Phil, the Groundling Theater was not yet open because we had to have off-street parking. Our small theater came under the same rules as the porno theaters. To keep them from trying to open in nice neighborhoods, they made a big rule about having to have off-street parking. We could hold our classes, and we could have Open Scene Nights where we could invite guests, but we couldn't charge money. It was quite some months before we could function as a real business.

Then, "one night, not too long after I joined the company," continues McClurg,

I did a satire of a Catherine Deneuve fragrance commercial, and we had a break half-way through, and we all went to the little bar across the street to have a drink. Phil was there and was so excited about what he was seeing. He made a point to talk to me specifically about doing imitations of famous people and their personalities. He was very excited about that. He was just so open and effusive in his praise. When he thought something was good, he told you. Sometimes when people think something is good, they're jealous. They'll look like they're giving you a nice compliment, and then they'll damn you with fake praise at some point. But Phil was never that way. If he loved it he told you so. He decided then he was going to come to classes, and maybe be in the shows when we opened, and that's what he did.

Hartman and McClurg became fast friends; they enjoyed working together and learning from one another. Says McClurg:

Phil always paid great attention to the details of his characters, not only having the right shirt or the right coat, but also how he wore his hair, what he wore on his head, even his shoes. I learned in costuming class when I was in college that the two most personal things about your personality is how you wear your hair and what shoes you wear. It says a lot about you. Phil changed a lot of things about himself in order to make his characters jump off the stage. He changed his style a lot. Sometimes he would dye his hair back to its natural brown, and other times he would sort of bleach it out. One time he kind of went red. You just never quite knew what style of clothing he was going to wear. One of the reasons Phil was so comfortable on stage is because he was always so well prepared. In class, we would improvise things and come up with new characters. He was such a good writer.

McClurg also found Hartman to be quite a character off-stage as well:

> He came in one night and he was wearing white slacks, a Hawaiian shirt, and a straw hat. He just
> kind of sauntered in and said, "Guess what I did today?" And I said, "Well, I'm lookin' at you.
> Did you go to the beach?" And he said, "I took a sailing lesson. I'm gonna learn how to sail." And
> he did love sailing. He bought a sailboat, and he would just go out into the Santa Monica Bay,
> drop anchor, and just lay there on the deck and look at the sky, feel the sun on his face, then
> come back in and go back to his life. But he just loved the silence of being out there on the
> ocean. He always had a big hello and a hug, and his own personal laugh, a boyish giggle, just like
> a happy little kid.

It was also at the Groundlings that Hartman met two men who would become life-long friends, fellow performers Jon Lovitz and Paul Reubens. It was with Reubens that Hartman would create the character of "Pee-wee Herman," which Reubens would breathe life into in a number of hilarious comedy sketches. The two men (along with scribe Michael Varhol) later wrote a feature script based on the character, titled *Pee-wee's Big Adventure*, which became a hit motion picture in 1985. The movie helped to launch the careers of star Reubens and first-time feature film director Tim Burton. Hartman had a small role as a reporter. In 1986, Reubens took Pee-wee to the small screen in a popular CBS children's series, *Pee-wee's Playhouse*. Hartman signed on to write for the program and also appeared regularly the first season as "Captain Carl."

But Hartman's career took off in another direction that same year when in the fall of 1986 he joined the cast of NBC's perennial late-night favorite, *Saturday Night Live*, where, as with the Groundlings, he would thrive as a creative force both in the writers' room and onstage. *Saturday Night Live* was still recovering at the time from the program's early-'80s ratings slump after the departure of executive producer Lorne Michaels and the entire original cast. By '86, under the supervision of new showrunner Dick Ebersol, the show was on the rebound (thanks in no small part to the emergence of young newcomer Eddie Murphy, whose tenure on the show began in 1981 and ended in the spring of 1984, when he left to pursue a feature film career). Hartman stepped into a talented troupe that included Dana Carvey, Nora Dunn, Jan Hooks, Victoria Jackson, Dennis Miller, Kevin Nealon, and Hartman pal Jon Lovitz, who had been recruited the previous season.

Hartman quickly became not only one of *Saturday Night Live*'s most prolific writer-performers, but an audience favorite as well. On stage, he would entertain viewers with a wide array of impressions, including Frank Sinatra, Ronald Reagan, Ed McMahon, Burt Reynolds, Jack Nicholson, Phil Donahue, Barbara Bush, and Bill Clinton. He also had a stable of recurring original characters, like the Frankenstein monster and the "Frozen Caveman Lawyer." Backstage, Hartman was well-regarded for his generosity in helping novice, incoming writers get their material on the air.

The popularity of *Saturday Night Live* allowed its cast members to spread their wings and find work in feature films. Dana Carvey found success by translating his *Wayne's World* sketches into a wildly successful movie in 1992; his co-star, Mike Myers, another Canadian import who joined the cast in 1988, starred in and directed 1993's *So I Married an Axe Murderer* and later *Austin Powers: International Man of Mystery* (1997). Even Lovitz worked steadily in features, like *My Stepmother Is an Alien* (1988) and *Mom and Dad Save the World* (1992). Hartman, too, was in demand, landing supporting roles in projects such as *Jumpin' Jack Flash*, *Three Amigos* (both in 1986) and *Blind Date* (1987). He also landed a number of voice-over gigs: Disney's animated big-screen venture *The Brave Little Toaster* (1987); a number of

Phil Hartman came to national attention as a cast member of NBC's *Saturday Night Live*. Pictured is the ensemble program's 1991–92 cast. From left: (back row) Hartman, Jan Hooks, Mike Meyers, (front row) Dennis Miller, Dana Carvey, Victoria Jackson, Kevin Nealon (courtesy NBC/Photofest).

cartoon series for TV, such as *DuckTales* (1987) and *Tiny Toon Adventures* (1990); and, most famously, a menagerie of characters for the FOX network's celebrated hit *The Simpsons*. Phil Hartman had quickly become a sought after commodity in the entertainment industry. His ambitions and hard work had paid off, and he had earned a reputation as being one of the most dependable and bankable names in the business.

Hartman's personal life, at least outwardly, also seemed to be coming together. Hartman had been twice divorced. His first marriage, to Gretchen Lewis in 1970, came to a quick end. He tried again in 1982, marrying real estate agent Lisa Strain. But the second go-around was only marginally more successful than the first, ending in 1985 after less than three years. Then, in 1987, the third time seemed to be a charm. That year Hartman wed Vicki Omdahl, who changed her name to Brynn Hartman after the ceremony. Brynn, 29, was a native of Thief River Falls, Minnesota. After graduating high school, she was married briefly, then did some modeling in Minneapolis before relocating to Los Angeles in order to pursue an acting career.

Brynn had her inner demons, however. She suffered from personal insecurities that were only magnified when she became part of the Hollywood system. She had turned to alcohol and drugs in order to cope, and was soon overtaken by her addictions. After marrying Hartman, it appeared for a while that she had cleaned up her act and become sober. But despite kicking her habits, she continued to be plagued by panic attacks brought on by her ongoing feelings of inadequacy. Although on the surface she and Phil appeared to be a happy couple, privately Brynn was still battling depression. Being married to one of the industry's brightest talents didn't help matters. Although she refrained from immediately returning to alcohol and cocaine, Brynn did seek out cosmetic surgery in hopes it would help her land more work. She did score a couple of minor roles, in the feature film *North* (1994) and two episodes of TV's *3rd Rock from the Sun* (1998). But true fame eluded her, and the pressure continued to mount.

The couple did find reason to celebrate. Bright spots in their marriage included the births of their two children: son Sean in 1988 and daughter Birgen in 1992. From the outside looking in, the Hartmans were living the American dream.

In 1994, Hartman announced he was leaving the cast of *Saturday Night Live*. He'd been with the show for eight years, the longest any performer had remained with the program up until that time. The following year he landed his first lead movie role, in *Houseguest*, as a husband and father whose perfect suburban existence is turned upside down by a conman (comedian Sinbad) who shows up posing as an old buddy. The film raked in only $26 million at the domestic box office, but it led to a series of bigger and better roles.

But Hartman wasn't yet finished with television. He still appreciated the quick pace and feeling of camaraderie that came with the medium of TV. Initially, he was offered the chance to do his own variety series. But when a similar venture by fellow *Saturday Night Live* alumnus Dana Carvey went belly up on ABC in the spring of '96, Hartman had second thoughts. Variety programs had seldom worked in prime time since the 1970s when *The Carol Burnett Show* ruled the airwaves. So Hartman decided to look for a scripted comedy instead. That spring he found a new home on the NBC sitcom *NewsRadio*. He immediately felt at home on the program's soundstage and in the character of news anchor Bill McNeal.

Actor Stephen Root, who co-starred with Hartman on *NewsRadio*, as WNYX station owner Jimmy James, recalls those earlier days on the show:

> I'd just done a series with Lloyd and Beau Bridges called *Harts of the West*, and was still doing a fair amount of auditioning. When I went in for *NewsRadio*, they were actually looking for a guy in his sixties, someone who could pull off a Mr. Carlson from *WKRP in Cincinnati* sort of thing. But I thought the material was a lot smarter than that, so I came in with my own interpretation of the character and worked closely on it with [director] James Burrows and [creator/executive producer] Paul Simms.

Root remembers being incredibly impressed by Hartman as they became acquainted:

> I hadn't known Phil before *NewsRadio*, but I was a fan of his work on *Saturday Night Live*. A couple of other *Saturday Night Live* people had done shows around that time that had tanked pretty badly, so Phil didn't want to head a show, he wanted to be part of an ensemble. *NewsRadio* really was an ensemble, and we were all on the same page from day one. That's how Phil got involved.

The only people that Paul [Simms] wanted for the show from the very beginning was Phil, Dave Foley, and Andy Dick, who he'd worked with before. The rest of us just came in and went through the basic audition process.

Everyone involved believed early on that *NewsRadio* was going to be special. Explains Root:

We knew the pilot was really good. The evening we shot it, we started at seven o'clock and finished it at nine-thirty. It was the easiest, fastest pilot I had ever done because all the people were right on the money, we were working together like clockwork, and of course we had Jimmy Burrows directing. We figured we'd at least get picked up and would have a pretty good chance. We were being geared for midseason, so we didn't have all the pressure that comes with being on in the fall. Then we just kind of slipped on in midyear and all the critics really liked us.

Back on the stages of *Saturday Night Live*, Hartman had earned the nickname "the Glue" for his ability to bring the cast closer together and hold them there. Likewise, Hartman became a central figure on the set of *NewsRadio*. Insists Root:

Everyone was in awe of Phil. It took a little while for him to really trust us, though, because he was coming from *Saturday Night Live*, where, from what he had told us, it was a very back-biting atmosphere. At *NewsRadio* we were all just trying to make a funny show, we didn't care who wrote it. It took Phil about a year to trust us. Before that it was like, "You want to rewrite what!?..." He was very cautious for a while.

Hartman's diplomatic nature also came in handy when personality conflicts would arise between cast members. Says Root:

It was hard for Phil and Andy Dick to work together. They were like oil and water. But they were still good on-camera together. They always got the job done. Phil's character and mine — ours were the most over-the-top. But that's what Phil was used to. He was used to doing many different characters, so doing just one on *NewsRadio* was something he could have done in his sleep. He was used to doing four or five characters a show on *Saturday Night Live*, and his stuff tended to get more outrageous, otherwise he'd get bored.

Veteran television director Tom Cherones, whose credits include NBC's *Seinfeld*, became one of *NewsRadio*'s most prolific directors. He, too, found working on the show, and with Hartman, one of the highlights of his career:

NewsRadio was the most enjoyable directing experience I've ever had. I enjoyed working with the actors, and with the head writer, Paul Simms, who was respectful of everybody's jobs. He showed respect all around — to the actors, the crew, to me...and I'd never had quite that amount of respect before from an executive producer. So it was my favorite experience. On *NewsRadio* we had a really good group, and Phil, of course, was the leader. Everybody looked up to him, and he was a great help in keeping the show running smoothly. Phil blended right in with the rest of the cast. Andy Dick was always a little bit of a problem because he was younger and kind of randy, but Phil was a big help in controlling him.

It was with Hartman that Cherones found the most in common:

Phil and I had a good time together; we were both airplane pilots, and we talked about flying planes and that sort of thing. Bill and I were the oldest people on that show, so there was some kind of bond there as well. He was a great guy, a very happy person. He had all the bells and whistles, he had toys, he had an airplane, he had bought an old Bentley and also had a pick-up truck. He was a happy guy. I didn't sense any personal problems with him.

But despite their admiration for Hartman, few people on the show felt they knew the *real* Phil Hartman. Perhaps hiding behind all those varied personas over the years provided Hartman with protection from insecurities of his own. Offers Root:

The large cast of NBC's situation comedy *NewsRadio*, shown in happier times, before the murder of co-star Phil Hartman. Pictured from left: Dave Foley, Khandi Alexander, Hartman, Vicki Lewis, Maura Tierney, Joe Rogan, Stephen Root, Andy Dick (hanging below) (courtesy NBC/Photofest).

I don't think anyone knew Phil really well, except perhaps those he came up with in the Ground-lings. Phil was one of those people who never seemed to come out of character. But he was never annoying. Phil would go into different characters all the time. The real Phil Hartman, from what I could see, was a guy who loved his kids and would have been happy to sit around and watch them play and draw. That was the real Phil Hartman, but he hardly ever let himself do that. He was brilliant at being these different characters; it was easy for him and a lot of fun for us.

Root did enjoy the time he got to spend with Hartman away from the show, and it did give him a little more insight into the man behind all those wonderful alter egos:

I did hang out with him because we both had kids that were real small. We'd go to Knotts Berry Farm. But none of us on the cast really spent that much time with him because Phil really preferred just to go home and spend time with his kids. I think Phil was a real happy person, a multi-talented guy, and a tremendous artist who was always doodling. He would do a lot of art for his kids, and he would show us that. He just had so many facets; he was a great mimic, a great sketch artist, and actor. He would have found his niche in films; he hadn't found it at that point. He was still doing kind of over-the-top characters in film. He hadn't really learned to trust himself. I think he would have found that if he'd had more time.

Unfortunately, time for Phil Hartman was running out.

By the spring of 1998, Phil Hartman's career was reaching new heights. On the big screen he was gaining momentum with appearances in such features as *Greedy* (1994), *Sgt. Bilko* (1996), *Jingle All the Way* (1996) and *Small Soldiers* (1998). On TV his series *NewsRadio* had just been picked up after narrowly escaping the network axe. On May 16, NBC had announced it was canceling the show. Then, on May 18, it reversed its decision and picked up *NewsRadio* for a full fifth season. The cast, then on hiatus, was overjoyed, and looking forward to returning to work later that summer on 22 new episodes. But nothing could have prepared them for the news they'd awaken to ten days later.

On the evening of May 27, 1998, actor Stephen Root had attended a party given by friends. He had a little too much to drink at the event and decided to spend the night. The next morning he got into his car and began the trek home. During the drive he switched on his radio and tuned to the news. "I was completely hung over," recalls Root, "and at first I thought they were talking about another Hartman." But it didn't take long for Root to realize that it was indeed his friend and costar Phil Hartman who was the topic of discussion on just about every station — radio and television — that morning. Hartman, 49, had been killed in the early morning hours of May 28, and just as shocking was the revelation that he had died at the hands of his wife Brynn in an apparent murder-suicide.

Continues Root:

Then I got home, and I began receiving so many calls from newspapers and media. I had no idea that my phone number was so not-private. It all started immediately, everybody asking for a quote. A friend came out and helped field a lot of those calls so that I could write something. But it was just a horrible, horrible morning.

Root was not alone in his shock and dismay. Not far away, Edie McClurg, too, was about to learn of her friend's passing:

When I first heard about it, I got physically sick. I was outside and I turned on the radio, and they said something about a murder on Encino Avenue, and then they said Phil Hartman, and I was just about ready to step into the hot tub, and I became physically sick. I just had to kneel down; it was so frightening. I thought, "What in the hell happened?" We had kept in touch over the years. I was shooting a show once on the same lot as *NewsRadio*; I was on a stage next door to his. So I just popped over to say hi, and, as usual, he was so warm. No matter where he got to in his career, his old friends were still his old friends. He was a good man.

The news of Phil Hartman's death dominated the airwaves that morning as fans across the country, along with Phil's friends and co-workers in Hollywood, mourned his sudden loss. As the day wore on, the facts of what happened slowly began to come to light, and only added to the horror of what was already evident.

The previous evening Brynn Hartman had been very upset and was drinking heavily. The binge was the result of marital problems, although the precise nature of her concerns remains a mystery, as only she and her husband knew the details. Some say she wanted a divorce, that she had been pressing Phil to end their marriage for as many as two years. But Phil had refused. Instead, he had convinced her to seek counseling, which for a time may have improved their relationship. Some accounts, however, implied that Phil may finally have had enough and told Brynn that he wanted out of the marriage. Several months earlier Brynn had spent time in a rehab center for her drug use. Whatever the truth may have been, Brynn had fallen off the wagon yet again. Not only had she been drinking, but a medical examiner's report would later reveal that she had also ingested cocaine and was taking the antidepressant Zoloft.

Between 2:00 and 3:00 A.M. the morning of Thursday, May 28, Brynn returned to the Hartman's ranch-style Encino Avenue home. She found her husband asleep in the master bedroom. She then reportedly pulled a Smith & Wesson handgun out of her purse and fired three shots into Phil as he slept beneath the covers, striking him in the forehead, the neck, and forearm. Based on the coroner's investigation, it was determined he died instantly, never regaining consciousness. Brynn then fled the scene, leaving the couple's two children, Sean (then 9) and Birgen (6), alone in the house with their father's body. She went to the home of a male friend, Ron Douglas, and confessed what she had done. He initially did not believe her, and after several hours the two drove back to the Hartmans' home together, where Brynn showed him the body.

A stunned Douglas first phoned Encino police and then woke the children and began to escort them from the house. As he was doing so, Brynn got hold of another handgun from somewhere on the property and locked herself in the master bedroom with Phil's body. Authorities arrived at approximately 6:20 A.M. and entered the home. Once inside, they attempted to talk Brynn out of the bedroom. By then she was in hysterics, crying uncontrollably. Negotiations quickly deteriorated, and moments later a gunshot rang out. Police immediately broke down the bedroom door. Inside they encountered a grisly scene: Brynn, dead from a self-inflicted gunshot wound to the head, was lying on the king-sized bed next to her husband.

Word began to spread, and it wasn't long before news crews were deluging the Hartmans' neighborhood.

NewsRadio director Tom Cherones recalls learning of Hartman's death and the immediate response of his co-stars:

> I'd been out to breakfast and had just come home, and I got a call from Kent Zbornak, the line producer, who told me what had happened. I was shocked, of course. I live in Oregon, and I immediately flew down to Los Angeles. Paul Simms had a gathering at his house. We all got there, and everyone was wondering whether the series should continue. And I said, "She [Brynn] has taken Phil from us, don't let her take the show from us too." All the cast was there, and we all agreed that we should continue, if we could, and of course we'd already been picked up for the next season.

The loss of Hartman affected not only *NewsRadio* but several other projects as well. He had made a guest appearance in the season finale of another NBC series, the comedy *3rd Rock from the Sun*. The episode, subtitled "Eat, Drink, Dick, Mary" (5/20/98), was the first of a two-parter intended to be resolved in the fall. The script for the conclusion had to be rewritten around Hartman's absence before being shot later that summer. Hartman had also just signed on to provide several voices — including that of the lead character — in a new animated series for Fox titled *Futurama*. Another actor was later signed for the part, but the show's protagonist was renamed Phillip J. Fry in honor of Hartman.

Several memorials were held for Hartman, including those by the Groundlings and his former *Saturday Night Live* costars. He was also nominated posthumously for an Emmy Award for his role as Bill NcNeal but lost out to actor David Hyde Pierce of *Frasier*. The official ruling regarding his death was that Phil Hartman had died as the result of a murder/suicide at the hands of his spouse, Brynn. During the investigation it was revealed that Brynn had told several friends that she felt odd after taking her antidepressants. Many believed her actions might have been the result of side effects from the drugs. Still others thought Brynn's jealousy over Phil's success was a contributing factor. "It turned out to be a big thing, her being jealous of him," says Root. "She just didn't have that kind of ability, and that, mixed with the drugs, put her over the edge; but nobody had any notion it was coming."

Both Phil and Brynn were cremated, and on Thursday, June 4, one week after the shooting, family members gathered at the Church of the Recessional at Forest Lawn Memorial Park to memorialize them. Both their children were in attendance. Afterwards, as outlined in Phil's will, their ashes were spread on Catalina Island, one of Phil's favorite places to sail his boat. It was decided that Brynn's sister and her husband in Wisconsin would raise Sean and Birgen.

In August 1998 the surviving members of the *NewsRadio* cast gathered to resume production on the program's fifth season. Over the summer, executive producer Paul Simms had recruited actor and comedian Jon Lovitz, who had previously made a couple of guest appearances on the show, to join the cast as Max Louis, WNYX's new on-air personality. Lovitz had been one of Hartman's best friends, and was still deeply wounded by his death. Signing on to *NewsRadio* was therapeutic, helping him to continue to feel connected to Phil. It was also a last favor for an old pal. The rest of the actors felt more comfortable with Lovitz than they would have been with a complete stranger coming into the mix.

Says Cherones:

> We all loved Jon. Jon had been there before, and we knew what he was doing. He was helping us get through this. It was really good of Jon to do it, and he did it because he was a friend of Phil's. He helped us through it, and we all enjoyed working together. And you have to realize, Jon was going through a tough time too.

Stephen Root agrees: "Jon was Phil's best friend at that point, and it was really nice of him to come in and attempt to fill his shoes."

One of the initial challenges of getting *NewsRadio* back up and running was figuring out how to deal with the loss of Phil's character. Executive Producer Paul Simms wrote that season's premiere script, "Bill Moves On" (9/23/98), in which it was explained that Bill had suffered a heart attack and died. Along with his will, Bill left behind a personal letter for each member of the staff. The episode then dealt with each character as they read Bill's final words to them.

Remembers Cherones:

> That first day back was very difficult. We all had a hard time. Paul wrote that very nice show where the character that Phil was playing died. Many of us have had deaths in our families, and, you know, we're all families when we do these shows. We're families for a short time; nevertheless, we're families. So it was difficult, and the actors had a hard time getting through that first episode. The way Paul had structured it was that Phil's character had written letters to each of the other characters, to be read after his death. So each had a turn dealing personally on-camera with his death.

After the murder of Phil Hartman, actor and comedian Jon Lovitz joined the cast of NBC's *News-Radio*. Lovitz and Hartman had been long-time friends, and had worked together as members of the Groundlings comedy troupe and on the NBC sketch comedy series *Saturday Night Live* (courtesy NBC/Photofest).

Stephen Root, too, vividly remembers walking back onto the set to resume shooting:

> The first day was the hardest for all of us because we had to do a show about Phil dying. We did
> the table read on Monday, cried through that, and then pretty much all agreed that we couldn't
> work on this during the week. We all felt that the best thing to do was to just go away, and then
> we'd come back in on Thursday and block it, then film it on Friday. But we'd be damned if we
> were going to rehearse it, and we didn't. We blocked it Thursday, then came in Friday and just
> shot it scene by scene, rehearsing it once in front of the audience, and then shooting it. We
> couldn't have gotten through it any other way. The audience cried through the whole thing; we
> cried through the whole thing. It was really the most difficult thing that I've ever done profession-
> ally.

Jon Lovitz's insecure, memory-impaired Max Lewis was hired in the next episode, "Meet
Max Louis" (10/7/98). Unfortunately, it became clear early on that Lovitz's brand of humor
wasn't compatible with that of *NewsRadio*. Explains Root:

> Jon did the best he could, but his rhythms were completely different from ours, or how Phil's used
> to be. Everyone pretty much accepted Jon coming into the show, although it did get a little tense.
> Jon and Andy had some personal problems. Jon found it a little hard to get into the ensemble
> mode instead of being the star of the show. It was kind of like, "You're part of an ensemble now,
> dude, we can't wait while you're on the phone. Come to the rehearsal now." So it was a little hard
> to get him into the groove, but he got into it by the middle of the year. He had to loosen up a
> bit, which he did. But it still wasn't the same.

The writing too, Root believes, was a little off that season: "The show wasn't retaining
its quality. It was a show with mostly the same people, but it wasn't the same show." Cherones
concurs:

> Jon was different, a bit broader than the rest of them. The show just didn't work the same way. I
> don't think the last season was as good as the rest of it, when Phil was there. It was as good as it
> could be, but I think we all missed Phil, including the writers. The fact that he wasn't there made
> my job harder, because Phil was a rock.

By the spring of 1999, with ratings slipping, it was clear the end was in sight. Based on
the show's history, Cherones held out hope, but he realized the odds were against *NewsRadio*
returning for a sixth season. "The truth is you never really know in network television,"
explains Cherones. "So you don't even think about it. You go on and do what you do, you
always try to do your best, and they'll either pick you up or not. In this case, they didn't."

NBC cancelled *NewsRadio* in May of 1999 after 97 half-hour episodes. Looking back,
says Root:

> It was a dream job, and they hardly ever come along, where the work and the people make you
> better because they're at the top of their game. It was a perfect ensemble, a perfect creative envi-
> ronment. They welcomed input on the floor. In the end, barring Phil leaving us, it was a great
> working situation. We all wanted the show to be the smartest show it could be, and it was for a
> while. It was a happy set for three years; the fourth year it was getting a little tenser; and then
> that spring Phil got killed, and the last year really was an unhappy year.

For both its cast and fans, *NewsRadio* remains a cause for celebration. Despite the loss
of a comic legend, the show stands as a visual testament to the remarkable skills of Phil Hartman, something to be enjoyed and admired, along with his other work, for years to come.

CHAPTER 12

The Royal Family
Redd Foxx

For a majority of TV viewers, Redd Foxx will always be remembered as cantankerous junkman Fred Sanford from the classic 1970s sitcom *Sanford & Son*. Foxx seemed to emerge from total obscurity when the NBC comedy premiered in January 1972. In reality, it had taken Foxx nearly five decades of hard living, adversity, and indignity to make his way from the streets of Chicago to the glamour of network television.

The journey began on December 9, 1922, in St. Louis, Missouri, when Mary Alma Sanford gave birth to her second son, Jon Elroy Sanford, who would someday grow into the man the world would know as Redd Foxx. Little Jon Elroy had an older brother, Fred Sanford, Jr. Their father, Fred Glenn Sanford, had walked out on the family three months before Jon Elroy's birth (Foxx would never meet his father). In 1923 Mary Alma relocated with her sons to Chicago and took a job as a domestic. The three struggled to survive during the difficult days ahead, including the Depression of the 1930s.

Jon Elroy never excelled academically and dropped out of high school after one year. Although lost in the classroom, he felt at home on the streets and spent many years as part of the city's 58th Street gang. When he wasn't holding people up at knifepoint, Jon Elroy was entertaining them. He and a group of friends formed a musical group called the Four Bon Bons and would perform on street corners.

In 1939 they hopped a boxcar to New York in search of stardom. After several months of struggling, they were offered a spot on the Major Bowes Radio Amateur Hour and took second place, a week's engagement at Harlem's Apollo Theater. Despite the break, long-term success eluded the four, and eventually the act broke up. While his friends returned to Chicago, Jon Elroy remained in New York.

Over the next few years he worked odd jobs and continued to hone his comedy skills by performing stand-up in local clubs. One of his day jobs was as a busboy and dishwasher at Jimmy's Chicken Shack, where he befriended a waiter named Malcolm Little, who would later change his name to Malcolm X and become a leading figure in the Civil Rights movement. They would hustle pool to make ends meet. Their red hair earned them the nicknames "Detroit Red" (for Malcolm) and "Chicago Red" (for Foxx). Jon Elroy would eventually adopt the moniker as part of his professional stage name, Redd Foxx (the Foxx came from pro-baseball player Jimmy Foxx).

Comedian Redd Foxx had a long and varied career, both on stage and with a number of best-selling adult party albums, before breaking into television with the NBC sitcom *Sanford & Son* in 1972.

In the 1940s Foxx teamed with fellow comedian Slappy White, and they soon found themselves on the "Chitlin" comedy circuit reserved for black stage acts. Their routines contained quite a bit of adult material, which further limited the number of venues at which they could appear. Vulgarity would become a trademark of Foxx's stage acts.

After a failed marriage in the late 1940s, Foxx made his way to Los Angeles, where he initially found things no easier than they'd been back east. He married for a second time in 1955, to Betty Jean Harris, a union that would last for two decades. That same year he landed his big break professionally when he signed with a minority-owned record label, Dooto Records, to record a party album (a "party album" was a recording that basically contained an adult-oriented monologue). The record, *Laff of the Party*, was laced with profanity and could be sold only from under the counter in most legitimate record stores. But it proved to be highly successful; Foxx would eventually record 54 albums in all, selling more than 20 million copies.

Having finally made a name for himself, Foxx was asked to appear on programs such as *The Tonight Show* and *Steve Allen*. He made his motion picture debut in the 1970 film *Cotton Comes to Harlem* (directed by Ossie Davis). His performance caught the attention of producer Bud Yorkin, which led to an offer to star in the sitcom *Sanford & Son*. Although he'd have to clean up his act for TV, Foxx saw it as a chance to gain national exposure and earn a great deal of money.

Yorkin had adapted *Sanford & Son* from the British sitcom *Steptoe & Son*, just as he and partner Norman Lear had previously developed the groundbreaking adult comedy *All in the Family* from the British series *Till Death Us Do Part*. On the show, Foxx played Fred G. Sanford, the ornery proprietor of Sanford & Son salvage, a junkyard in the ghettos of Watts. Young newcomer Demond Wilson was cast as Lamont, Fred's thirty-something son, who reluctantly did the legwork and heavy lifting but was always on the lookout for a way to better himself and get away from the junk business. The father/son chemistry between Foxx and Wilson was instant and believable.

When it came to the development of *Sanford & Son*, Foxx was allotted a great deal of input. The title character was named in memory of Foxx's older brother, Fred G. Sanford, Jr., who had died in 1963 from diabetes and kidney disease. Sanford was also said to be a native of St. Louis, just as Foxx had been. He even cast his old stand-up partner, Slappy White, as a regular during *Sanford & Son*'s first season.

Sanford & Son premiered on January 14, 1972, and was an immediate hit, becoming the number six show on television by the end of its first season. By the end of its second year, in the spring of 1973, the show was in the number two position, right behind *All in the Family*. Initially there had been doubt that Foxx could be funny under the restrictions set forth by NBC's Standards & Practices office. After all, *Sanford & Son* was airing at 8:00 P.M., a time-slot set aside for family programming. Foxx surprised everyone by turning Fred G. Sanford into an endearing old grouch the entire family could enjoy. One of Foxx's funniest bits on the show involved clutching his chest in moments of crisis and calling out to his late wife Elizabeth, "I'm coming to join you, honey!"

During the run of *Sanford & Son*, Foxx continued to perform his live act in Las Vegas, which led to a lot of embarrassment and anger when parents would bring their children to the theater expecting to see Fred Sanford. On stage, Foxx would revert back to the type of blue material that had made his albums so successful, causing many shocked families to run for the nearest exit.

Sanford & Son continued its reign on television for six seasons, five of those spent in the top ten. Finally, in the spring of 1977, ratings began to drop. It finished the 1976-77 season ranked number twenty-seven. The show was still winning its timeslot, however, and NBC was prepared to renew the show for a seventh season. But ABC had been wooing Foxx for some time with a big-money offer to do a one-hour variety series. With his NBC contract about to expire, Foxx announced he was leaving *Sanford & Son* to headline his own program for the alphabet network. *Sanford & Son* aired its final original episode on the evening of March 25, 1977.

Unfortunately for Foxx, he would soon regret his decision.

The Redd Foxx Comedy Hour premiered on ABC on Thursday, September 15, 1977, with incredible fanfare. Regular skits on the program included "The History of the Negro in America," in which Foxx and the cast would reenact famous historical moments the way they "really" occurred, and "Redd's Corner," which allowed Foxx to give airtime to some of his old friends from the Chitlin comedy circuit. Among the regulars on the series were Slappy White and future *Family Matters* star Jo Marie Payton. One interesting concept that emerged on the show was a skit in which Foxx and Payton would portray a squabbling married couple named Alphonse and Victoria (characters which Foxx and Della Reese would eventually play on Foxx's final project, *The Royal Family*.) Despite the enormous amount of publicity that initially surrounded the series, *The Redd Foxx Comedy Hour* floundered in the ratings and was cancelled after only 13 episodes.

For Foxx, the failure was a huge setback.

Foxx had made a great deal of money during his heyday on *Sanford & Son*, but he also indulged in an extravagant lifestyle. He was known for his opulence — he owned homes in Beverly Hills, Las Vegas, and St. Louis, as well as other real estate in the Los Angeles area (including a four-story office building from which he did business). He was also extremely generous, and whenever a friend was in need, Foxx would be there. He'd happily hand over thousands of dollars in cash and never ask for a penny of it to be repaid. His closest friends, such as Slappy White, received expensive cars and luxurious homes.

As a consequence, as the years passed, Foxx racked up a great deal of debt, never quite willing to believe the ride might eventually end. In order to pay off his delinquent alimony to second wife Betty Jean Harris (the marriage had ended in 1975), Foxx was forced to sign away his residual rights to *Sanford & Son* reruns. (A third marriage lasted from 1976 to 1981.) On top of the support he was paying to three ex-wives, he also had failed business ventures

Redd Foxx is best remembered for his role as ornery junk dealer Fred G. Sanford in the hit NBC sitcom *Sanford & Son.* He's pictured above with co-stars Don "Bubba" Bexley (left) and Demond Wilson (right).

to cope with. In the 1970s he had opened the Redd Foxx Club in Los Angeles. Foxx had spent much of his life on nightclub stages but knew little about running them.

On top of everything else, Foxx had also been having trouble with the Internal Revenue Service, dating back as far as the late 1970s. The agency claimed that Foxx owed nearly three million dollars in back taxes for income he'd failed to report on his tax returns. Foxx maintained that he was unaware of any wrongdoing. While Foxx had grown up street-smart, his lack of a formal education had forced him to put his financial interests into the hands of others. Foxx was merely told where to affix his signature, and did so without asking too many questions so long as funds continued to be readily available.

During his heyday on *Sanford & Son,* Foxx could afford to weather such financial woes. But as his career began to falter in later years, it all caught up with him. In 1983 he was forced to declare bankruptcy. Even then, Foxx continued to live the high life, spending money as quickly as he could earn it.

The failure of *The Redd Foxx Comedy Hour* had a drastic affect on Foxx's TV career and his ability to get other projects off the ground. In 1980 NBC, desperately in need of a hit, convinced him to revive the character of Fred Sanford. They offered him $50,000 an episode, which Foxx couldn't refuse. He needed some way of satisfying his debt to the government, and *Sanford* was it. The IRS wasted no time in garnishing a good portion of Foxx's salary, collecting it directly from Yorkin and Lear's Tandem Productions before Foxx would see a penny. What was left over, plus what Foxx made on weekends in Las Vegas, allowed him to continue living some semblance of his former lifestyle.

Sanford was given a mid-season birth on NBC's Saturday night schedule beginning on March 15, 1980. This time around, Foxx went it alone without Demond Wilson. Although no official reason was given for Wilson's absence from the cast, several theories have been put forth. One was that Wilson had insisted on the same $50,000 an episode that Foxx was receiving, a salary demand that NBC couldn't match. Some suggested that Foxx and Wilson had had a falling out over a failed stand-up routine that Wilson had attempted in Las Vegas after *Sanford & Son.* Others simply felt that NBC didn't feel it could mine gold from the same concept twice, and therefore felt the need to take *Sanford* in a different direction, mainly by giving the junkman a white partner (played by character actor Dennis Burkley).

Despite a lot of publicity, *Sanford* failed to draw a large audience and struggled through its abbreviated first season. When the show returned for a second season in January 1981, a number of cast changes had occurred. In an effort to boost ratings, LaWanda Page's Aunt Esther began to appear regularly, and many old faces from *Sanford & Son* began to show up on a recurring basis, including Whitman Mayo (as Grady Wilson), and actors Howard Platt and Hal Williams, as L.A.P.D. officers Hoppy and Smitty.

With the IRS refusing to cut him any slack, and *Sanford*'s dismal ratings, the pressure began to take its toll on Foxx. Veteran director Jim Drake recalls working with Foxx on the show:

> He smoked like a chimney, but had begun to wean himself off the cigarettes. But I can't say he was on the straight and narrow. Redd wouldn't eat. He used to go back to his dressing room, and when he came out for that second show, he would have a lot of life to him. So there was something that was being taken, ingested, whatever you want to say, backstage. I was never aware of it, and I didn't feel it was my place to ask.

During production of one episode, "The Still of the Night" (3/29/80), Foxx managed to shock everyone with his behavior during taping. The plot involved Fred and his new partner Cal discovering a fountain of youth formula that invigorates its users. Recalls Drake: "During the first taping, after taking a drink of this elixir, Redd just kind of hopped up and down and did a little dance. But on that second show, Redd actually climbed up onto the stove and over a twelve foot wall in the kitchen and off the set." NBC eventually cut away from the take because, according to Drake, "it would show that Redd was doing something or taking something [in his dressing room] that gave him that much energy."

Unfortunately, the change to *Sanford* did little to improve ratings. One episode of note did air that season, subtitled "Fred Has the Big One," broadcast on January 16, 1981. In that episode Fred finally suffered the heart attack he had feigned so many times in the past, clutching his chest and falling to the floor in a very dramatic scene. Rather than calling to his late wife Elizabeth, he instead cried out to Lamont. Suffice it to say, Fred survived but *Sanford* didn't. After four telecasts in its new Friday night timeslot, NBC cancelled the program. Seven already completed episodes would be telecast by NBC later in the season, bringing the series' final tally to only 26 half-hour segments.

It would take Foxx five years to get another shot at series television. In 1986 he returned to the airwaves in the ABC sitcom *The Redd Foxx Show*. This time around, Foxx portrayed Al Hughes, owner of a small diner in New York City who adopted a young white girl (played by Pamela Segall) whom he discovered living on the streets near his business. The ratings were disappointing, and after only a handful of episodes Al shipped his young ward off to boarding school. Actress Beverly Todd (*Roots*) was then added to the cast as Al's ex-wife Felicia, who demanded half of Al's business. Comedian Sinbad also joined the cast in one of his first professional acting jobs, as Byron, Al's new foster son. The new characters couldn't save *The Redd Foxx Show*, and it ended its run after 13 episodes.

It was Foxx's third failed series since *Sanford & Son* left the air in 1977, but it was only the beginning of his problems.

On the morning of November 28, 1989, Redd Foxx's world — excesses and all — finally came crashing down on him. He was staying at his home in Las Vegas when, early that morning, he was awakened by a loud banging on his front door. When he answered it, he found a small army of IRS agents on his doorstep, ready to seize all of his personal assets. It turned out Foxx was in debt to the government to the tune of almost three million dollars.

Foxx sat on his front lawn, at times barely holding back tears, at other moments seething with anger, as agents spent hours going through his home removing anything of value — furniture, paintings, bottles of rare wine, memorabilia — and loading them into trucks. Fifteen of Foxx's vehicles were also taken from the property, including several red pick-up trucks that had been used in the production of *Sanford & Son*.

News crews began to show up, focusing their lenses on Foxx, who was being stripped of all his material possessions.

Even after they finished seizing additional assets from his homes and properties in Los Angeles and St. Louis, Foxx still owed a huge sum to the government, with interest and penalties compounding daily. On top of that, the IRS also began to garnish his wages. Perhaps most damaging to Foxx on a personal level was the fact that none of his friends or business acquaintances, those he'd been so generous to over the years, ever called with a word of encouragement, let alone an offer of financial assistance. He felt alone and abandoned.

Foxx finally found an ally in comedian and actor Eddie Murphy (*48 Hrs.*, *Beverly Hills Cop*), who, in 1989, offered him $500,000 to co-star in his directorial debut, the feature film *Harlem Nights*. Foxx acted alongside Murphy and fellow performing legend Richard Pryor in the period comedy about an illegal gambling casino in the 1920s, and the gangsters and police corruption that accompanied it. Foxx spent a great deal of his screen time acting opposite actress Della Reese (*Chico and the Man, Roots: The Next Generations*). While in character, Foxx and Reese were constantly bickering. But between shots they would share incredible stories of growing up in poverty and struggling to make their way as black performers before and during the Civil Rights era. Reese had also guested on a 1975 episode of *Sanford & Son*. Murphy was so impressed with their camaraderie that he decided to create a TV series for them once production wrapped on *Harlem Nights*.

The result was a domestic sitcom titled *The Royal Family* (Murphy developed the concept, with input from Foxx). Foxx and Reese were cast as Alfonso ("Al") and Victoria Royal, a loving couple who could still go toe-to-toe when the situation called for it. As the series opened, Al was looking forward to retiring from his job as an Atlanta mail carrier when suddenly the couple's daughter, Elizabeth, showed up at the front door, her three young children in tow, and announced that her marriage was over and she was moving back in. The pilot was sold to CBS and placed on their fall 1991 schedule.

Foxx saw *The Royal Family* as not only an opportunity to get his career back on track, but to totally turn his life around. Of course, for Foxx there had always been a blurred line between the two. His work was his life, and both were in disarray. Now he finally felt optimistic again after years of insecurity, that same insecurity he'd grown up with and had fought to escape from. Ad buyers were predicting that *The Royal Family* would be the biggest hit of the upcoming season. Foxx, with the promise of a successful new series, plunged ahead full steam. The IRS was still nipping at his heels, still garnishing Foxx's wages; but with the new show and Foxx's weekend engagements in Las Vegas, it seemed Foxx might finally be able to get out from under. He was so confident that, on July 8, 1991, just before production commenced on the first regular episode of *The Royal Family,* Foxx married Ka Ho Cho, a Korean woman in her 30s, whom he'd fallen for. By all accounts, the two were truly in love and happy together.

It seemed like a new beginning for the 68-year-old Redd Foxx.

Veteran television producer Greg Antonocci was hired by Eddie Murphy Productions to oversee the day-to-day operations of *The Royal Family*. Antonocci admired Foxx's past work, but being a fan of Foxx was different than working with him creatively, and the producer was concerned about whether Foxx would be easy to control on the set. He was pleasantly surprised at how amenable Foxx was. Antonocci recalls:

> It was the first time I'd gotten to work with Redd, and I was just amazed at both the energy he had at his age, and the way he used it to electrify a room. At the readings we had a little game we played. I was in charge of the writing, and what I'd do is hold back a joke or two and just write it in his script, so that at the reading he could crack everybody up because they didn't see it coming. That's how he was, and that to me is not someone who was losing interest in his work or the ability to do it. He was performing even when we were just reading the script, which is a gift. Believe me, I've spent decades in half-hour comedies, and half the people want to walk through it; but Redd would see it as a chance to perform. I grew to have a real great affection for him.

Foxx seemed to have a new foothold on success. For the first time in years things were once again going his way. But behind all that newfound optimism all was not well with Foxx. What he wouldn't admit, or failed to accept, was that he was experiencing health problems. Producer David Steven Simon (*Full House, The Fresh Prince of Bel-Air*) recalls working with Foxx on *The Royal Family*:

After a career slump in the 1980s, Redd Foxx seemed on the verge of a comeback with his 1991 CBS comedy series *The Royal Family*. Pictured: Foxx and his co-star Della Reese (courtesy CBS/ Photofest).

He had a minion of people around him who were always handing him the next cigarette. He was just a ticking bomb waiting to happen. Lord knows how he passed the physical. When we used to go the table to read scripts, you could barely hear him talk he had so much phlegm in his chest. It was impossible to understand him sometimes.

Antonocci didn't see Foxx's health concerns as being quite as serious as Simon remembers, but realized that Foxx was showing signs of age.

I don't know if he was in really bad shape. It seemed to me he had to find a rhythm because he hadn't done a series in a while. He was still doing Vegas on the weekends, and I think that sort of stress just wore him down. He was 68 years old at the time. We tried to pace things because we realized he was an older performer and not someone who was a spring chicken, so we weren't going to go out there and drive him in every scene.

On most situation comedies, a dress rehearsal is usually done the day before filming, followed the next day by two live performances in front of a studio audience, one in the afternoon and another later in the evening. To ease the burden on Foxx, that schedule had been amended. Instead, producers would actually film the dress rehearsal, then the next day hold one live performance before a studio audience. Then editors would cut and combine the best of both shows into a final version of the episode. This was much less strenuous for Foxx.

What became apparent to everyone, however, was the incredible amount of pressure that Foxx was under because of the IRS. The harder Foxx worked, and the more money he earned, the more the government demanded from him. Antonocci admired the way Foxx handled it. He never let it affect his performance or get his spirits down, at least not openly. But it was still obvious that the situation was getting to him.

Antonocci felt sorry for Foxx because he believed the actor's situation with the IRS was not his fault. Antonocci insists:

He was not a devious guy, that I can tell you from being in this business for so long and growing up in the street. He was not just another high-priced performer trying to get away with something. He came up on his own talent without schooling. He was an uneducated guy who got himself into a fix because he had to trust somebody. I don't think the IRS ever took that into account. But I do know he wasn't a devious guy; it was not in his makeup.

Foxx got along well with his *Royal Family* co-stars. Besides Reese, the rest of the cast included Mariann Aalda as Al and Victoria's daughter Elizabeth; Sylver Gregory as Elizabeth's 16-year-old daughter Kim; Larenz Tate as 15-year-old son Curtis; and Naya Rivera as 4-year-old Hillary. Foxx, who hadn't worked with young children before, got along surprisingly well with the young actors.

Mariann Aalda (*1st and Ten*, *The Edge of Night*) also became close to Foxx during their time together on the series. She fondly recalls meeting Foxx for the first time after landing the role of Elizabeth. "I'd never met Redd and he wasn't at my screen test," she remembers. "I didn't meet him until we shot the pilot. We had a photo shoot after it got picked up, and I had this really lovely Laura Ashley dress that I thought was quite fetching. It wasn't from wardrobe, it was my own dress, but the stylist agreed it was just right for the occasion."

But before the photo shoot could begin, Foxx's irascible side brought the proceedings to a halt. He looked over at Aalda and asked, "Can't we get her something better than this to wear?"

"Redd, this is my dress," Aalda replied.

Foxx turned to the assembled crew and said, "Well damn, let's take up a collection and buy this girl some clothes."

He looked back to Aalda and said, "You've got a nice shape, you've got nice legs, but you can't see it in there. This is show business, baby, you've got to show them something."

Foxx had the wardrobe stylist step in and pin back the dress. "You see, now that's better."

But he wasn't finished yet. He next turned his attention to Aalda's chest.

"Can't we get her some socks or something?"

Moments later Aalda's bra was padded full of socks.

Foxx looked on gleefully. "See, now that's the look."

Then, referring to Sylver Gregory, the amply endowed actress playing Aalda's 16-year-old daughter, Foxx continued, "It's a damn shame when the daughter has more than the momma." Then, motioning to Aalda's breasts, he added, "You know, they only cost $1500. I'll buy you some."

Aalda was far from embarrassed, however. She says:

> He used to tease me and razz me. But he was a very loving and generous person. He used to get into arguments with the producers, saying, "You know, I'm a star, I've made my career, you don't have to give me all the lines. Give these other children some lines." And he included me as one of the children. So he was very, very generous that way. You know, on a lot of shows the star wants to hog all the lines. He was not like that at all. He loved that show, he wanted it to be a legacy of a black family that had love and warmth, and he really fought hard for the integrity of the show.

Production on *The Royal Family* continued through late summer 1991. The anticipation continued to grow as the show's debut approached. Greg Antonacci was extremely happy at how well the program was coming together, particularly the relationship between his two leads. Early on, there was some apprehension as to whether Foxx and Reese, two individuals with such strong opinions, could work together without getting on each other's nerves. The question was quickly answered. Says Antonocci:

> What they had was wonderful. There were two very strong personalities there. I think there was an urge on Della's part to be sure that she didn't stand in Redd's shadow. She was a pro. Every show is a growing process, and we were really growing and starting to learn how to write the show.

The Royal Family premiered on CBS on the evening of Wednesday, September 18, 1991, and lived up to its expectations. The ratings were spectacular. In the following weeks those numbers dropped a bit, as is the case with most new show, but never enough to qualify the series as anything but a hit. The cast and crew were thrilled and began to settle in for a long, memorable run. Redd Foxx, in particular, seemed to have an extra little bounce to his arthritic step.

Then one October day, without warning, everything fell apart. On the afternoon of October 11, 1991, executive producer Greg Antonacci was in his office when the phone rang. He listened intently to the panic-stricken voice on the other end of the line, then began to hurriedly make his way down to the *Royal Family* soundstage. With each step he took, the magnitude of the horrifying events unfolding on the set was filling him with dread.

The day had started off typically. Seven episodes of *The Royal Family* had been completed by that time, and the cast was busy rehearsing show number eight, which was to be filmed that evening. Redd Foxx had been particularly busy. The previous day, he and his youngest costar, Naya Rivera, had made a personal appearance on *The Arsenio Hall Show.*

Della Reese and Redd Foxx, co-stars of the CBS sitcom *The Royal Family*, enjoy a leisurely moment together onscreen just weeks before Foxx collapsed on the set with a fatal coronary (courtesy CBS/Photofest).

Foxx was doing a lot of publicity for the series, and that Friday was no different. Even though the cast was preparing for a dress rehearsal and the actual taping later that day, Foxx was whisked away from the set for more on-camera interviews. It was an exhausting schedule to keep.

At about 4:00 P.M., Foxx returned to the soundstage and re-joined the rehearsal. The scene was fairly straightforward. Foxx, as Al Royal, was to enter the living room from the kitchen, ready to sit down and relax in his favorite armchair, only to find that someone had stacked some boxes on it. The joke was that, in the Royal household, no one ever sat, or put boxes, in Grandpa's chair. In the character's typical fashion, he was supposed to lose his temper and chastise the rest of his family. As the director called action, Foxx entered the living room on cue and moved toward the chair. He then suddenly clutched at his chest and dropped to the floor. The cast and crew spontaneously burst into laughter. They thought Foxx was pulling his old heart-attack routine from *Sanford & Son*. Slowly, the onlookers began to realize that Foxx was not joking. Aalda sadly recalls:

> We all thought that Redd was doing a pratfall because he came in and kind of like just slid down. We were just laughing, and a considerable amount of time passed. He was a comic, so he was going to work it, so it was at least ten or fifteen seconds. And then Della said, "Get up, Redd." He didn't, and she repeated, "Get up, Redd." So it was a good twenty seconds before we realized what had happened. It was so hot that I thought he had fainted. I ran to the refrigerator and got some ice and brought it back. I don't think anybody knew what was going on. Then somebody said, "Get the paramedics."

By most accounts, it took paramedics ten to fifteen minutes to reach Foxx. In the meantime, Della Reese, a very religious woman and minister of her own church, formed a prayer circle around Foxx. As the cast and crew joined hands and prayed, Reese sat on the floor and cradled the dying Foxx in her arms. The crew tried to shield the children in particular from what they were witnessing. "It was traumatizing for them," recalls Aalda. "The youngest, Nira Rivera, didn't really know what was going on. Her mother was on the set and protected her. But the older kids, they knew, and it was really devastating to them, to both Sylver and Larenz."

By the time Greg Antonacci reached the soundstage, paramedics who were on duty at Paramount had arrived and were working on Foxx. County paramedics arrived soon afterwards. They were able to revive Foxx, and he regained consciousness briefly. He was taken to the Queen of Angels Hollywood Presbyterian Medical Center where emergency room doctors began working on him. States Antonocci:

> It was pretty stunning. There is just something about those classic performers, you kind of feel that they're invincible, they're bigger than life. You don't think about them being mortal. I know that sounds crazy, but it's Redd Foxx; this guy is such a life force, he can't die.

Members of the cast and crew all got into their cars and followed the ambulance to the hospital. Aalda recounts:

> We just sort of hung out there; we didn't know what else to do or where to go. A couple of hours later someone came out and confirmed that he had had a massive coronary, and everyone broke down in the room. Della led us all in prayer. Then they said, "There's nothing you can do; we'll keep you posted." And we all kind of went home. I remember there was a lightning storm that night, and this is Southern California, so you don't get lightning storms that much. There was a lot of lightning in the sky that night. I got a phone call about eleven o'clock that evening from Shelley Jensen, who was one of the producers on the show, and he said that Redd had passed.

[He'd actually been pronounced dead at approximately 7:45 P.M.] We were all devastated, we really did pull together like a family, and had lost grandpa.

Antonocci had remained at the hospital at the request of Foxx's wife Ka Ho Cho to await word on his condition. He explains:

I was the last one who stayed there with his wife and waited. Her grasp of English wasn't the greatest, but she asked me if I'd stay with her and try to translate for her, which is really pretty peculiar because I didn't know Korean. Then they sent out a middle–European doctor, and it was a real vaudeville act trying to get information from him and make it clear to her. I could barely understand what the doctor was saying to me, and was then barely able to translate to her. I thought this is just perfect, Redd would be here laughing; it felt like a bad Lucy routine, moving from one to the other with everyone speaking a different language."

The punch line, ultimately, was no laughing matter. Foxx was gone.

Redd Foxx was put to rest at the Palm Memorial Park in Las Vegas. Thousands showed up for his memorial service, including old friends like Slappy White, LaWanda Page, and Lola Falana. The cast of *The Royal Family* was there, along with Eddie Murphy. Foxx's widow, Ka Ho Cho, read an unfinished poem that Foxx had written in which he reaffirmed his love for her despite their difference in age. Della Reese provided the eulogy.

Despite the fact that he'd been starring in a hit sitcom, Foxx was so broke at the time of his death that Eddie Murphy had to step in and pay for his funeral. He did, however, leave behind a rich legacy of comedy. He had succeeded in lifting himself up literally from the depths of poverty and achieved his dreams. All those whose lives he touched with his comedy would fondly remember him. In May 1992 he was inducted into the St. Louis Walk of Fame as a gesture of gratitude by his hometown.

For those involved with *The Royal Family*, Foxx's sudden death was a severe shock. But they found solace in their memories of him. Insists Aalda:

Redd really fought hard for the integrity of the show. He really believed in it and wanted to present a black family in a strong, positive way. The good thing is that, first of all, he suffered his fatal heart attack to the sound of thunderous applause, so he kind of went out with his boots on. And he owed the IRS money, so it was like, did they get it from him then? We've all got to go, does it get much better than that? You go with your boots on like an old gunslinger and owing the IRS money, and, knowing Redd, I'm sure he took great satisfaction in that.

With Foxx gone, decisions had to be made quickly about the future of *The Royal Family.* There were only three remaining unaired episodes. Everyone agreed that Redd Foxx could not be replaced as Al Royal; the question was whether another actor could come in and fill the void left by his absence. Initially, the idea of adding an uncle was considered. Actors John Amos (*Good Times*) and Sherman Hemsley (*The Jeffersons*) were seriously considered before CBS and Paramount decided to go in an entirely different direction. It was soon announced that actress Jackee (*227*) would join the cast as Victoria's half-sister, Ruth. It was believed that fans would simply view adding a new male actor to the cast as an attempt to replace Foxx. A female addition to the show might stand a better chance of being accepted by viewers.

Jackee was thrilled to be asked to join the show, and was particularly enthused about working with Reese, but was concerned about stepping into the series under such painful circumstances. She had met Foxx at an Ebony/Jet Showcase event and would run into him at different Hollywood functions. She thought he was an amazing performer, and had been crushed by the news of his death. To her surprise, less than a week after his passing, she got the call from CBS to help *The Royal Family* deal with his loss. She explains:

> I was scared. It's like, "I know I can't replace Redd Foxx." But I thought joining the show was still a great opportunity. All those things go through your mind. You know you're not going to actually replace anyone, but you're still sad about the person dying.

Her first few days on the set were emotionally draining. When she arrived, the cast and crew were still mourning Foxx's loss. "The mood was bad; they were devastated," remembers Jackee. "They just cried and cried. When I got there, they were still shaking when they talked about him. They'd start trembling."

There was also concern about their futures. Offers Jackee:

> A lot of people don't think about it, but when somebody dies in the cast of a show, right away you know that it may not go on. People don't want to think that way, but it's a reality. It's not like a government institution where they'll just bring somebody else in to take over. When you do something creative, you've written it with that person in mind, and sometimes they're irreplaceable. And people know the show might not go on. So all of that is on their mind — doubt,

After star Redd Foxx died from a heart attack he suffered on the set of the CBS sitcom *The Royal Family*, actress Jackee Harry (pictured) was signed to play the late character's oldest daughter (courtesy of CBS/Photofest).

fear, and sadness. And then they're hopeful; it's a crazy business. So they were sad. All I could do is come in and do my job. We had fun, I met a lot of great people, and it was not a bad experience at all.

Redd Foxx's final episode of *The Royal Family*, subtitled "Educating Al," was broadcast on the evening of November 20, 1991. The following week, CBS telecast the first post–Foxx program, "New Beginnings" (11/27/91). The episode opened on a typical day at the Royal home. Then the doorbell rings and Victoria answers it to find several of Al's friends from the post office bearing bad news: Al has passed away suddenly. Among the actors portraying Al's friends were old Foxx cronies Don Bexley and Prince Spencer. The heartbreaking episode featured an incredibly moving performance by Reese. Jackee's character of Ruth then appeared to help her sister and her family through the transitional period to come.

As expected, the episode drew interest from a good sampling of viewers. What was unexpected was CBS's next move. After the "New Beginnings" broadcast, the network pulled *The Royal Family* off their schedule. Many times when a network places a series on hiatus, it's an unofficial declaration that the program has been cancelled. But CBS made it clear to those involved that the show was not dead; production was to resume, with a promise that the series would return to the schedule during the current broadcast season.

Production on a new batch of episodes continued through the holidays and into the early months of 1992. As promised, *The Royal Family* did return to the CBS line-up on April 8 in the same 8:00 P.M. Wednesday timeslot it had occupied the previous fall. One notable revision had been made to the format: due to the age difference between Della Reese and Jackee, the latter's character, Ruth, was no longer Victoria's half-sister, but her oldest daughter. The change had both a positive and negative effect on the show. On the plus side, Jackee was now a viable foil for Mariann Aalda's character, Elizabeth. But on the downside, that left Reese with no one to squabble with. The result was that Foxx's absence was being felt now more than ever.

The ratings for the spring episodes never matched those of the Foxx-era episodes, but were still respectable. The momentum of the show slowed once again when it was unexpectedly preempted on April 29 when riots broke out in Los Angeles due to the beating of Rodney King by L.A.P.D. officers. *The Royal Family* ended its season on May 13, 1992 (two episodes remained unaired at the time). CBS continued to express enough interest in the show that, initially, the cast had reason to hope for a second season. Ultimately, those hopes were dashed, and *The Royal Family* was cancelled after its first and only season of 15 episodes.

Summing up his experience with Redd Foxx and *The Royal Family*, executive producer Greg Antonocci says:

> I feel that it was a tremendous opportunity missed. I would love to have seen where we could have gone with it. Personally, it's a great loss not to have been able to work with Redd for a longer time. I learned a lot from him. It was a very, very tough loss for me. I really connected with Redd. It's something in my life that I'll look back on with a smile. I did get to meet some terrific people, and I was glad to have done that.

Although *The Royal Family* did not turn out to be the long-running hit that many had hoped for, it did allow Redd Foxx to regain some of the optimism and vigor that was so much a part of his personality in the past. Thanks to perpetual reruns of *Sanford & Son*, Foxx will continue to be a source of joy and laughter to each new generation. To those who knew him personally, Jon Elroy Sanford will always be Redd Foxx — an outstanding comedian, an outspoken professional, a dirty old man, and a dear and generous friend.

CHAPTER 13

The Sopranos
Nancy Marchand

HBO's edgy crime drama *The Sopranos* has become one of the most influential series in television history. Yet when it premiered in January of 1999 the show's prospects were iffy at best. Airing on a pay cable channel meant *The Sopranos* would not be limited by FCC regulations concerning content the way that programs playing the broadcast networks are. This was of particular importance, given the show's genus. But this freedom would come at a price.

The Sopranos was the story of Tony Soprano, a middle-aged family man and capo of the New Jersey mafia. When the mob's current don is diagnosed with terminal cancer, it's decided Tony will eventually fill his position. The mounting pressure both at home and at work — of dealing with two highly dysfunctional "families" — drives Tony to seek professional help from a psychiatrist, a move that in and of itself could prove fatal. The show was laced with profanity, sexuality, nudity, and a great deal of graphic violence. While many viewers might be drawn to the show for this type of gritty realism, the danger was that others might just as easily be offended and tune out.

While its presence on HBO allowed the show to thrive creatively, there were possible drawbacks. One was that HBO was available in only about one-third of U.S. homes, severely limiting the potential size of its audience. Another downside was that a full-season order for a cable television series usually consists of only 13 episodes, unlike the standard 22 segments that are ordered for most network programs. That meant that a hiatus of close to one year could be expected between seasons, which might lead to audience erosion.

Still, HBO rolled the dice — and, fortunately, won big.

The Sopranos beat the odds and became a runaway hit with both critics and viewers alike. Fine writing, an incredibly talented cast, and gritty realism (the show was filmed on location in New Jersey) led to the type of mass appeal that was unheard of for pay-cable programming at that time. HBO's viewership rose dramatically; tens of thousands were subscribing to the channel simply to watch *The Sopranos*. There were weeks when the show would actually out-draw its network competition by literally millions of viewers.

The Sopranos, together with HBO's original comedy series *Sex and the City*, revolutionized the way the industry viewed original pay-cable projects. HBO in particular would become a magnet for some of Hollywood's top talent, and would regularly top all competitors when it came to Emmy recognition.

The Sopranos was created by writer/producer David Chase, a veteran showrunner whose past credits include such hits as *The Rockford Files* (NBC, 1974–80) and *Northern Exposure* (CBS, 1990–95). When he began piecing together *The Sopranos* in 1997, he realized authenticity would be a key element in making the show work. That meant no cutting costs by substituting locations in and around Los Angeles or Canada. Chase insisted on setting up shop on the actual streets of New Jersey that were populated by the real-life inspirations for the characters he'd developed.

The lead role of Tony Soprano went to James Gandolfini, an Italian-American actor born in Jersey who'd begun his career on the New York stage and crossed over into supporting roles in films like *Get Shorty, The Juror*, and *Crimson Tide*. The rest of the Soprano family included Edie Falco (*Oz*) as his addled wife Carmela; Jamie-Lynn Sigler as daughter Meadow; Robert Iler as son Anthony, Jr. (A.J.); Dominic Chianese (*The Godfather, Part II*) as Tony's uncle, Corrado "Uncle Junior" Soprano; and Michael Imperioli as nephew Christopher Moltisanti. Tony's mob family was comprised of Tony Sirico as Paulie "Walnuts" Gualtieri; Vincent Pastore as Salvatore "Big Pussy" Bonpensiero; and musician Steven Van Zandt (of Bruce Springsteen's E-Street Band) as Silvio Dante. Actress Lorraine Bracco filled the role of Tony's analyst, Dr. Jennifer Melfi, who eventually learned of Tony's real line of work (on paper he ran a waste management company) but continued to treat him anyway.

Rounding out the cast was actress Nancy Marchand as Tony's mother, Livia Soprano. Marchand was a well-known and respected performer whose career had spanned close to half a century and included the stage, film, and television (the latter in the Emmy-winning role of Mrs. Pynchon on CBS's *Lou Grant*). Her work on *The Sopranos* proved to be a far cry from the type of portrayals she'd been known for. Throughout her long tenure as an entertainer she was often called on whenever the need for a grand and aristocratic female character arose.

The relationship between Tony and Livia was the cornerstone of the series. There had never been a mother-and-son story quite like theirs told on television before. Tony's father, Johnny Boy Soprano, had once been a mob boss before being sent to prison, where he died. His fate was preferable to growing old with Livia, whose cold, vindictive, even homicidal nature had made life a living hell for her family. Livia and Tony's relationship had always been volatile, particularly after Tony's father went to prison. Tony's need to enter therapy was deeply rooted in his tumultuous ties to his mother. The decision to make Tony the new boss did not sit well with either Livia or Uncle Junior (he'd expected to fill the position himself). They soon conspired together, with Livia putting out a contract on her son's life.

Marchand cherished the character of Livia. It was a drastic departure for her, and she embraced the opportunity. Eventually, the part would become much more than a career challenge. Diagnosed with terminal cancer, Marchand would use the role as a lifeline during the final days of her life.

Nancy Marchand was born on June 19, 1928, in Buffalo, New York, and was incredibly shy as a child. Her mother had studied at Julliard and later taught piano, a rarity for a woman at the time, and felt that the arts would be a good way for Nancy to open up and become less awkward. She enrolled the preteen Nancy in an acting workshop, where she blossomed.

Nancy graduated high school early and entered Carnegie Tech at age sixteen to study drama. Acting had not only opened her eyes to the world, but had become her life's ambition. After college she joined the Brattle Theatre in Cambridge, where she met her future husband, Paul Sparer. Paul was a Harvard grad who had originally planned to be a psychologist, but, like Nancy, became hooked on acting. They married in June of 1952 and had three

In 1999, despite her ongoing battles with emphysema and lung cancer, actress Nancy Marchand joined the cast of HBO's critically acclaimed crime saga _The Sopranos_. She is pictured above with star James Gandolfini (courtesy HBO/Photofest).

children, David, Katie, and Rachel. The couple struggled to keep the family afloat while pursuing full-time acting careers.

Nancy found her niche appearing at such prestigious theaters as the Long Wharf at Yale, The Lincoln Center Repertory Company and the Goodman Theater in Chicago. She appeared in productions featuring the works of Shakespeare, Chekhov, and Shaw. She also ventured into the new medium of television, the center of which was New York at the time. She landed

Broadcast live on the evening of May 24, 1953, NBC's *Goodyear Television Playhouse* production of *Marty* featured Nancy Marchand appearing alongside Rod Steiger (courtesy NBC/Photofest).

the role of Clara in the live TV production of Paddy Chayefsky's *Marty* in 1953, and made over a dozen appearances on *Kraft Television Theatre*.

Her children recall their mother's dedication to her career and family. "Acting was a huge part of her life," says son David, now a trial attorney. "It was her big creative outlet, just about the most important thing in her life, that and her family." Adds daughter Katie, also an actor:

"Acting was everything to her. She had a tremendous drive." Youngest daughter Rachel, an opera singer living in Switzerland, says:

> It was extremely important. She never made it seem that it was more important than family, but it was who she was, her essence. I don't believe that fame was what she was after, however. It was the process, the work, that mattered to her. She was lucky, but also good, and with the two combined she became famous, but that was never her goal.

Nancy's husband Paul worked mostly on the stage, where he was nominated for a Tony in 1962 for *Ross*. In addition, he found success as a commercial voice-over artist and soap opera star. During the '50s and early '60s, as the children were growing up, it was Paul who was the primary breadwinner for the family. Even when both parents were working, however, they struggled financially. Says Katie:

> We were not at all wealthy. My parents slept on a fold-out couch in the living room until my brother went to college. My sister and I shared a room, my brother had his own. There were times when my dad used to have a bum coat, where he would actually steal food. In the 1960s, my father started getting work on soap operas, as well as his voice work, and things were easier.

Despite their career commitments, Nancy and Paul were certain never to neglect their children. They arranged it so that one parent would always be at home with the children, which often cost them jobs. For better or worse, they also tried their best not to worry their children with the concerns of their careers or the monetary crunches their professions frequently inflicted on the family.

Of her mother, Rachel says:

> I'm sure it was difficult balancing her two lives, but one of the most important things to my mom was never letting her children see her worry, or to see her and my father discuss money problems. My parents never let on that life was hard or expensive. They hid all that from us, and it was a bit of a shock to grow into adulthood and face those realities.

It wasn't until all three of the children were grown and out of the house that Marchand's career took another turn. Her move into television would introduce her to an entirely new audience beyond the theater community. She would become a familiar fixture on both afternoon soaps (*The Edge of Night*, *Another World*) and nighttime TV (*Beacon Hill*, *The Adams Chronicles*) before landing the prominent role of Mrs. Margaret Pynchon on the CBS series *Lou Grant* (1977–82). She would garner five consecutive Emmy nominations — and take home four statues — for her role as the headstrong publisher of the fictional *Los Angeles Tribune*. The show brought her the fame and recognition that she had never really sought, and sometimes despised, and the money which would finally make life more comfortable for her family.

Lou Grant was a spin-off of the long-running comedy classic *The Mary Tyler Moore Show*. The unusual aspect of *Lou Grant* is that it was an hour-long drama spun-off from a half-hour sitcom. When *The Mary Tyler Moore Show* ended its run of original episodes in the spring of 1977, CBS immediately approached co-star Edward Asner about doing his own show. Asner was interested so long as he could bring along Allan Burns and Jim Brooks, the creators and showrunners on *Mary Tyler Moore*.

Asner, Burns, and Brooks went to CBS with the idea of doing a one-hour drama about print journalism. CBS was a bit leery at first, figuring Asner's fans would be more accepting of him in another comedy. CBS relented in order to keep Asner on board, and he agreed to reprise the character of Lou Grant to hook viewers.

One important asset that helped *Lou Grant* become a hit was the presence of Gene

Reynolds, a former actor who'd become one of the most respected producer-directors in the business (he would later serve as President of the Directors Guild of America from 1993 to 1997). His credits included *The Andy Griffith Show*, *Hogan's Heroes*, and *Room 222*. His most prominent achievement, though, was adapting the 1970 motion picture *M*A*S*H* into one of the most successful series on television. After its premiere in the fall of 1972, Reynolds stayed with *M*A*S*H* long enough to aid in its transformation from a standard military-issue comedy to an award-winning drama laced with moments of poignant humor. He left in 1977 to help the fictional Lou Grant make a similar transition from one genre to another.

One of Reynolds' earliest decisions was to hire Nancy Marchand as Lou's publisher, feisty Margaret Pynchon, who'd inherited the *Tribune* from her late husband and stepped into his shoes despite the skepticism of the all-male editorial staff. Remembers Reynolds:

> We had great difficulty finding a woman to play Mrs. Pynchon. What we needed was a woman of intelligence, a woman who was well-educated and appeared to have a certain kind of American aristocracy. We looked at a lot of women in Los Angeles, but we just couldn't find her. Then the casting director said that Nancy Marchand was in Los Angeles doing another show, and when he mentioned her I said, "God, it would be wonderful if we could get her to come over and meet everybody."

Reynolds was familiar with Marchand. He remembered her from *Marty*, and had seen her in a show with Fritz Weaver about the life of Frederic the Great. Reynolds was a big fan. He eventually coaxed Marchand over one day after she'd finished work on another project. She read for the part in front of Reynolds, Burns, and several other writers for the show. Reynolds had a habit of never making casting decisions in front of actors, preferring to let the actor go and then comparing notes with others on his staff before hiring anyone. Marchand's reading was "beautiful," he recalls. Reynolds had based the character on Katharine Graham of the *Washington Post* and Dorothy Schiff of the *New York Daily News*. "The idea of a woman publisher, a woman of real character and strength and determination and smarts, was a wonderful part," insists Reynolds.

After her reading, Marchand left the room. Immediately, Reynolds and his staff began to confer. Reynolds recounts:

> We all sort of said to one another, "Gosh, we really love her." I don't know if we had to go to the network or not; I kind of doubt it. But we noticed that she had left some glasses at the reading, so rather than run down there and tell her she's got it, we wrote a little note and stuck it in the case with her glasses that said, "We love you, and we want you." And so we ran down and gave her the glasses, and she said, "Oh, thank you very much," but she didn't bother to look at the glasses. Somebody was driving her and off they went. But I don't think she ever found the damn note because eventually her agent said, "They want you for the part," and she was surprised.

Lou Grant premiered on September 20, 1977, running on Tuesday nights at 10:00 P.M. In January 1978 it was moved to Mondays at 10:00 P.M., where it would remain for the rest of its five-year, 114-episode run. It was never a major hit, but performed well, ranking number 27 during its fourth season. It won the Emmy for Outstanding Drama Series for the 1978–79 and 1979–80 seasons. Asner, who had received seven straight Emmy nominations for Best Supporting Actor in a Comedy for *The Mary Tyler Moore Show* (with three wins), received an additional five consecutive nominations for *Lou Grant*, this time as Outstanding Lead Actor in a Drama (he won twice). Marchand, too, would receive five consecutive Emmy nominations for Best Supporting Actress in a Drama as Mrs. Pynchon. She won four of those years, losing out only once, during the show's second season, to Kristy McNichol for ABC's *Family*.

During the course of the show's run, Marchand and Asner became close. Says Asner:

I had worked with her in Stratford in my earlier days, and that's how I came to realize what a fantastic actress she was. Nancy was great, and that gave me a great buffer to bounce against. And with my playing of the rough and ready tradesman-like persona, the old free press-type journalist coming against aristocracy, we had great sport in entrusting ourselves to one another. I learned from her every time I worked with her. With her intelligence and her talent, I felt she could do no wrong.

Asner recalls fondly their time not only on the set but socially as well:

One night I invited her to my home for dinner. I said, "Follow me on the freeway." Little did I know that she was such a cautionary creature in terms of driving. Her car would get too close to mine, and she would start to drop back. She'd slow down to the point where I'd be losing her. So if I was doing forty, she'd begin doing thirty; I'd start to slow down for her, and she'd slow down even more. And it was the most arduous trip I've ever had in my life, trying to keep her in my rear view mirror and trying not to go too slow on the freeway. I really needed a stiff drink by the time we got to the house for dinner.

A bold decision at the end of *Lou Grant*'s fourth season put Marchand to the test. In that year's final episode ("Stroke," 5/4/81), Mrs. Pynchon suffered a debilitating stroke that left her partially paralyzed and unable to speak. She stubbornly refused to retire, however, and returned to her post at the *Tribune*. She continued to struggle with her affliction throughout the show's fifth and final season, earning Marchand accolades for her realistic and sensitive portrayal of a person living with a disability. The show ended its celebrated run on September 13, 1982, because of declining ratings, according to CBS. Asner and the producers, however, maintained that the show's cancellation was retaliation against Asner's outspoken, left wing political stances. "Essentially, I think it was my own personal notoriety at the time," claims Asner, "becoming involved in El Salvador, and William Paley's not wanting to antagonize the Reagan administration, that lead to our cancellation."

By the time *Lou Grant* ended, Marchand was in great demand, and afterwards worked steadily in television and films. Her credits included period dramas, such as the TV miniseries *North and South, Book II* (1986), and the feature films *The Bostonians* (1984) and *Jefferson in Paris* (1995). She appeared in such high profile movies as Harrison Ford's *Sabrina* (1995) and director Garry Marshall's *Dear God* (1996). She also attempted to break away from her WASPy image by taking roles in the slapstick comedies *The Naked Gun: From the Files of Police Squad!* (1988) and *Brain Donors* (1992).

In the late 1990s health problems began to slow her down a bit, although retirement was never an option. Then, in 1998, already suffering from emphysema, she was diagnosed with terminal lung cancer and given six months to live. She and her husband withheld the news from their grown children for a few months before finally sitting down with them and broaching the subject. Daughter Katie recalls that day:

My mom said, "I have cancer." I flipped out; my brother and my sister are pretty different temperamentally. Obviously, we were all shocked and upset, but to them it wasn't totally unexpected, because she had been smoking since she was twelve. My mom was someone who always had a terrible cough, who always had a terrible cold; in the winter she would be huffing and puffing.

Katie feels certain it was her mother's smoking that caused her cancer. Her father, too, was a chain smoker, and even Katie herself took up the habit for a time when she was younger. She says, emotionally:

They were smokers, smokers, smokers. I mean, that's how I remember my mother putting me to bed at night: we'd be in the dark, with her making pictures with her cigarette butt in the dark. I know that she tried to stop smoking, and my brother David was really much more adamant about it—he tried to get them both to stop when he was a teenager. But they smoked like many people of their generation. At least she quit cold turkey when she was diagnosed, which not everybody does.

Despite her dire diagnosis, Marchand was determined to continue practicing her craft. Not being able to act was one of her greatest fears, even when she was facing the end of her life. "I think it did scare her," explains Marchand's youngest daughter, Rachel. "I remember her asking, 'Why did I get this awful illness?' But she was a fighter." Marchand would snap out of it when the next possibility presented itself. Then came *The Sopranos*, just when she needed it most.

When David Chase began casting *The Sopranos*, word went out to all the major talent agents in New York and Los Angeles. Although Chase had decided to populate the show with primarily Italian-American actors, he left open the possibility of hiring any actor who truly fit the role. Chase had seen literally dozens of actresses, but hadn't yet found his Livia. Then one day his casting director walked in the room and announced, "Nancy Marchand is here."

Chase recognized her immediately, was familiar with her stage and television work, and was particularly fond of her turn in the *Naked Gun* film. He claims he wasn't put off at all by Marchand's image as a high-society grandee. Explains Chase:

That didn't deter us in the least. What happened was we had read I don't know how many actresses for the role, and we were getting very close to shooting. We were actually at a loss, because no one came even close to understanding the part or interpreting it. We really had no one. So at those junctions in time, you're thinking, "Well, maybe it's the part itself, it needs to be rewritten," or, "Oh my God, what are we going to do?" We were in casting; they were bringing in one person after another. Then she just showed up, and she did it and she just nailed it.

Although Marchand made it clear she was experiencing health problems, she didn't give them the full story up front. It soon became obvious that she was seriously ill. Says Chase:

We didn't know just how ill. She seemed a little winded when she got to the casting office; we were on the third floor in this hot little office. She seemed a little off, but we heard she might have emphysema. We didn't realize how ill she was when we hired her, though. But we found out soon thereafter; by the time we started to shoot we kind of knew.

Chase decided to keep her on for two reasons: one, he loved her performance, and two, his original storyline called for Livia to die at the end of the first season of thirteen episodes, so it was a limited role anyway.

Marchand threw herself into the role. Despite the fact that she was one of the few performers in the series who wasn't Italian-American, the rest of the cast readily accepted her into the family. Says Chase:

No, she wasn't Italian-American, but she was a trained professional, a great actress; and I never heard her express anything to me about being uncomfortable. All she ever said was that she

Opposite, top: Nancy Marchand won four Emmys for her portrayal of publisher Margaret Pynchon in the CBS newspaper drama *Lou Grant.* Here she is pictured with co-stars Edward Asner (left) and Mason Adams (right) (courtesy CBS/Photofest). *Opposite, bottom:* Nancy Marchand (right, pictured here with Melissa Errico) once again took to the stage in director Tony Walton's 1996 Off-Broadway revival of *The Importance of Being Earnest* (courtesy Photofest).

enjoyed doing it. She never had to ask advice on how to portray the character. Although in one instance, she was calling Tony "Antony," like that. I said, "I think you should just say Anthony." And she replied, "Well, this Italian lady in my building says that." And we talked about it more, and I said, "I'm from an Italian family and I never heard that. I think that's a New York thing." She thought about it or maybe asked the lady, and said, "You're right," and just called him "Anthony." That was the sum total of our discussion about the role.

Dominic Chianese, who played "Uncle Junior" Soprano, Livia's cohort in her plot to kill Tony, shared the most screen time with Marchand. The two became very close. Chianese had seen Marchand on stage many times, himself being a long-time theater actor. He and Marchand would sit together during table readings. He remembers:

> The magic between us started on the first day. I knew I was sitting next to a great actress; we really had great chemistry together. We had an unspoken comradery. There was a complete trust, which really helped me tremendously. I did notice that every once in a while if I said something in Italian she would listen closely — she was very absorbing as an actress. She knew that she was dealing with a culture that she was not entirely familiar with; but then, living in New York, she understood the mannerisms and stuff like that. But great actresses take risks, and she took risks and it worked.

Her work on *The Sopranos* gave Marchand the strength to get through the chemotherapy that was a part of her cancer treatment. Working had a profound effect not only on her spirits but also on her health. Originally diagnosed with only six months to live, Marchand was still going strong a year later. "As far as I know, once they found the cancer it never really spread outside her lungs," says Katie. This allowed Marchand to turn her full attention to her performances.

Her children were delighted to see their mother reveling in her work only months after fearing they would soon lose her. Says her son David:

> I liked her role as Livia on *The Sopranos* because it wasn't like her at all. Her role as Mrs. Pynchon on *Lou Grant* was very good, but she was kind of portraying herself. *The Sopranos* offered her something different. Not that I liked the character — she was pretty obnoxious — which is what made it such a wonderful challenge for my mother. I knew she could do it because she was a very good actress, and it was a pleasure to see her doing something different. She got a big kick out of it. I remember her describing Livia as being "almost like an animal," incredibly inconsiderate and self-centered; and she got a kick out of being this awful person.

The Sopranos premiered on HBO the evening of January 10, 1999, and changed the face of television. The series became an immense hit with both critics and viewers, and in doing so made pay cable a viable new source of original programming. Although HBO had been producing both original series (*Dream On*, *The Larry Sanders Show*) and movies (*And the Band Played On*, *Barbarians at the Gate*), along with live sports and concert events, it was the powerful strength of programs like *The Sopranos*, *Sex and the City*, and *Oz* that ushered in a new era for the network.

The Sopranos did generate controversy from advocacy groups that objected to what they considered to be the stereotypical portrayal of Italian-Americans. Even Frank Renzulli, who served as co-executive producer during *The Sopranos'* first two seasons, initially had second thoughts about working on the series. He recalls:

> When I first came onto that show during production of the pilot, I was reluctant. I didn't want to write anything about Italian-Americans and gangsters and all that stuff. As an Italian-American involved in my community growing up, I always found these things offensive. David opened my eyes that what I was reacting to was the bad writing and not the subject matter. Things like,

"Hey, boss, so Mr. Gotti would like to see you." I'll give you a fucking thousand dollars if you find one wiseguy who ever referred to a cop or anybody as "mister." But David had it grounded in such a way that it really appealed to me, and I said "Yes."

As production drew to a close on *The Sopranos'* first season, Chase faced a difficult decision about what to do with Marchand's character. As the storyline played out, Tony had learned of his mother's scheme to have him killed, and the two spent the remainder of the season at war. Tony even forced her out of her house and into a nursing home. In the season finale, according to Chase's original plan, Tony was to go to the nursing home with the intent of murdering his mother.

Chase remembers his dilemma concerning Livia's fate:

In the first season she was obviously extraordinarily important, her relationship with Tony and Junior. Tony's complete internal dynamic was about his problems with his mother. The plan at the end of the season was for Tony, when he found out that Livia had been involved in the attempt on his life, to go back to the nursing home to smother her. But when he got there, she was already going to have been dead from a stroke, cheating him of his satisfaction.

But two things happened. Chase explains:

Nancy was so good that we just didn't want to let that happen. The other reason that made us decide to continue was by that time we knew her condition was pretty serious, and it seemed that killing that character would have had a negative impact on her health. That may be overestimating the importance of the show, but Nancy did say, "Please let me keep working." She did say that to me once. She was not someone who talked a lot, but she said that to me and I didn't probe; I took that to mean she wanted to keep going. And I'm glad we did.

Marchand couldn't have been more pleased when she got word that her contract with *The Sopranos* would be extended.

But just as Marchand was again finding some peace, her life was shattered in September 1999, just as production on the second season of *The Sopranos* got underway. Marchand found her husband Paul, then 75, unconscious on the floor of their New York apartment. He was rushed to Columbia Presbyterian hospital, where it was discovered that he, too, had lung cancer that had metastasized to his brain. He underwent brain surgery and then began radiation therapy.

He was later able to return home and seemed to be getting better. His family was hopeful, recalls Katie Sparer. "Perhaps I was in denial, but I thought, 'My mom's been all right, she's been through this and she's living her life and working. She's not doing great, but she's going along here, and he'll do the same.'" But by early October Paul was back in the hospital, and his condition continued to worsen; his weakened immune system was unable to fight off an infection. He lay in the hospital for over a month, growing weaker. He lost consciousness and became critical. Finally, on November 19, 1999, his family made the painful decision to remove him from life support.

The emotional impact of Paul's death sent Marchand into a deep depression. While she continued to work on *The Sopranos*, the strain of her loss had a dramatic impact on her health. Though the chemotherapy successfully kept her cancer from spreading, her emphysema grew worse, and she had to keep an oxygen tank nearby at all times to help her breathe. "That first year, *The Sopranos* was a godsend," insists Katie. "My mom had the show, her husband, her children and grandchildren, and the house she loved in Connecticut; so I think she was okay until my dad died. And then that was it; it all caught up with her."

Nancy Marchand and husband Paul Sparer share a happy moment together on the sun porch of their Connecticut home in the summer of 1998 (courtesy David R. Sparer).

David Chase was determined to make Marchand as comfortable as possible on the set. He sometimes changed the shooting schedule to accommodate her chemotherapy treatments, and arranged for a nurse to pick her up each morning and stay with her the entire day. Says son David:

If she hadn't had that level of attention, she couldn't have pulled it off. But I think from her own personal point-of-view, it was worth every bit of trouble. It didn't surprise me at all that she wanted to keep working. Her ideal thing almost would have been to die on stage.

Co-star Chianese remembers how difficult it became for Marchand on the set:

At some point she did have the oxygen thing with her, and she'd wear that when she wasn't on screen. That was tough on her. She had COPD [Chronic Obstructive Pulmonary Disease]. She never asked for any favors or anything like that; she was very stoic. She got pretty bad after a while. But when she acted, you never knew she was sick. You never could tell. She never let it bother her. That happens with actors, especially those with stage training. Something happens when you get on stage; your will is so strong you sort of forget other things for a while. You're living the character. You find the strength psychologically somehow, and then when you're finished, you feel the pain again.

Katie Sparer agrees that her mom was never one to complain. She laughs:

She was a tough old WASPy broad. She was an excellent homemaker, both my parents were, but they weren't huggy, kissy parents. I think that's one reason why my mother probably needed the stage. She came from that WASPy background where you didn't display emotions. When my father died I was the one who was carrying on, but my mother never shed a tear. I know at one point I felt sad about something, and her reaction was to just clench her fist and say, "Don't." But again, that was just a part of her personality, the way she had been brought up and lived her life. The stage, and her screen work, offered her some escape from that.

Marchand's condition continued to go downhill; eventually the decision was made that she'd be better off in an assisted living apartment where medical attention would be available around the clock. Looking back, Katie feels the decision may have been the wrong one, but at the time they didn't know what else to do. The move was very hard on her mother. Says Katie:

> That was done with the best of intentions, but I really think it was not a good thing for her. She had a very lovely room that she liked very much, but I think that it was so difficult for her not to be in her own home. She was still working, but was in the hospital a lot. And then at the very end she was in the hospital for quite a while, and it got to a point where there was nothing else we could do. There was some thought to putting her in a hospice, but I said absolutely not.

Despite her personal problems, Marchand was nothing but a total professional on the set of *The Sopranos*. Her performances never suffered. A second season of 13 new episodes premiered on January 16, 2000. While much of the season dealt with the FBI's attempts to bring down Tony, now officially the head of his New Jersey crime family, the writers continued to delve into the relationship between Tony and his mother. Chase and the other writers tried their best to keep Livia involved in the family, despite her actions of the past season. Explains Chase:

> Obviously it created problems, because if a mother has tried to kill a child, the fact that they would ever have a relationship again is impossible. So you think to yourself, "Well, OK, so what are we going to do with her the second season, since she can't interact with Tony, because he would have nothing to do with her?" Which, in fact, did happen. But we still found ways to have her interact with the grandchildren and annoy Carmella and things like that. It wasn't like it was the first season, but we decided to still go on because she was so great.

The season finale ("Funhouse," 4/9/2000) featured an open-ended storyline in which Livia is caught trying to board an airplane using a stolen airline ticket that can be traced to Tony. The FBI quickly moves in, and we're left wondering whether Livia will turn on her son and cooperate with the feds.

In June of 2000, after production had ended on the second year of *The Sopranos*, Marchand's emphysema grew worse, and it became more and more difficult for her to keep her lungs clear. The result was that the rest of her body continued to weaken. Dominic Chianese visited her in the hospital:

> The thing that hurt Nancy the most, I think, was when her husband died. I went to see her at Columbia Presbyterian, and she was resting in bed. I told her my whole life story just to keep talking and say something, and she was concerned about me. She was so sweet. She said, "I hope you find the right wife this time," that sort of thing. I felt so bad for her, and I just kept talking. I said to her, "You'll be back, you'll be back." And she looked at me like she wasn't sure. That was the last time I saw her.

Finally, on Friday, June 16, 2000, Katie had her mother taken by ambulance from Columbian Presbyterian hospital back to her beloved home in Stratford, Connecticut. "I figured that would be best, for however long she had left, however many weeks or months," she says. The end of Nancy Marchand's life would come much quicker. Back in the familiarity and comfort of her home, Marchand passed away two days later, on Sunday, June 18, 2000.

She was 71 years old. "She was able to be at her house here," adds Katie, "and that was like a gift. In the end, it wasn't the cancer that got her; she died from a combination of a broken heart over losing my father and the emphysema."

Marchand's children knew what her acting meant to their mother, and credit *The Sopranos* with making her final days much easier. "She did stay alive for four-plus years after being diagnosed," comments David Sparer, "a lot longer than they thought she would be able to." Adds Katie: "She went out with her boots on. What better way to go? It kept her going, kept her alive. There's no question in my mind." Marchand's youngest daughter Rachel had just left for a trip to Switzerland when her mother passed away. "I sometimes wonder if she would have died when she did if I had not gone away. I think I grounded her to this world, but at the end she had little joy in her life, and I was happy that she was released from her suffering."

Marchand was cremated, and her ashes were mixed in with those of her late husband Paul. Their remains were then spread over a variety of their favorite locations in life.

Her loss to her television family was equally felt. Says Chase:

> Everyone loved her, all the other actors looked up to her as a real pro. We had a fairly young cast, and her reputation proceeded her, and they all looked up to her as a role model. Her character was extremely important to my original vision of the show; it's a loss from which the show has never recovered.

Recalls Frank Renzulli:

> It was painful for us on a personal level; she was a sweet woman. Talk about the traditional show business trouper. I don't think they make many more like her, when you think how frail and fragile some of these actors seem to be. A blister on their foot can hold up production. But Nancy was from the old school. I can't imagine how much discomfort and pain she endured while working, but she never complained.

Dealing with her loss on the show presented problems. The series had relied heavily on the relationship between Tony and Livia, between mother and son, as dysfunctional as that relationship may have been. Insists Renzulli:

> Nobody has a fucking impact on a human being like a mother. My mother is 85 years old, and when I hang up from talking to her sometimes I can't explain why I want to kill the goldfish or throw something through a fucking window. And then you ask yourself, "What did she say? Well, she asked me about the dry cleaning. It's the third time she's asked me about it, and I know there's more than she's saying." How can you explain all the guilt that a mother can give you with a well-placed pause in a sentence? What power to give a person. So when we lost Nancy, not only did we lose a great actress, but we lost a great motivational engine for making Tony Soprano the man he is.

Complicating matters even more was that Marchand's character was in the midst of a major storyline when she died, leaving the writers scrambling for a way out. There was never any thought given to replacing her with another actor in the role of Livia. The most likely scenario would have been for Livia to die off-screen during the series' hiatus. But Chase thought there might be another option, one unique to television. He decided that, despite Marchand's death, perhaps it would be possible to give Livia one last screen appearance to wrap up loose ends. The result drew mixed reactions from fans, critics, and even from the cast.

Chase wrote one last episode for Livia, including a confrontational scene between her and Tony. Sitting in for Marchand was a body double, draped in a turtleneck sweater, who delivered her lines and elicited the necessary responses from actor James Gandolfini. Once the footage was completed, a computer effects team was brought in, at a cost of over $200,000, to superimpose Marchand's head onto the stand-in's body. The headshots of Marchand were taken from earlier performances, utilizing bits of old dialogue. The finished scene was a bit eerie: despite the hefty price tag, the effects shots looked odd, artificial. The composites of Marchand's head were far from seamless. Even more, it was debated whether the scene was necessary. Tony demanded to know whether Livia planned to testify for the FBI, but she never did give him a straight answer. Tony then stormed from the room, telling her to do whatever she wanted. In the completed episode, "Proshai, Livushka" (3/4/2001), Tony learns later that evening that Livia died in her sleep after their argument.

Chase will be the first to admit the scene didn't live up to his expectations. He concedes:

> We realized we might have oversold ourselves with it when we saw the final result and saw how it looked. You know, when you work on anything you just get involved with the tiny problems of it all, the whole process; so when you start at something bad and bring it to something good you think you've succeeded, but that's because you've been embroiled in the process. Because of where you started out, it looks pretty good. It wasn't quite that successful. I don't regret it, though. It was important to finish off her storyline, to see her death register on Tony.

Marchand's children understood and supported Chase in his decision. Says David Sparer:

> That scene was weird, but I feel positive that she would have been glad they did it. Because "the show must go on" was really her way, and somehow they had to deal with the fact that she wasn't there. So it was one way of doing that. As her son, it was a little creepy to watch. It's the kind of thing where I didn't want to watch, but, of course, I had to.

Katie remembers Chase explaining to her and her siblings what would be happening. "I know I have seen it, but I had my hands over my eyes," she says. "I honestly can't watch my mother or my father on television. I haven't been able to, I still am so cut up about them in some ways."

The Sopranos went on to become HBO's most honored series. Despite the fact that Marchand appeared in only the first two seasons, her contributions to the program are still recognized and remembered by everyone involved. Just as important are their sustained memories of their friend and costar. Recalls Dominic Chianese:

> One time, while we were in a car, some guy from my old neighborhood came up and said, "Hey Dominic, how you doing? You remember me?" Blah, blah, blah... And I said, "Oh, yeah." And Nancy was sitting in the front seat, and I caught her eye. She looked back at me as if to say, "What a pain in the ass this guy is." I'll never forget that look. She hated that small-talk bullshit. Maybe her sickness made it tougher for her, but it also put her right where she needed to be for the role. At that last part of her life, I'm glad that she finally got a chance to be recognized as the great actress she was.

Chase also recalls the admirable way in which Marchand faced her illness and yet continued to live life:

> I remember one time I went to her trailer while we were shooting the pilot to tell her that she was done for the day. And she said, "Oh sweetie, I'm sorry I didn't do a very good job today," because she was tired. And it really made my heart expand that she called me sweetie, because she was a fairly reserved woman. She was extremely, extremely funny and acerbic, and smart about everything. But she played it kind of close to the vest. The other thing I remember is that the role of Livia was extremely particular. I think history has borne out that there has never been a mother character like that on television, and I guess Nancy picked up the idea somehow that this was probably based on my mother. We never discussed it, but as Livia started making all of these insane, bizarre, ludicrous statements and engaging in this terrible behavior, Nancy said to my

wife one time, "I trust that the person this is based on is dead." And my wife said, "Yes, she is." And it was based on my mother. My mother wasn't a murderer, obviously, but a lot of the dialogue came from things that my mother said, as well as some of the physical mannerisms, the damp Kleenex always clutched in her hand, the threadbare bathrobes, and that sort of complete, amazing, narcissistic solecism — my mother had that tendency. And Nancy understood that, she harnessed it and ran with it.

Marchand's passion was always her acting, and she spent her life pursuing it without compromise. Katie remembers when her mother was first hospitalized and unable to speak: "She was able to write, and the first thing she wrote wasn't 'Will I live?' It was 'For fifty years I was an actor — no more.' So obviously that's what kept her going." She did return to acting, albeit for a brief time, but the legacy she created in those twilight hours of her career will define her for generations to come.

CHAPTER 14

Bonus Chapter

Unfortunately, the unlucky thirteen series covered in-depth in this book are not alone in the tragedies that befell them. This chapter includes a list of other programs that dealt with the death of a primary actor during production. In each case, the loss of the actor — and the character — was handled in a different way. Often the era during which the show was being produced had a significant effect on the path that was taken. Death on television was much more difficult to deal with in the '50s and '60s than it was in later decades. Ironically, if an actor left a series in a contract dispute, such as Kathy Nolan did when she departed *The Real McCoys*, death was considered a viable option for the character. However, if an actor passed away in real life, dealing honestly with his or her death was typically ruled out. More likely, as was the case with actress Bea Benedaret, who died during the run of *Petticoat Junction*, her character was simply never again mentioned. Regardless of how their deaths were handled onscreen, these actors have the distinction of being remembered by fans who decades later still relish the wonderful memories of their performances — memories that need not fade in time, thanks to the fact that they were captured on film and can be relived over and over again.

Barney Miller (ABC, 1975–1982) Hal Linden played Captain Barney Miller, who oversaw a motley crew of detectives working out of a Greenwich Village police precinct. Among the large ensemble cast of this workplace sitcom was stand-up comedian and character actor Jack Soo (*The Green Berets*). Soo passed away from cancer of the esophagus on January 11, 1979, at age 62. It was explained on the series that his character, Detective Nick Yemana, had also died. A tribute episode dedicated to Soo aired on May 17, 1979, in which the cast members stepped out of character and recalled fond memories of their late friend (including flashbacks to previous episodes).

Bewitched (ABC, 1964–1972) Long-running domestic sitcom with a supernatural twist. Elizabeth Montgomery played Samantha, a beautiful young witch who married Darrin Stephens, an advertising executive who was mortal. The newlyweds did their best to keep the magic in their marriage while keeping the witchcraft out. When the series premiered in the fall of 1964, actress Alice Pearce played the Stephens's nosy next-door neighbor, Gladys Kravitz. Pearce was diagnosed with ovarian cancer shortly after production began, but producers allowed her to continue working while undergoing treatment. Sadly, she lost her battle with the disease on May 3, 1966, after production had wrapped for the show's second season. She was awarded a posthumous Emmy Award for her role as Gladys, which was accepted by her husband, Paul Davis. Actress Sandra Gould assumed the role of Gladys Kravitz in the fall of 1966 and remained with the show for the remainder of its run.

Cosby (CBS, 1996–2000) Four years after their groundbreaking collaboration on NBC's *The Cosby Show*, Bill Cosby and Phylicia Rashad returned to television as husband-and-wife Hilton and Ruth Lucas. Hilton had just turned sixty and been laid off from his job of thirty years at an airline. Getting used to being a househusband didn't sit well with him. Ruth worked part-time at a flower shop. During the second season, the Lucases' daughter Erica (T'Keyah Crystal Keymah), a lawyer who quit practicing to become a chef, moved back into the house. The family also took in a boarder, Griffin Vesey (Doug E. Doug). Actress Madeline Kahn (*Paper Moon, Blazing Saddles*) played Ruth's best friend and business partner, Pauline Fox. During the final season, she and Ruth bought the flower shop, as well as the bookstore beside it. Kahn passed away from ovarian cancer on December 3, 1999. The December 29 episode, subtitled "Loving Madeline," was a tribute to the actress that included clips from her past performances on the show. *Cosby* ended its run the following spring.

Dennis the Menace (CBS, 1959–1963) Jay North starred in this adaptation of Hank Ketcham's cartoon creation. The series' primary focus was on young Dennis Mitchell, who served as a constant annoyance to his elderly neighbor, Mr. George Wilson (played by actor Joseph Kearns), who wanted nothing more than to enjoy a peaceful retirement with his wife Martha (Sylvia Fields). Kearns died unexpectedly of a heart attack on February 17, 1962, midway through the series' third season. To compensate, George was sent off on a trip, and his brother John Wilson came to stay with Martha in his absence. Veteran character actor Gale Gordon was cast in the new role. Thus, Dennis still had his Mr. Wilson. When the series returned for its fourth season in the fall of 1962, John Wilson (now with his own Mrs. Wilson, played by Sara Seeger) took up permanent residence next door to the Mitchells. George and Martha were never again mentioned. An interesting side note is that a recurring character on this series was named Theodore Mooney. When *Dennis the Menace* ended its run in 1963, Gordon immediately stepped into his most memorable role, that of banker Theodore J. Mooney on *The Lucy Show*.

The District (CBS, 2000–2004) Fresh off his nine-season stint as Coach Hayden Fox on ABC's *Coach*, actor Craig T. Nelson made the switch to drama for this hour-long political series. Nelson played Jack Mannion, newly appointed chief of police in Washington, D.C. Lynn Thigpen co-starred as Ella Farmer, a computer analyst who provided Mannion with statistics and forecasts that aided him in his fight to clean up the inner city. Thigpen was a highly respected African-American actress with an extensive resume: stage, both on–Broadway and off (she was both a Tony and Obie award winner); film (in *Tootsie* and *Lean and Mean*; her last film, *Anger Management*, with Jack Nicholson and Adam Sandler, was released after her death); and television, where she was Emmy-nominated for her role on *All My Children*. In early March 2003, Thigpen began experiencing severe headaches; she died of a cerebral hemorrhage on March 12. On the series it was explained that Ella had died from a stroke. For the remainder of the season Mannion failed to accept her death, and refused to allow anyone to clear out her office. He finally came to terms with her loss in the season finale.

Dragnet (NBC, 1952–59, 1967–70) Sgt. Joe Friday had two primary partners during his tenure as TV's most by-the-book police detective. In the show's 1950s incarnation, Ben Alexander played Officer Frank Smith. When the series was revived in the late 1960s, Harry Morgan was cast as Officer Bill Gannon. But trivialists may note that Friday's first partner was Sgt. Ben Romero, played by actor Barton Yarborough. Yarborough died of a heart attack on December 19, 1951, after completing only two episodes. Two other actors did temporary duty alongside Webb for the remaining eleven episodes of *Dragnet*'s first year. When the series returned for a second season in January 1953, Alexander had been added permanently to the cast.

Harry and the Hendersons (Syndicated, 1990–93) Based on the 1987 feature film, this half-hour comedy series told of the Henderson family, who happened upon a Sasquatch during their vacation and ended up accepting him into their family. Of course, keeping him secret from their neighbors was a constant struggle. Kevin Peter Hall, who at 6'9", again assumed the role of the Bigfoot. Harry had donned the furry suit for the movie. Hall's previous credits include the series *Misfits of Science* and the sci-fi film *Predator*, in which he played the alien who battles it out with Arnold Schwarzenegger. In 1991, during production of the series' second season, Hall announced that he was suffering from AIDs. He succumbed to the disease on April 10, 1991, at age 35. Dawan Scott assumed the role of Harry for the remainder of the season, with Brian Steele stepping in for the third and final year.

Hill Street Blues (NBC, 1981–87) This hour-long dramatic series revolutionized television in the early 1980s with its gritty setting and hand-held camera angles. Hill Street Station was a police precinct in a crime-infested inner city neighborhood (the city was never actually given a name). In many cases, the officers of the precinct were almost undistinguishable from the criminals they were trying to collar. The series was an early effort from famed producer Steven Bochco, co-created with Michael Kozoll. Among the outstanding ensemble cast was actor Michael Conrad, a noted character actor equally at home going for laughs as he was at tackling drama. Conrad played Sgt. Phil Esterhaus, who briefed the Hill Street officers each morning before they headed out on patrol. "Let's be careful out there," became his catchphrase. Conrad developed urethral cancer during the show's third season. His screen time diminished as his disease worsened; onscreen, his dramatic weight loss could not be hidden. He died on November 22, 1983, at age 58. Robert Prosky was added to the cast as Sgt. Stan Jablonski, who assumed roll call duties for Sgt. Esterhaus. It was explained that Esterhaus had died during sex with his fiancée.

Hotel (ABC, 1983–88) Loosely based on writer Arthur Hailey's best-selling novel, this series might be described as a land-based *Love Boat* (Aaron Spelling and E. Duke Vincent produced both). The series, starring James Brolin and Connie Sellecca, followed the exploits of the staff and clientele of the prestigious St. Gregory Hotel in San Francisco. Bette Davis originally signed to play the hotel's owner, Laura Trent, but after completing the series' two-hour pilot she fell ill and had to bow out. Anne Baxter then joined the cast as Laura's sister-in-law, Victoria Cabot, who assumed the day-to-day operations. On December 12, 1985, Baxter died suddenly of a brain aneurysm. Rather than bring in another replacement, Brolin's character inherited her half-share of the St. Gregory, and he ran the hotel for the remainder of the show's five-year run.

Law & Order: Trial by Jury (NBC, 2005) NBC may have gone to the well one too many times with this fourth installment of creator Dick Wolf's popular *Law & Order* series franchise. This one dealt with the complexities of the New York City jury system. Actor Jerry Orbach had spent twelve seasons as the star of parent series *Law & Order* before stepping down in 2004 after being diagnosed with prostate cancer. He was clearly losing his battle with the disease when he approached Wolf with his desire to keep working during the final months of his life. Wolf arranged for Orbach to reprise his character, Detective Lennie Briscoe, in a supporting role on *Trial by Jury*. Sadly, Orbach died after completing only two episodes. The series itself was cancelled after 13 episodes were filmed.

Love and War (CBS, 1992–95) Susan Dey starred in this sitcom as recently divorced socialite Wallis "Wally" Porter, who bought into a seedy New York restaurant/bar called *The Blue Shamrock* and then attempted to add a touch of class to the establishment. Jay Thomas also starred as Jack Stein, a brash columnist for *The New York Post* who was a regular at the *Shamrock* and fell head over heels for Wally, despite his opposition to the changes she was making to his favorite watering hole. John Hancock was cast as the bar's original owner, Ike Johnson. A familiar African-American character actor who'd previously held recurring roles on several series, including *Family Ties, Hardcastle & McCormick,* and *L.A. Law,* Hancock died of a heart attack on October 12, 1992, only three weeks after the premiere of *Love and War.* It was explained on the show's November 16, 1992, episode, subtitled "For John," that Ike (like Hancock) had died of a heart attack. Two weeks later, actor Charlie Robinson (*Night Court*) showed up as Abe Johnson, Ike's brother, who assumed Ike's duties at the bar. A photo of Hancock remained on display behind the bar for the remainder of the program's three-year run.

Mr. Ed (syndicated, spring 1961; CBS, fall 1961–65) One of the more absurd comedies in TV history, Mr. Ed told the tale of Wilbur Post (Alan Young), an architect who bought a new suburban home only to discover a horse in the barn out back. An even bigger surprise was that the equine, Mr. Ed, could speak—but only to Wilbur. Once Wilbur got past the notion that he might be going insane, his primary concern became keeping his and Ed's secret from his wife Carol (Connie Hines) and their neighbors Roger and Kay Addison (Larry Keating and Edna Skinner). Your typical '60s-era nosy next-door neighbor, Roger was always walking in unannounced at the most inopportune moments. Larry Keating developed leukemia in 1963 and died shortly after production began on the series' fourth season. No explanation was ever offered for Roger's abrupt disappearance. Actor Jack Albertson was briefly added to the cast as Paul Fenton, Kay's brother. In December the Posts got new neighbors altogether. Leon Aames and Florence MacMichael joined the cast as Gordon and Winnie Kirkwood. They remained for two years. When the show played out its abbreviated final season, the Posts were finally free of any annoying neighbors, but Wilbur and Ed still found ways to get into weekly scrapes all on their own.

Night Court (NBC, 1984–1992) Harry Anderson starred in this underrated sitcom as Judge Harry T. Stone, who sat on the bench of a Manhattan night court. The show was a surprise hit in the spring of 1984 and ran for nine seasons. Behind the scenes, however, the laughs were overshadowed by not one, but two, tragedies. Actress Selma Diamond was originally signed to play court matron Selma Hacker, a curmudgeon who chain-smoked and always got the last hysterical word in. Diamond passed away on May 13, 1985, of lung cancer, shortly after production wrapped on the second season. When the series returned for a third season that fall, Florence Halop had been added to the cast as Florence Kleiner, Selma's replacement; it was announced that Selma had died over the summer. Diamond and Halop were remarkably similar in their appearance; both were short and ornery, and possessed gravelly voices. They were so alike that the casual viewer might not have even noticed the switch. Tragically, Halop, too, passed away after only one season on the show. She died of breast cancer on July 15, 1986, shortly before production was to resume on *Night Court*'s fourth season. This time the producers took no chances, choosing stand-up comic Marsha Warfield, a much younger woman, to assume duties in Judge Stone's courtroom. She remained with the show until it folded in 1992.

Petticoat Junction (CBS, 1963–70) The Shady Rest Hotel in the small town of Hooterville (the rural community also featured in *The Beverly Hillbillies* and *Green Acres*) was the setting for this low-key family sitcom. Widow Kate Bradley (Bea Benadaret) ran the Shady Rest, with the help of her three beautiful daughters and the girls' scheming uncle Joe, (Edgar Buchanan). Benadaret was a respected voice artist who had worked extensively in both radio and television. She provided the voice of Betty Rubble on *The Flintstones*, and was also a regular on *The George Burns and Gracie Allen Show* and *The Beverly Hillbillies* before landing the lead in *Petticoat Junction*. Despite the laughs onscreen, off-camera, Benadaret was waging a brave battle with breast cancer. She was written out of much of the fifth season (it was explained Kate had gone to visit her sister). Feeling stronger, she returned in the season finale, "Kate's Homecoming" (aired March 30, 1968). Unfortunately, it was to be her final appearance. Her conditioned worsened over the summer, and she was again absent when the show returned for its sixth season that fall. Benadaret died on October 13, 1968, at age 62. Shortly after her death, June Lockhart was added to the cast as Dr. Janet Craig, Hooterville's new female M.D.

Phyllis (CBS, 1975–77) After *Rhoda* was successfully spun-off from *The Mary Tyler Moore Show* in 1974, CBS quickly made the decision to do likewise with *Phyllis*. Everyone involved had high hopes for the venture. Award-winning actress Cloris Leachman had played Phyllis Lindstrom for five seasons on *Mary Tyler Moore*. On the new show, recently widowed Phyllis and daughter Bess (Lisa Gerritsen) set off to make a new life for themselves. Unfortunately, the show was plagued by tragedy from the start. On July 24, 1975, after only three episodes had been completed, actress Barbara Colby, who'd been cast as Phyllis's new boss, Julie Erskine, was brutally murdered. The crime was never solved. Liz Torres took over the role for the remainder of the season, after which the character was dropped in a change of format. Early in the second season, elderly characters Sally "Mother" Dexter (played by 86-year-old Judith Lowry) and her boyfriend Arthur Lanson (portrayed by Burt Mustin, age 93) became engaged, and were married on December 6, 1976 (in the episode subtitled "Mother Dexter's Wedding"). Sadly, Lowry died of a heart attack on November 29, eight days before the episode aired. Mustin's health also began to fail, to the point that he was unable to view the episode. He died on January 28, 1977. After two low-rated seasons, *Phyllis* was cancelled a few months later.

Suddenly Susan (NBC, 1996–2000) Brooke Shields starred in this workplace sitcom modeled after *The Mary Tyler Moore Show*. In the pilot, Susan Keane (Shields) dropped her rich boyfriend after deciding she wanted to prove she could make it on her own. She landed a job as a columnist for a San Francisco magazine, *The Gate*. Nestled comfortably in a pre–*C.S.I.* Thursday night timeslot, *Suddenly Susan* finished its first season ranked the number three series on television. A move to Monday nights the following season proved disastrous, however, and the show never recovered. It did manage to limp along for three more years before NBC finally pulled the plug. Late in the series' third season, actor David Strickland, who played music critic Todd Stites, committed suicide. On March 22, 1999, after suffering from years of deep depression, he hung himself in a Las Vegas motel room. Devastated, the cast and crew of *Suddenly Susan* dedicated the season finale to the young actor. In the unusual episode, Todd's character disappeared, and his friends went searching for him. Along the way, they discovered a variety of touching facts about his life that they'd been unaware of. At the end of the episode, still having not found him, they received a call from the police. The exact nature of that call was never explored, but Todd was missing from the office when the show returned that fall for its fourth season. It was cancelled unceremoniously that December.

Wagon Train (NBC, 1957–62; ABC, 1962–65) This popular early western series followed a wagon train as it traversed the Wild West. At the beginning of each season a new assortment of pioneers would depart Missouri and spend the TV season braving the wilderness, only to arrive in California each spring. Ward Bond portrayed Major Seth Adams, the experienced wagon master to whom the travelers entrusted their lives. Bond died of a heart attack on November 5, 1960, as production was underway for the series' fourth season. Veteran western star John McIntire joined the cast in the spring of 1961 as the new wagon master, Christopher Hale, who led the move west for the remaining four seasons.

The Waltons (CBS, 1972–81) One of the most popular family dramas in history, *The Waltons* was creator Earl Hamner, Jr.'s somewhat semi-autobiographical account of growing up in the depression era hills of Virginia. The Walton family included parents John and Olivia (Ralph Waite and Michael Learned), grandparents Zeb and Esther Walton (Will Geer and Ellen Corby), and eldest son John Walton, Jr. ("John-Boy," portrayed by Richard Thomas). John-Boy, an aspiring writer (and Hamner's alter-ego), also narrated the stories. In 1976, Ellen Corby suffered a debilitating stroke and was absent from the series until the spring of 1978, when she returned for the season finale, "Grandma Comes Home" (aired March 30, 1978). The episode featured an amazing performance by Corby, who returned in a partially impaired state, paralyzed on her right side and unable to speak. Grandma came home from the hospital but felt unnecessary because her family, concerned she would overexert herself, prevented her from participating in the everyday activities of the household. At the end of the episode, a heartbroken Grandma Walton finally manages to convey two words to the others: NEED ME. Unfortunately, the episode would prove to be Will Geer's final appearance. Just when it seemed the Walton family had been reunited, Geer passed away suddenly from a heart attack on April 22, 1978. When the show returned that fall, the family was still mourning his loss. It was explained Grandpa had died (like Geer) from a heart attack and had been buried atop Walton's Mountain.

The West Wing (NBC, 1999–2006) This NBC political drama centered on the presidency of liberal Democrat Josiah Bartlet (Martin Sheen) and his White House staff. The series became a huge hit both with viewers and critics, placing regularly in the top-ten for several seasons early in its run. Among the show's talented ensemble cast was actor John Spencer in the role of Chief of Staff Leo McGarry. Spencer earned five consecutive Emmy nominations as Best Supporting Actor, taking home the trophy once, in 1999. When the program returned for its final season in the fall of 2005, President Bartlet's last term in office was about to expire, and Leo was persuaded to run for Vice President alongside new Democratic hopeful Matthew Santos (Jimmy Smits). Just as the fictional presidential campaign was beginning to heat up onscreen, Spencer died of a massive heart attack on December 16, 2005. The writers wrote around his absence for several episodes leading up to the election. On the show, Santos and McGarry won their bid for the White House in *The West Wing*'s April 9, 2006, telecast, subtitled "Election Day (Part 2)." But Leo never lived to enjoy the victory. The episode's storyline included his death (of a heart attack) on the eve of the election, before all the votes could be counted. The following week's episode, "Requiem" (4/16/2006), served as a memorial to Spencer, as cast members past and present paid tribute to Leo.

List of Interviews

1— 8 Simple Rules for Dating My Teenage Daughter

Earl Hamner, Jr., 2/3/05
Tracy Gamble, 2/20/05
David Steven Simon, 2/23/04
James Widdoes, 3/17/05 & 3/24/05
Joyce DeWitt, 3/21/05

2 — Alias Smith & Jones

Alexander Singer, 2/10/04
Ben Murphy, 3/9/04
Roger Davis, 3/12/04
Jo Swerling, Jr., 3/15/04
Glen A. Larson, 4/7/04

3 — Bonanza

Richard Collins, 3/10/04
Robert Blees, 3/24/04
David Dortort, 3/24/04 & 3/26/04
Ken Howard, 4/22/04
Wally McCleskey, 4/22/04
David Canary, 5/21/04
Tim Matheson, 7/21/04
Mitch Vogel, 7/28/04

4 — Cheers

Shelley Long, 3/1/05
Ted Danson, 4/4/05
Ken Estin, 4/14/05
Peter Casey, 4/20/05

Rhea Perlman, 5/5/2005
Dean Hargrove, 6/29/05

5 — Chico and the Man

Ed Scharlach, 3/3/04
Peter Baldwin, 3/9/04
Alan Sacks, 3/25/04
Isaac Ruiz, 4/25/04 & 7/14/04
Hal Kanter, 5/1/04
Gabriel Melgar, 5/13/04
Ray Andrade, 6/14/04
Danny Mora, 10/14/06

6 — Cover Up

Bob Shayne, 3/19/04
Brian Lane, 4/1/04
Glen A. Larson, 4/7/04
Bob Murray, 4/11/04
Richard Anderson, 5/5/04
E.G. Daily, 6/23/04
James D. Parriott, 6/29/04
Guy Magar, 7/7/04
Meeno Peluce, 7/10/04
Eric Paulsen, 8/2/2004

7 — Dallas

David Jacobs, 5/12/04
David Paulsen, 7/1/04
Steve Kanaly, 7/8/04
Camille Marchetta, 10/13/04
Larry Hagman, 12/1/04

8 — Eight Is Enough

Bob Shayne, 3/19/04
William Blinn, 5/14/04
Dick Van Patten, 7/7/04
Dianne Kay, 7/19/2004
Randal Kleiser, 10/19/04

9 — Gimme a Break!

Lauri Hendler, 5/12/04
Lara Jill Miller, 5/16/04
Hal Cooper, 9/1/04
Rod Parker, 9/2/04
Jim Drake, 9/15/04 & 1/15/05
Brigit Jensen-Drake, 9/15/04
Telma Hopkins, 10/25/04
Joel Thurm, 1/19/2007

10 — Lime Street

Raymond Austin, 2/23/04
E. Jack Kaplan, 4/24/04
Mart Crowley, 4/25/04
Julie Fulton, 4/27/04
Harry Thomason, 5/21/04
Jane Smith, 10/12/05

Quote: "It's in her genes..." "The Women In My Life," *Ladies Home Journal*, Sep. 1985, p. 34.
Quote: "When kids are that young..." "Still Mourning Samantha Smith, Robert Wagner Decides That His *Lime Street* Show Must Go On," by David Wallace, *People* magazine, Nov. 1985, p. 81.

11 — NewsRadio

Stephen Root, 9/19/06
Tom Cherones, 10/17/06
Edie McClurg, 10/23/06

12 — Royal Family

David Steven Simon, 2/23/04
Mariann Aaida, 6/23/04
Jim Drake, 9/15/04 & 1/15/05
Jackee Harry, 10/18/04
Greg Antonucci, 12/2/04

13 — The Sopranos

Frank Renzulli, 12/3/04
Gene Reynolds, 12/10/04
Edward Asner, 12/20/04
David Sparer, 2/21/05
Katie Sparer, 2/22/05
Rachel Bersier, 2/27/05
David Chase, 6/16/05
Dominic Chianese, 6/16/05

Other References

Episode titles, airdates, and names of certain guest stars and characters were sometimes drawn from the websites *epguides.com*, and *imdb.com*, *tv.com*, as well as from the acclaimed book *The Complete Directory to Prime Time Network and Cable TV Shows* (1946–Present, Eighth Edition), by Tim Brooks and Earle Marsh.

Index